Communication of Information Technology
Project Sponsors and Managers in Buyer-Seller Relationships

by

Ralf Müller

ISBN: 1-58112-198-9

DISSERTATION.COM

USA • 2003

Communication of Information Technology
Project Sponsors and Managers in Buyer-Seller Relationships

Dissertation.com
USA • 2003

ISBN: 1-58112-198-9
www.Dissertation.com/library/1121989a.htm

COMMUNICATION OF INFORMATION TECHNOLOGY PROJECT SPONSORS AND MANAGERS IN BUYER - SELLER RELATIONSHIPS

A thesis submitted for the degree of
Doctor of Business Administration

by

Ralf Müller

Henley Management College
Brunel University

July 2003

COMMUNICATION OF INFORMATION TECHNOLOGY PROJECT SPONSORS AND MANAGERS IN BUYER - SELLER RELATIONSHIPS

Ralf Müller

Abstract

Communication is frequently identified in the literature as a major factor impacting Information Technology (IT) project failure. The importance of communication is amplified in buyer - seller relationships through the long-term impact of project failures on the future business of IT vendors with their customers.

The formal communication between IT project sponsors from buyer firms and project managers from IT vendor firms within business to business markets is investigated through this study. Typical communication patterns between project sponsor and manager in high and low performing projects are identified. The antecedents of these patterns are assessed and the effectiveness of project sponsor - manager communication investigated. A multi-method approach is used with a quantitative analysis of a worldwide survey with 200 responses, followed by a qualitative analysis of three interviews with pairs of project sponsor and manager, each pair from the same project.

Results show that project sponsors expect more analytic and verbal communication from project managers. A model shows the development from frequent informal communication to formal communication between project managers and sponsors. A second model shows how communication in high performing projects is determined by the level of collaboration between project managers and sponsors, as well as the degree of structure in project execution. Effectiveness of project sponsor and manager communication is found to be decreased through written statements about recent achievements, and increased through face-to-face meetings of the parties. A series of recommendations is provided to improve project sponsor - manager communication.

Table of Contents

List of Tables

List of Figures

ACKNOWLEDGEMENTS

There are a number of people who supported me during the present study and deserve my deepest thanks.

Financial support for the study was made available by Peter Jørgensen and Søren Dyhrberg from NCR Systems Engineering Copenhagen, Denmark. Their support and trust in my work sustained even through rough economic times.

My Supervisors Professors Rodney Turner and Arthur Money made this study an exciting and stimulating experience through their deep insights in their subject areas, the inspiring and constantly high value of their feedback, as well as their patience and guidance.

Support through Dr. David Price, the Henley Doctoral Office with Jackie Coleman, Veronica Clarke and Louis Child, together with the lecturers from the Henley Research Methodology and Research Techniques workshops provided the foundation and guidance for progressing.

Last, but certainly not least, I like to thank my wife Renate and my son Jonas for their patience and continuous motivation to finish this project.

Thank You !

CHAPTER ONE – INTRODUCTION

Communication is certainly the essence of civilization. Without communication we could neither recognize nor share common interests, which means we could not easily cooperate in achieving mutual goals. The quality of one's communication skills is probably the most important of all traits (PMI 1987, p. H1).

Communication is at the heart of all managerial activities. The above statement from the Project Management Institute's (PMI) *Guide to the Project Management Body of Knowledge (PMBoK)* is representative of a large amount of research studies and practitioner articles which show the importance of proper communication for successful project management. Along with its importance communication is frequently identified as a major determinant for project success or failure. Hartman (2000, p. 11) concluded from his research at the University of Calgary, Canada:

From the numerous failed projects examined by us, the ultimate cause of failure was always the same. Cost overruns were due to poor estimates, missed elements of scope, and more; but in the end all was due to inadequate communications. Schedule overruns were due to work being more complex than anticipated, resources not being available, the scheduler being too optimistic, and more. Yet again, when we checked, there was a breakdown in communication at some point in all cases.

A related and spectacular example is the American National Aeronautic and Space Association's (NASA) loss of the Mars Climate Orbiter, which was caused by an error in the formal communication between two geographically separated teams. While navigating the spacecraft close to the Mars surface one team used metric units and the other team English units without formally communicating the units (only the numbers). Through that the spacecraft was brought below the minimum distance to the Mars surface, where it collapsed (NASA 1999).

Studies on the reasons for failure of Information Technology (IT) projects repeatedly show similar patterns. Examples are Oz & Sosik (2000), who identified five major factors that lead to cancellation of IT projects, with one of them being poor communication. Similarly the Standish Group (1998) compares project success with a three-legged stool, with one of the three legs being communication. Other research showed that communication beyond the boundaries of the project team has a larger impact on financial results than project team internal communication (Jiang et al. 2000, Keller 2001). Hutinski et al. (2001) identified a possible reason for this by showing that complexity levels of communication are highest during requirements specification stages and implementation stages of IT projects. In their research more than 50% of the respondents indicated moderate to great communication difficulties during these stages. An initial research on 34 IT projects during the early stages of the present study indicated that communication has the most significant impact of all PMI defined knowledge areas (i.e. in management of integration, scope, time, cost, quality, human resources, communication, risk and procurement) on cost variances in IT projects (Müller & Turner 2001). Despite communication's importance for project results the empirical research by Partington (1997) showed that projects often lack good communication beyond the boundaries of the project team.

PMI estimates that project managers communicate approximately 90% of their time (ESI 1994, citing PMI). However, a search for 'Communication' at the PMI online bookstore revealed only three books with the word 'Communication' in their title, with one addressing presentation techniques, another business writing and the third one data communication. The relation between importance of communication for project results and the quantity and quality of supporting literature in project management seems to be out of balance.

Research on communication maturity identified IT firms as being especially low in their communication maturity when compared with firms from engineering and construction, information management and movement, as well as high-tech manufacturing industries. This lack of maturity was in line with overall low project management maturity in the IT industry (Ibbs & Kwak 1997).

The present study aims to improve the effectiveness of formal project sponsor - manager communication by deepening the understanding of the complex processes underlying this communication. Effectiveness is defined as the mutual fit of communication requirements and capabilities, as outlined in Chapter 3 (Bensaou & Ventkatraman 1996, Tushman 1979). Formal communication occurs through the official communication channels given by the buyer-seller relationship (Mullins

1999a), i.e. between the project sponsor and manager as representatives of their respective organisations. Their formal communication reflects the official authority structure between the organisations, through which they provide each other with needed information in a timely manner (PMI 2000) and reduce the communication contents to project related matters concerning the organisations (Johnson 1993), thus their formal communication should follow an expressed purpose and agenda (Cooper 2000). PMI (2000) defines e.g. reports and briefings as indicative of formal communication, whereas ad-hoc conversation is seen as informal communication. Formal situations and the associated communication are often referred to as regimented, deliberate and impersonal in nature; as opposed to informal communication which occurs in situations of behavioural spontaneity, casualness, and interpersonal familiarity (Morand 1995). Speakers in formal communication situations are more committed to the topic they communicate than to the relationship between the communicating parties, whereas in informal communication they are more committed to the relationship than to the topic (Mead 1990). While formal communication is perceived as slow in speed and high in accuracy, informal communication is seen as high in speed and low in accuracy (Mullins 1999a). This is supported through research by Johnson et al. (1994), which showed that formal communication is perceived as being more credible than informal communication. This also explains research results which showed that managers receiving formal project reports feel more 'in control' of the project (Kraut & Streeter 1995). A summary of the differences of formal and informal communication is provided in Table 1-1.

Peoples' perceptions about what constitutes formal communication, as opposed to informal communication, are formed through context factors such as culture and the situation within which their communication occurs (Mead 1990). That implies that the borderline between formal and informal communication in the daily work of project sponsor and manager is blurred. As will be seen this is also supported by the results of the study. To identify those communication practices yielding highest credibility and accuracy the study excludes, to the extent possible, informal communication, which among others include body-language, grapevine, rumors, and politics. The study focuses on formal communication as described above, being aware that a distinction from informal communication is often subjective and situational.

Characteristic	Formal communication	Informal communication	Source
Situation	Regimented, deliberate, impersonal	Casual, spontaneous, interpersonally familiar	Morand (1995)
Commitment	Higher for topic than for relationship	Higher for relationship than for topic	Mead (1990)
Credibility of contents	High	Low	Johnson et al. (1994)
Style	Reports, briefings, etc.	Ad-hoc conversations, memos, etc.	PMI (2000)
Speed	Slow	Fast	Mullins (1999a)
Accuracy	High	Low	Mullins (1999a)

Table 1-1: Differences between Formal and Informal Communication

The study uses two complementary methodologies. A quantitative methodology based on a worldwide survey and a subsequent qualitative methodology with a set of structured interviews. The triangulated results show opportunities for improvement of communication effectiveness, because of project sponsors' significantly higher preference for analytic contents and verbal media. Antecedents for the choices of contents, frequency and media differ. Sponsors choices are driven by past experiences and managers' by project risk. Effectiveness of communication is negatively impacted by qualitative statements about *status and recent achievements* in written reports send by project managers, and positively impacted by face-to-face meetings between the two individuals. A model for buyer-seller communication identifies communication along a continuum of increasing sponsor - manager collaboration. High performing projects exhibit an additional dimension reflecting the level of rigid operational structures within a project. These two dimensions are balanced through a written communication between sponsor and manager in 2 - 4 weeks intervals. The model provides guidance in identifying reasons for deviations from this balance.

The findings of the study accumulate in a series of recommendations that can be used by project sponsors, managers and IT firms to improve their communication practices in order to prevent from project failure and provide for long lasting, profitable business relationships.

1.1 Background

The importance of communication is not new. Already the first article on *The Project Manager* in Harvard Business Review (Gaddis 1959) identified the need for careful preparation and explanation of all communication in order to achieve acceptance from those involved in a project. Since then project management has developed into a worldwide profession with several Bodies of Knowledge (BoK) (Turner 2000). These BoK's describe the generally accepted knowledge and practices applicable to most projects most of the time (PMI 2000). The definitions of the terms project and project management vary among the different BoK's and along the timely evolution of the project management profession. The most recent definition of a project integrates the common view of projects as unique undertakings with recent organisational developments in the industry towards more project oriented organisation and management structures (Turner & Müller 2003, p. 7):

> *A project is a temporary organisation to which resources are assigned to undertake a unique, novel and transient endeavour managing the inherent uncertainty and need for integration in order to deliver beneficial objectives of change.*

Project management is defined as the application of management techniques, knowledge, skills and tools to achieve a project's objectives (IPMA 1999, PMI 2000).

Along with its professional development project management became the basic building block in the strategic management of products and services firms (Cleland, 1991). Projects are the object of exchange, where buyer firms procure complete technological solutions as projects to address their business problems. These buyer - seller relationships involve not only the exchange of products and services for money, but also social interaction and other interactive processes (Halinen 1997).

The responsibility for a project's success within a buyer firm lies typically with the Project Sponsor, who holds the business case (Morris 1998) and provides the link between the project and the customer's senior management (Wideman 2000). Partington (2000) defines two roles of a project sponsor. These are a) to ensure the project aligns with the firm's strategy from inception of the project and throughout its lifecycle, and b) to accept primary responsibility for the delivery of the project. For that the project sponsor provides the financial resources for a project, accepts project milestones and project completion (PMI 2000), and is accountable to the buyer organisation's management for the investment in the project. He or she monitors and approves forecasts and plans (Harpham 2000) and eventually receives the value of the project (Turner 2000). Research by Crawford and Brett (2000) showed that sponsors take on additional responsibilities in form of political support of the project, consultation prior to project manager decision making and subsequent ratification, provision of objectives and resources, responsibility for project scope and to a minor extent management of issues and risks. The project manager of the selling organisation acts on behalf of the sponsor and manages the planning and implementation stages of the project. Through that the project sponsor delegates the responsibility for the day-to-day management of the project to the project manager. While monitoring the project manager the sponsor takes on a mentor role which requires the belief in the project manager's ability to manage the project, patience in watching execution, and the vision to differentiate between one-time and mortal failures of project managers (Nonaka & Takeuchi 1995, citing Lee, 3M). Project Managers are the individuals to manage the project towards the agreed objectives (APM 2000, PMI 2000). So *why* the project is done is a sponsor responsibility, and *what* the implementation entails is a project manager responsibility (Partington 2000).

IT seller firms establish project teams as temporary agencies to achieve project specific objectives, and appoint project managers to manage the projects on their behalf, often at the customer's site (Turner & Müller 2003). The respective position of buyer and seller in a project leads to different perceptions of the project (Bacharach & Lawler 1980). The meanings generated by the representatives of these positions are found to be unique and not identical (Shulman 1996).

The project manager's organisational position relative to the employing organisation, the customer and the project, is one of in-between the employing organisation and the customer, but close to the project. This creates a perspective of 'customer-focused delivery of what is contracted' for the project manager, which is different from the buying firm's project sponsor perspective who perceives the same project from an intra-company change management perspective (Partington 1997), of which the IT system may only be a minor part and required to be flexible in adapting to the higher objectives of the overall project. This conflict needs to be solved through communication. As representatives of their respective organisation project sponsor and manager have overlapping membership in both organisations (Eisenberg et al. 1985) and need to integrate different requirements stemming from their different perspectives. Through their mutual communication they balance their organisation's requirements.

1.2 Scope and Underlying Assumptions of this Study

The unit of analysis is the formal communication of project managers from IT vendor firms with project sponsors from buyer firms. The scope of the study excludes all non-project and non-work related communication, as well as a detailed investigation in informal communication. As such the scope is constraint to communication that officially takes place between buyer and seller and, at least in case of written communication, is stored on enduring media where it remains auditable e.g. in case of litigation or legal actions between the parties.

Two assumptions underlie the present study. First, that the project manager and sponsor have free access to the three media types assessed, these are personal communication, verbal communication and written communication, with the latter one including electronic mail. This follows earlier studies in media usage (Rice & Shook 1990).

The second assumption is a sufficient level of computer literacy and technical proficiency on the side of project sponsor and manager to handle e-mail, voice mail and possibly video-conferencing. The study's scope is limited to IT projects only, so a minimum level of computer literacy can be assumed both on the buyer as well as the seller side.

1.3 Organisation of this Study

The study is executed in a nine step process derived from Remenyi et al.'s (1998) eight step process. Figure 1-1 shows the three main phases of preparation, execution and conclusion, which were operationalized through nine distinctive steps in a partly iterative manner.

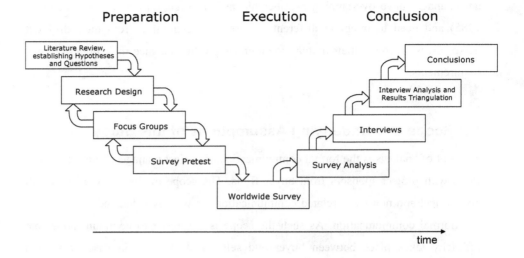

Figure 1-1: Research Process

The preparation phase consisted of the literature review with subsequent development of research questions, hypotheses and research model. Two focus groups were setup to validate the research model and survey instrument, as well as to pre-test the questionnaire. During the execution phase a worldwide Internet based survey and subsequently three interviews with pairs of project sponsor and manager of the same project were held and the collected data analyzed. The conclusion phase comprised the triangulation of the results and the development of conclusions and recommendations for project sponsors and managers for the improvement of their communication.

The organisation of this thesis follows the research process described above. Chapter 2 starts with an outline of the buyer – seller theories underlying this study. A subsequent literature review summarizes the recommendations for sponsor - manager communication from the existing project management literature. This is followed by a review of organisational communication research as well as organisation structure theory as it relates to communication. Within Chapter 3 the research model, research questions and hypotheses are developed. Chapter 4 describes the methodology used and the survey sample. The chapter starts with the methodology selection and the associated philosophical basis. The execution of the research model is described in the remainder through the work with the focus groups, the development of the survey instrument and interview questions, as well as the quantitative and qualitative approaches to analyze the data. Furthermore, the data collection process, sampling frame and sample are described. Chapter 5 provides the quantitative and qualitative analyses of the data. The interpretation of the analyses results is done in Chapter 6, where also the study's contribution to knowledge is outlined. Chapter 7 concludes the study by summarizing the results and linking them to prior research. The chapter also provides a series of recommendations for project sponsors and managers on how to improve their communication for the benefit of their joint projects. The study closes by outlining the strength and limitations of the research, as well as the implications for further research. The survey instrument, interview guide, as well as the tables and figures from the quantitative and qualitative analyses are provided in the Appendices.

CHAPTER TWO - LITERATURE REVIEW

This chapter reviews and summarizes the literature on formal buyer – seller communication in project management. The chapter starts with a review of two buyer – seller theories to establish the initial perspective of the research. This is followed by a review of literature from project management, organisational communication and organisational structure theory as it relates to the communication problem stated in Chapter 1.

The terminology used follows Wideman's (1991) suggestion with the buyer organisation being represented by a project sponsor, and the seller – or implementer – organisation being represented by a project manager. The terms *buyer - seller* and *project sponsor - manager* are therefore used synonymously throughout the study.

2.1 Inter-firm Relationship Theories

To address the complex issue of research in inter-firm relationships it is helpful to refer to existing theories which explain the factors that govern these relationships. As outlined in the Introduction, this study's unit of analysis is the communication between project sponsor and manager during IT project implementation in a buyer – seller relationship. Established inter-firm relationship theories that match this level of analysis are Transaction Cost Economics and Agency Theory (Williamson 1995). They are introduced in the following sections.

2.1.1   Transaction Cost Economics (TCE)

TCE focuses on the level of individual transaction which converts 'input' to desired 'output', e.g. the implementation of a new IT system to improve a company's internal efficiency. TCE is rooted in economic theory and explains the decision to 'make' a product in a firm's own hierarchy or 'buy' it in the market. The former case provides for better control of 'fit for purpose' or lowering of maladaptation costs of the product at generally higher management costs, whereas the latter case provides for lower prices through economies of scale and price competition in the market. According to

Williamson (1975) the make or buy decision is based on the combined ramifications of:

- the degree of asset specificity as the main influential factor. This is the extent to which the object of the transaction is specific (or unique) to the individual transaction and can not be redeployed in future transactions

- the degree of uncertainty which arises a) from a lack of communication or conscious supply of false and misleading signals, preventing a decision maker finding out about the plans made by others in the transaction; and b) the general uncertainty in human behaviour; as well as c) the general risk of the undertaking

- the frequency of the transaction. TCE was originally developed for repetitive, routine transactions, undertaken by the classically managed organisation in functional and hierarchical structures. Within these repetitive transactions no specialized governance structures are required, whereas highly unique transactions demand specific management structures.

Through that TCE 'regards a firm as a governance structure, rather than a production function' (Willimason 1985, p. 387). The costs for governing these transactions are defined as transaction costs, where:

> Transaction costs are economized by assigning transactions (which differ in their attributes) to governance structures (the adaptive capacities and associated costs of which differ) in a discriminating way (Williamson 1985, p. 18).

TCE proposes that firms adapt their governance structures to achieve the lowest expected transaction costs. Transaction costs are regarded as the economic equivalent to friction in physical systems, stemming from the complexity of the relationship between buyer and seller organisations and the impossibility to develop and agree on contracts comprehensive enough to structure the relationship in an all comprehensive manner. To economize on transaction costs TCE proposes that high levels of asset specificity, uncertainty and contract incompleteness lead to 'make' decisions, whereas low levels lead to 'buy' decisions (Adler et al. 1998).

A central issue in TCE is the difficulty of mutual assessment of the performance of transaction partners (Rindfleisch & Heide 1997). The need for performance assessment and control derives from the buyer's desire to control progress (Levitt et al. 1999). The procedural mechanism to satisfy this need is through formal communication between representatives of the buyer and seller organisation, which are the project sponsor and the project manager respectively. The extent of their collaboration and mutual satisfaction of communication requirements determine the transaction costs to a large extend. That identifies the relationship between project sponsor and manager as a major factor impacting transaction costs. A specific dimension, covering the relational aspects of TCE was developed by Heide & John (1992) through their concept of Relational Norms. Here norms are defined as at least partially shared expectations about behaviour within a group of decision makers. Relational exchange norms are

> ...based on the expectations of mutuality of interest, essentially prescribing stewardship behaviour, and are designed to enhance the wellbeing of the relationship as a whole (Heide & John 1992, p. 34).

Evidence from their research shows that 'relationalism' is built through three different though related domains, such as:

- flexibility, which is the bilateral expectation of willingness to make adaptations as circumstances change

- solidarity, is the bilateral expectation that a high value is placed on the relationship and that the behaviours of buyer and seller are directed towards maintenance of the relationship and avoidance of behaviour detrimental to the relationship

- information exchange, is the bilateral expectation that parties will proactively, frequently and informally provide information useful to the partner.

Relational norms are the mechanisms that provide the *ability* to implement governance structures in projects, whereas the TCE domains of asset specificity, uncertainty, and frequency are the mechanisms to *motivate* firms to structure their relationships in a particular way (Heide & John 1992).

Even though TCE is criticized for its crudeness in the form of primitive models, underdeveloped tradeoffs, severe measurement problems and too many degrees of

---

freedom (Williamson 1985) it is frequently used as a theory to address research issues and explain marketing phenomena.

A complementary and conceptually closely related approach to TCE is that of Agency Theory, which will be described in the next section.

2.1.2 Agency Theory

TCE and Agency Theory both explain transactional governance mechanisms in relation to transaction costs. The focus of agency theory is the potential for conflict of interest that arises in a principal and agent relationship. This potential conflict arises when one party (the principal) depends on another party (the agent) to undertake some action on the principal's behalf (Bergen et al. 1992, Jensen 2000). The delegation of decision making authority from principle to agent is assumed problematic because:

- the interest of principal and agent will typically diverge if both are utility maximizers

- the principal cannot perfectly and costlessly monitor the actions of the agent

- the principal cannot perfectly and costlessly monitor and acquire the information available to or possessed by the agent (Barney & Hesterly 1996, Jensen 2000)

Agency theory includes employment relationships, e.g. a project manager employed by an IT vendor. The management of project managers, especially when working at remote customers sites, therefore becomes an agency problem. Agency theory addresses the problem of conflicting interests as a contracting problem between principal and agent. Two scenarios are distinguished, these are

- the pre-contractual problem when a principal has to select and offer a contract to an agent suitable for the task. This is often referred to as a 'hidden information', *ex ante*, or adverse selection problem. It addresses information asymmetries between principal and agent, where the principal is assumed to know the nature of the task the agent should perform as well as the personal characteristic needed to perform this task.

- the post-contractual problem of incomplete information on the side of the principal about the agent's actions on the job, as well as the agent's higher level of task related information which the principal would like to obtain. This is often referred to as the *ex post* or moral hazard problem. It arises from the agent's closer involvement in e.g. project tasks and the principal's dependency on the information flow about the project's status from the agent.

An agency problem arises when self interest causes the agent to withhold information or even send false information to the principal. This is addressed in Agency Theory by attempting to realign the interests of the principal and agent through contracts that either specify actual behaviour of agents or the outcomes of tasks. The contracts should be designed that the actions regarded as most appropriate by the principal yield the highest payoff for the agent (Bergen et al. 1992).

Even though TCE and Agency Theory share the same fundamental principle of transaction cost they differ in perspective and unit of analysis. TCE takes an incomplete-contracting view and uses the individual transaction as unit of analysis, thus focuses mainly on the *ex post* transaction costs. Agency Theory adopts an *ex ante* view of the relationship between principal and agent, and focuses mainly on the individual agent as the unit of analysis.

Agency theory has been criticized for taking an inherent investor view only and for assuming that humans are primarily motivated by financial gain. However, the *'empirical evidence is on balance supportive of agency theory'* (Barney & Hesterly 1996, p. 128)

Research by Turner & Keegan (2001) confirms the complementary nature of TCE and Agency Theory in project based organisations. Their research showed the difference in governance structures depending on a firm a) serving a few large clients or many small clients, and b) undertaking few large projects, programmes or many small multi-projects. The results of the research show that in project based firms new governance structures evolve that require two additional roles, those of Broker and Steward. Here the seller firm's Broker is responsible for the long-term relationship with the buyer, while the Steward assembles the resources to deliver the project.

In Agency Theory, the role of the Broker is that of a representative of the interests of the buyer within the seller firm (a quasi principal), especially in projects with high asset specificity. The role of the Steward is to deliver the project (as a quasi agent) with the project manager being the agent on the site of the project. The quasi roles are therefore the internal representatives of the project within a seller firm. The real principal and agent roles are executed by the sponsor and project manager at the project site. Here the principal assigns the agent as the Chief Executive of the agency (project team) that brings about the desired change through the project, manages the project's inherent uncertainty and utilizes the required resources (Turner & Müller 2003). The literature's recommendation for their communication is discussed in the next section.

2.2 Project Management Literature on External Communication

Communication is the fundamental activity through which social interaction is accomplished (Orlikowski & Yates 1994). Definitions of Communication are manifold and range from the interchange of information to that of a social discourse (Oxford 1996). The variety of definitions is also reflected in the changing nature of communication as a subject in project management literature. Here earlier definitions of communication management referred to mechanistic sender - receiver structures (PMI 1987), which are often described through communication models as the basic components of communication (Krone et al. 1987). These models consist of:

- message – the verbal and non-verbal cues each communicator conveys

- channel – the vehicle or medium in which a message travels

- sender and receiver – being the message's source and destination respectively

- transmission - the actual sending and receiving of messages through channels

- encoding and decoding – the process of creating, transforming or deciphering of a message

- meaning – interpretation of the message contents

- feedback – a response to the initial message

- communication effect – the outcome or general result of the message exchange process.

The transmission of information through a channel is typically described in the literature as a sequence of Input – Coding – Channel – Decoding – Output, with Noise causing disturbances during transmission through the channel (Parry 1967).

More recent definitions (e.g. PMI 2000, p.117) refer to:

... the dynamic processes for planning, information distribution, performance reporting and administrative closure, together with the social and integrative characteristics of communication, which link people, ideas and information necessary for project success.

Four major processes are described by PMI (2000) for managing communication:

- Communications planning, i.e. determining the information and communication needs of stakeholders. It includes communication requirements, technology, constraints and assumptions, as well as tools and techniques for communication planning, and the outputs from communication planning, e.g. a communications management plan.

- Information distribution, i.e. making the needed information available to project stakeholders in a timely manner.

- Performance reporting, i.e. collecting and disseminating performance information. This includes status reporting, progress measurement, and forecasting.

- Administrative closure, i.e. generating, gathering, and disseminating information to formalize phase or project completion.

An analysis of the two leading academic journals in project management, PMI's Project Management Journal (PMJ) and IPMA's International Journal of Project Management (IJPM), as well as PMI's widely distributed *PM Network* showed low attention in the literature to project communication. Between 1990 and 1999 communication was the topic of five articles, or 2.5%, of the combined PMJ and PM Network articles, and 1 article, or 0.2% of the IJPM articles (Morris 2000).

The literature reviewed for project sponsor – manager communication can be classified in methodologies, maturity models (terms explained below), BoKs, project management books, articles and papers from academics, researchers and practitioners. Methodologies, BoKs and textbooks provided the majority of specific suggestions for communication frequency and contents, whereas other literature stressed the importance of good communication processes and practices without giving 'tangible' advice *how to* communicate.

Project Management Maturity Models, i.e. tools to benchmark and identify strengths and weaknesses of a firm's project management practice (Jugdev & Thomas 2002), do not recommend specific communication frequencies or contents.

Morris (1994) says that successful project realization involves striking the right balance between sponsor and project manager. The interaction between them can take on many different forms, but should be planned and managed, e.g. through a simple communication plan showing the type of information, method, media, timing and responsibility in the interaction (Calvert 1995, PMI 2000, SEI 2002, APM 2000). Formal interaction should be through meetings, where the project manager's reports are discussed (Turner 1999). Here the current, integrated analysis of progress against plan and predictions for the remainder of the project should be communicated (Archibald 1976).

2.2.1 Frequency of Project Sponsor – Manager Communication

This refers to the number and timing of formal communication events between project manager and sponsor during the implementation of a project. It includes all media and possible communications contents.

A review of four widely used project management methodologies showed that recommendations for formal project sponsor – manager communication are often linked with formal reporting. Methodologies are applied to reconcile the different perspectives of the parties involved in a project and to guide the project through a controlled, well managed, visible set of activities to achieve the desired results. Methodologies also identify how much responsibility, authority and accountability the individuals in a project have (CCTA 2000). The methodology serves as a guideline throughout the project and supports the Project Manager in his or her day-to-day work, e.g. in the communication with the Project Sponsor. Methodologies' recommendations on communication frequencies differ and are either on a weekly or monthly basis, or dependent on milestone or stage achievements, supplemented by intermediate reports in case of longer stages. Milestones are significant events in a project, usually the completion of a major deliverable (PMI 2000). Stages are groupings of activities in projects. A stage starts with a decision point for management where the risks of the upcoming stage are evaluated and resources allocated and authorized for the stage. Especially projects that cannot be planned in detail upfront require these decision points to review and authorize the detailed plans of the coming stage, so that the project manager can continue with the project (CCTA 2000).

Phases are logical groupings of project activities, usually culminating in a major deliverable (PMI 2000). Depending on the type of a project's phase the deliverable of that phase can e.g. be a conceptual document in the concept phase or an IT system at the end of the implementation phase. Depending on the project type different phases are used in projects. NCR's GlobalPM project management methodology (NCR 1997) defines five phases for IT delivery projects. These are:

- Concept phase: where the feasibility of the potential project is assessed, a decision is made to proceed, and a Project Manager is assigned

- Pre-contract planning phase: where a core Planning Team is assembled, that plans the activities necessary to support proposal development and contract negotiation. The Pre-contract Planning phase ends with the buyer and seller firm's signature of a joint contract

- Post-contract planning phase: this is after the contract, or other authorization to proceed pending receipt of the contract, is received from the customer. The project manager assembles the full project team, which then develops and creates the integrated project plan. Ultimately, the customer reviews the baseline project plan, which is finalized, agreed to, and signed off on, before project implementation.

- Implementation phase: the time the project team carries out the project according to the baseline project plan. The phase ends with the buying firm's signature for complete delivery of the IT system.

- Close-out phase: where the Project Manager closes out the project by ensuring that all documentation is completed and that open items are resolved. The project manager also reviews the final status of the project with the project team, and conducts a lessons learned session.

The sum of all phases constitutes the project life-cycle, which defines all activities from start to end of a project.

The methodologies reviewed were four of the leading methodologies from industry and Government:

- PRINCE 2 from the UK – a mandatory project management methodology for all Government projects in the UK (CCTA 2000).

- V-Model – a mandatory project management methodology for all Government IT projects in Germany (BWB 1997).

- PROPS – a commercial project management methodology developed by Ericsson, Sweden for product development and customer delivery projects. The methodology is widely adopted by larger companies, mainly in Northern Europe (Ericsson 1999).

- GlobalPM – a commercial project management methodology, developed by NCR Corporation, USA together with ESI, USA. This methodology was adopted by AT&T and Lucent Technologies (NCR 1997).

Table 2-1 lists a comparison of the methodologies' suggestions on reporting frequency and contents during project implementation (details of *contents* are described in the next section). Even though a variety of terms are used the recommended reports are all written and due either weekly, monthly, or at milestone, stage or phase achievement, and at project end.

	PRINCE 2	V-Model	PROPS	GlobalPM
Reports	Stage end report, Mid-stage report, Project closure report	Progress reports, Project end report	Progress report, Final report	Management status report, Earned value report, Close-out report
Non-mandatory reports	Highlights report, Checkpoint report	Case reports, Protocols, Internal message Memo		Weekly status report (only for roll-out projects)
Frequency of reports	Monthly, at stage end, and project end	After milestone achievement and at end of project	Monthly and at end of project	Weekly (for roll-out projects) and at end of project
Control method	Earned value	Earned value	Earned value	Earned value

Table 2-2: Reporting Recommendations of Four Project Management Methodologies

These recommendations are not without critics. Lipman (1996) classified status reporting as periodic and static, which contrasts the dynamic and continuously evolving nature of project progress, with the potential to adversely affect a project's success. Pinto and Kharbanda (1996) as well as Partington (1997) found that companies try to lower their levels of bureaucracy and minimize formal reporting and reviews of projects. Tan (1996) supports this and suggests less formal documentation and reports, but more frequent meetings or phone conversations. This is contrary to methodologies' suggestions to use written media for formal communications (e.g. in CCTA 2000).

Project management textbooks, as well as practitioner and academic articles often recommend adjustment of sponsor – manager communication frequency to the individual project's requirements. If project specific agreements are lacking the literature suggests a variety of communication frequencies, which can be seen on a continuum, ranging from communication only after the achievement of major events in a project, i.e. at variable timely intervals, via fixed timely intervals (e.g. monthly), to continuous communication on a daily basis. These categories are described below.

Communication at project phase end, phase transition, or project end
This is the least frequent communication between project sponsor and manager. It occurs only at the transition from one phase to the next or at the end of project phases.

This communication is recommended by all four methodologies reviewed to evaluate the results of the recent phase and authorize the plans and resources for the next phase.

Communication at Milestone achievement

Morris (1994) recommends milestone reviews as the minimum of communication between project managers and sponsors. This communication takes place after major planned events in a project happened, usually after hand-over of a major deliverable (BWB 1997). Milestones are often communicated to interested parties outside the project team (i.e. stakeholders) to communicate project progress or when major risks occur (Turner 1993).

Monthly communication

This communication frequency is most often recommended, usually in form of a monthly report or face-to-face meeting (Archibald 1976, Morris 1994, CCTA 2000, Ericsson 1999).

Bi-weekly communication

Turner (1999) suggests reporting every fortnight. For stability in reporting he strongly recommends that the work element reported against should be roughly equal in duration to the frequency of reporting.

Weekly communication

Lock (2000a) recommends this frequency for very short projects and Turner (1993) recommends it for high risk or almost finished projects. NCR's methodology (NCR 1997) suggests weekly reporting especially for roll-out projects, i.e. large quantity hardware delivery, which require less development but more logistic and team management.

Daily or Continuous Communication

Turner (1993) recommends daily reporting for projects at high risk or those close to finish. Other proponents of this communication frequency recommend using Internet technology and corporate-wide intranets for real-time access to project data, where

The Internet is the global connection of servers [computers] linked to share information and communicate either on a personal level or company basis. The intranet is a corporate environment set up to facilitate the sharing, communication, and use of applications within the corporate community with access to the internet (Lucas 1997).

This technology enabled and timely unlimited access to databases with project related information - such as data on cost, timing, achieved functionality, and subcontractor delivery status etc. - allows provision of up-to-the-minute status information to project manager and sponsor simultaneously. This supports the industry's desire for quicker and low cost access to project information (Barkowski 1998, Barry & Pascale 1999, Lipman 1996, Lucas 1997, Timmons 2000).

PMI's (1999) research about the future of project management identified more than two dozen commercially available software tools that provide collaboration capabilities over the Internet, allowing joint report development and real-time updates. In line with business needs of the industry the study anticipates cybernetic communication and control systems that enable project teams to amalgamate their capabilities quickly, easily and at relatively low cost. An approach supported by Griffin's (2002) taxonomy of Internet Applications for project management communication. According to this taxonomy a formal project sponsor – manager communication via the Internet is best accomplished using e-mail and audio/video-conferencing. Formal stakeholder communication, which involves a wider audience, may also use web-sites, web-based group-ware tools and text conferencing tools.

The aim for more and faster technology is not always seen as sufficient for better communication. The problem of communication lies in understanding *what* is communicated, not *how* a message is communicated (Celestino 1995), and technology only provides the opportunities for communication, but not communication *per se* (Shulman 1996). Researchers found that problems of communication are more in un-stated assumptions among the people involved (Parry 1967), unwritten customer expectations (Hartman et al. 1995), the inability to satisfactorily define the needs of the users (Burns & Stalker 1994), as well as poor generation and management of expectations (Shulman 1996). These problems are not solved by better and faster communication technology. With up to the minute information about project status sponsors in buyer organisations easily feel attracted to micro-manage their projects and thereby get in the way of their project managers. A balance is required which provides enough information to the sponsor to trust the project manager that the project is progressing according to plan and will deliver the desired results. For that the project manager needs to be empowered to manage the project, but also needs to send regular progress reports so that the sponsor does not need to be involved into operational decisions. This requires mutual awareness of individual communication expectations of the parties, as well as discipline and time to assemble, structure and transmit information so that the communication requirements of the receivers are fulfilled.

2.2.2   Contents in Project Sponsor - Manager Communication

This refers to the information content exchanged between project manager and sponsor at each formal communication event. Report contents, as suggested by the literature, should be based on the project plan and use defined control criteria for measuring progress against objectives, calculate progress and forecast time and cost for completion (Turner 1999). The review of project management literature showed that six different categories of formal communication contents are suggested. The following lists and describes these categories. In the interest of clarity and space the references are provided in the subsequent Table 2-2.

Status and achievements
Reporting of status and achievements should be based on the project plan and report project plan adherence in terms of schedule, budget, and implemented functionality. This is the traditional triple-constraints (budget, time, and functionality) and most basic form of status reporting.

Changes to the project
This includes changes in scope, plan, risks, quality requirements etc. It encompasses any changes triggered by any of the project partners or the project context, which lead to a change in scope which requires a change of contract or special agreement between the parties.

Issues and open items list

This is a continuously maintained list of current issues and 'open items' that need to be resolved for project delivery.

Next steps in the project

An update for the project sponsor on the near term activities within the project. It is the forward looking update and complements the backward looking status and achievement reports.

Trends in the project

These are tendencies within the project detected through analysis, e.g. increasing schedule deviation over time, often calculated from the project's quality and progress measures.

Quality and progress measures

This includes the agreed upon quality metrics, e.g. Defect Measurements like rate of software defect discovery and total defects. It also comprises integrated project performance measures, e.g. Earned Value Management, which integrates scope, schedule and resource for performance measurement. The Gower Handbook of Project Management (Turner & Simister 2000) defines earned value as:

> *... a methodology for comparing the achieved value of work in progress against the project schedule and budget. It can be performed at the single activity level but its maximum benefit depends on looking at all activities and rolling the results up through the hierarchy of the work breakdown structure. As with any measurement technique, earned value analysis is not a progress control tool in itself. It can only highlight a need for corrective action by indicating trends. The method does, however, have the advantage of being able to show trends fairly early in the project life cycle* (Lock 2000, p. 494).

Frame (1987) recommends earned value especially for larger projects, because of the accumulation of large quantities of task related data. For reporting purposes these quantitative measures should be complemented by qualitative information about quality problems, external delays, problems - anticipated and present - and risks (Turner 1999).

© Ralf Müller 2003   Literature Review   Page 24

The references for the six contents categories are listed in Table 2-2. Status, quality and progress measures and changes are most often recommended as communication contents.

	Status and achievements	Changes	Issues & open items	Next steps	Trends	Quality and progress measures
Methodologies						
PRINCE 2 (CCTA 2000, Duhig-Berry 1993)	X	X	X	X	X	X
V-Model (BWB 1997)	X	X			X	X
PROPS (Ericsson 1999)	X	X	X		X	X
GlobalPM (NCR 1997)	X	X	X	X	X	X
Maturity Models						
CMMI (SEI 2002)	X	X		X	X	X
ESI (ESI 1999)	X		X	X	X	X
SMART (Hartman 2000)	X	X	X	X	X	X
BoKs						
Guide to the PMBoK (PMI 2000)	X		X	X	X	X
Handbook of project based management (Turner 1999)	X	X	X			X
IPMA Competency Baseline (IPMA 1999)	X					X
Articles and books						
(Archibald 1976)	X	X				X
(Bissett & Weil 1989)	X	X	X			
(Pinto 1998)	X				X	X
(Turner 1993)	X				X	X

Table 2-3: References for Formal Communication Contents

Depending on project size the use of different control systems is suggested for multi-project environments (Payne 1995, Payne & Turner 1999). It allows for optimisation of the fit between project and control system, but adds a layer of complexity at the management level, because of the need to understand and compare information from different systems (Payne 1995). This potentially impacts the contents and frequency of sponsor – manager communication.

A specific problem in project reporting is the incompatibility of data formats between the accounting systems used in buyer and seller organisations. This is caused by different cost classifications and aggregation levels of data, which historically developed when organisations created their unique costing structure to control and analyse their projects (Frame 1999, Schneider et al. 1995). These classifications range from simple cost accounts to complex coding and breakdown structures. Aligning the data formats and with it the communication between different organisations can become a costly issue (Milinusic 1999). The same problem applies to corporations that change their organisation structure towards smaller and more independent project teams. Here the accounting systems must be adequate for the revised business practices and give a true picture of results and profitability (Selin 1991). Newer accounting standards like activity-based costing or events-based accounting are a step towards more project-related accounting, but are still not compatible with data from earned value measures (Schneider et al. 1995).

For the project manager the problem of incompatibility of earned value numbers and accounting systems applies in two ways, first in obtaining required data for reports from the seller's project accounting systems, and second providing data to the sponsor at the risk that the data are not usable in the accounting system of the buyer organisation. This questions the value of earned value data beyond the level of performance evaluation of individual projects, and suggests a more comprehensive reporting and information exchange between the organisations involved in a project.

The next section addresses the impact of risk on communication between sponsor and manager.

Communication and Risk

PMI's study on the future of project management (PMI 1999) anticipates an increase in project control due to the concern over project risks. The increasing size of projects and the pace of technological advancement, which make new products obsolete by the time they reach the market, are seen as a major driver for increased concern over risk.

The link between communication and project risk was identified by Turner and Cochrane (1993). Their Goals-Methods matrix classified project risks by levels of unclearness of project goals and unclearness of methods to achieve those goals. These risks are reduced through communication. Within a 2 by 2 matrix four different project types and risk types are defined (see Table 2-3). Higher levels of unclearness in goals or methods constitute higher risk.

		Goals well defined	
Methods well defined	No	**Type 2** Product Development	**Type 4** Research & Organisational Change
	Yes	**Type 1** Engineering	**Type 3** Application Software Development
		Yes	No

Table 2-4: Goals and Methods Matrix (Turner & Cochrane 1993)

The four different project types are:

Type 1: Projects with well defined goals and well defined methods to achieve those goals. These projects are of low risk, usually engineering projects, with project plans stating sequences of well defined activities.

Type 2: Projects with clearly defined goals, but poorly defined methods. These projects are usually product development projects of medium risk. They are planned in terms of the final deliverables, with the method of achieving them being planned on a rolling wave basis, i.e. incremental throughout the project, as new information becomes available.

Type 3: Projects with poorly defined goals, but well defined methods. These are often IT application development projects of medium risk. They are planned in terms of life-cycle stages, where goals are defined in conceptual terms, but their specification is refined through the stages of the project.

Type 4: Projects with both poorly defined objectives and methods. These are often research or organisational change projects. These projects are of highest risk and need to go through iterative stages of definition of goals and methods. Through that a project is likely to move in either the Type 2 or Type 3 quadrant where it can be managed as a project of this type.

The impact of risk on project sponsor's and manager's choices in communication frequency, contents and media is not yet researched. Media selection theories from organisational communication theory address the impact of unclear messages, such as in case of unclear objectives or methodologies, on the media choices for communication. These theories are outlined in the next section.

The review of external communication suggestions in the project management literature shows a lack of consistent recommendation on *how* project sponsor and manager should formally communicate with each other during project implementation. Earned value is generally recommended to report project progress, but its data are not usable beyond the boundary of a project because of incompatibility with existing accounting standards and systems. The important area of effectiveness in sponsor – manager communication for project success is not addressed and appears to be an under-researched area in project management.

In the next section the focus is widened from project management to organisational communication theory to identify the underlying factors and theories that drive the communication between sponsor and manager.

2.3 Organisational Communication

A wide variety of communication related research topics developed over time, trying to understand organisational communication from many different perspectives. Organisational communication became a subject of research starting in the 1920s and was shaped in the beginning by interests in business and industrial communication. In the 1980's the focus shifted towards 'the study of messages, information, meaning, and symbolic activity' that constitute organisations (Putnam et al. 1996).

From an organisational communication perspective human communication, such as between project manager and sponsor, is said to occur only when certain conditions are met (Dance 1967, p. 85):

The sufficient condition for the occurrence of communication is therefore some model or construct, within the person's psychological system, of the relationships between some aspect of himself and some aspect of the objects or people or ideas of his world with which he is about to deal.

A basic distinction is made between contents of communication and the way a message is transferred. Dance (1967) distinguishes between communications and communication. Here communications refers to discrete messages, whether transmitted by sound, light, touch, or some other mode, and communication refers to the study of theory and principles underlying the origination, sending, receiving, and interpreting of messages. He categorized communication in three levels, namely intra-personal, inter-personal and organisational. The intra-personal level refers to a person's neurophysiological basis for communications. Next is the level of interpersonal communication, where face-to-face communications are seen as the basis of all human speech communication. Extensions through electronic or other means are only effective relative to the closeness with which the dyadic communication is duplicated. Level three refers to person-to-group communication. Openness or congruence in interpersonal communication leads to openness between the communicating parties. Interpersonal relationships between communicating individuals are impacted by the level of congruence of experience, awareness and communication, to the extent that increasing congruency leads to more accurate mutual understanding, improved psychological adjustment, and mutual satisfaction in the relationship (Dance 1967).

This mutual adjustment is especially important at the interface between project manager and sponsor. Several studies showed the criticality of this interface by observing that performance is higher when 'gatekeepers', such as project managers, assume primary responsibility for coupling the project to other parts of the organisation (Allen et al. 1980, Katz & Tushman 1981, Tushman & Katz 1980, Tushman & Scanlan 1981).

Allen et al. (1980) showed the importance of balancing these procedural aspects with the social aspects in external communication. This is supported by Barry and Crant (2000) who developed the concept of Interactional Richness. This purely theoretically developed concept classifies the dyadic communication (like that of sponsor and manager) along a continuum from expressive to instrumental attributes of a relationship, which explains an interaction partner's behaviour in terms of perceptions of the parties' motivation to maintain the relationship. Expressive attributes refer to the belief that the relationship exists primarily to derive emotional satisfaction, whereas instrumental attributes refer to the parties' motivation to maintain the relationship to fulfil role demands or meet organisational obligations. The model foresees communication mismatch in cases of mixed attributions in the dyad, i.e. one party perceiving the relationship as expressive and the other party as instrumental. Congruent perceptions about the relationship lead to efficiency in communication, better coordination, and higher accuracy of reception and interpretation.

Research on social aspects of communication practices found that organisations use 'genres' of communication. Genres are *socially recognized types of communicative actions'* (Orlikowski & Yates 1994, p. 542), which structure the expectations in interactions through norms in the why, what, how, who/m, when and where of communication (Orlikowski & Yates 1998), e.g. the genre for communication in academic communities is reflected in the media, form and structure of this thesis. Another example is the use of memos or meetings in firms depending on the decision making style – autocratic or democratic – within an organisation. Genres tend to stabilize the communication within and beyond organisations, but can change due to time pressures or other changes in circumstances. Once changed a new genre is added to the existing ones and a repertoire of genres is build up (Orlikowski & Yates 1994).

Huber and Daft (1987) showed that individuals have difficulties anticipating the communication needs of their communication partners. Communication patterns in organisations are based on the organisation's 'sensable' representations of their external environment, i.e. a perception of the environment and not the environment itself. Just like a photograph represents an event, but isn't the event itself. This finding is supported by Maturana & Varela's (1980) *Theory of Autopoeisis and Cognition* which says that externally triggered activities within a living system are not triggered directly by the outside world, but by the living system's internal representation of the outside world.

Translated into project environments this means that project manager and sponsor would not necessarily communicate what the other party expects. Rather than that, communication content, frequency and media would be determined by a representation one party has of the other party's information needs. If this representation is equivocal or non-existing the resulting communication is not likely to meet the receiving party's expectations. This is amplified by the uniqueness in meanings and opinions, which cannot be identical because they are shaped by an individual's position in an organisation. Therefore 'shared' understandings are at best transitory (Shulman 1996). An effect like this is described by Burns and Stalker (1994) as a breakdown in communication between higher levels and lower levels of a company's hierarchy because of substantial differences in technical knowledge, expressed in the use of technical terms that were not understood by higher level managers. The difference in technical knowledge does not inhibit communication *per se*, but the false representation of the information needs within the sender caused a wrong choice of detail in technical discussions.

Given these findings from organisational communication research it is unlikely that a high level of congruence in preferences for communication contents, frequency and media between project managers and sponsors exists.

A central subject in organisational communication research is how senders of information select their media. This is described in the next section.

Communication Media
Communication media refers to the way a message is conveyed from project manager to sponsor and vice versa.

From the dyadic focus of project sponsor – manager communication two broad perspectives of media selection theories exist, these are media richness perspective and social presence perspective (Fulk & Boyd 1991, Trevino et al. 2000, Yoo & Alavi 2001). Media richness perspective focuses on the characteristics of media, such as bandwidth, communication cues and feedback speed (Yoo & Alavi 2001). Social presence perspective advocates that media choice is dependent on the social meaning associated to a medium, i.e. individuals select media based on the value others assign to a medium (Schmitz & Fulk 1991). This is exemplified in the paragraph above about genres through the prevalent communication patterns in organisations and their impact on choices of communication media.

Research studies combining variables from social presence and media richness theory, e.g. Symbolic Interactionism (Trevino et al. 1987), identified the complementary nature of both perspectives (Sitkin et al. 1992). All three theories are described below.

Media Richness Theory
This theory is based on a media's information transfer capabilities. In this theory the concepts of equivocality and uncertainty are theorized as determinant for media selection. Within this context, equivocality is defined as the existence of multiple and conflicting interpretations of an issue, i.e. the ambiguity of a message, whereas uncertainty is the gap between the data that is needed and the data currently available. Media richness is defined as a medium's capacity for transmission of multiple cues and rapid feedback. Following that face-to-face interactions are classified as the richest medium, followed by telephone, and finally written communications as the leanest medium. Rich media are best suited for high equivocal messages where communicators must develop shared meanings in order to communicate effectively, whereas routine messages with clearly understood issues require less rich media (Daft & Lengel 1986, Huber & Daft 1987, Russ et al. 1990).

Equivocality arises within project sponsor - manager communication when project goals are unclear or only ambiguously agreed upon, i.e. the project issues and objectives can be interpreted in multiple ways. This eventually leads to conflict and can end up in project failure (Oz & Sosik 2000). Projects with unclear objectives or methodologies are classified by Turner & Cochrane (1993) as risk projects and are described above. The application of media richness theory to this risk classification indicates a relationship between project objective equivocality and use of rich media. Similarly, the extent of clearness of methodology used (combined with the methodologies general recommendations for written communication) indicates a relationship between methodology clearness and use of written media.

Media richness is the most popular theory for research in media selection which among other results showed that:

- Preference for rich media increases with non-routine management problems, and high performing managers are more sensitive to the richness requirements in media selection than low performing manager (Lengel & Daft 1988)

- Accounting/finance managers have a lower demand for rich media. Their relative independence from other organisations require fewer face-to-face meetings (Donabedian et al. 1998)

- Individual differences in media choice appear more in low equivocality communication. High equivocality masks these individual differences (Trevino et al. 1990). This was criticized for ignoring factors like communication comprehension and self-monitoring, which were found significantly related to media selection (Alexander et al. 1991).

A meta-analysis of over 40 studies showed that managers in higher levels of the organisation prefer richer media over managers at lower levels (Rice & Shook 1990). This complements research by Lee and Heath (1999) on media attitudes on the side of message receivers which showed that managers preferred richer media for keeping up-to-date on immediate and relevant issues. Managers' response to external information was done through phone calls in 98.5% of all cases.

Social Presence Theory

This theory was developed as a response to the criticism media richness theory received for ignoring the contextual aspects of media choices. Media choice in group communication was found to be based on media richness as described above, but also socially influenced through co-worker and Supervisor attitudes towards a specific media (Schmitz & Fulk 1991). Social influences were consistently stronger when individuals were highly attracted to their work groups (Fulk 1993).

Symbolic Interactionism

In an attempt to mix media richness and social presence Trevino et al. (1987) showed that media richness, symbolic values of communication media, and situational pressures are related. Their findings showed that:

- face-to-face communication is used for difficult ambiguous non-routine messages, discussions, and to express emotions

- written media is used to show authority, lack of urgency, get attention, make strong impressions, be official, or to comply with protocol. However, written media requires shared meanings to exist, which are often established through prior face-to-face communication

- telephone and electronic mail is used when communication is constrained by time and distance pressures. In addition electronic mail is also used because of individual preferences

- Media choices are made based on geographical or timely constraints first, followed by content or symbolic reasons, with a tendency towards higher priority for contents variables.

Trevino et al. (2000) showed that people select media that they believe are liked by the message recipient. Furthermore it supported the complementary view of social and media richness perspective, with the former primarily influencing media choice and the latter media attitude.

The review of media choice theories indicated that the popular media richness theory and the Goals - Methods concept of project risk are both based on the concept of unclearness of messages and lack of required data. The concepts of media richness and risk have not yet been applied together, so that there is no indication how project risk impacts the choice of media in project sponsor - manager communication.

The review of organisational communication theory in the context of dyadic buyer-seller relationships showed that sponsors and managers are not likely to have similar requirements for contents, frequency and media in their formal communication. That has a potential impact on the effectiveness of their communication and the outcome of projects. The review did not provide an answer to the research problem stated in Chapter 1 and needs further research.

The next section reviews the literature on the often cited impact of organisation structure on communication.

2.4 Organisational Structure and Communication

Organisation is a means to achieve co-operation between the members of a firm. Setting up an organisation confers and defines certain rights to control the activity of one self or others and to receive information, together with obligations to accept, control and transmit information (Burns & Stalker 1994).

The purpose of structuring organisations is to divide the work among the members of an organisation and to co-ordinate the members' activities so that they can be directed towards the organisation's goals. An organisation's structure defines the relationships among the positions in the organisation and among members of the organisation. Structure creates a framework of order and command, which provides for the planning, organizing, directing and controlling of tasks (Mullins 1999b).

The literature suggests different communication needs for different organisation structures, due to their differences in information processing capabilities and requirements (Galbraith & Lawler 1993, Nonaka & Takeuchi 1995).

Research literature on organisational structure, as it relates to communication, can be categorized in three parallel streams, which are all pursued at present and findings of one stream can be applied in the others (McPhee &Poole 2000):

1. The traditional *dimensional* approach, which identifies structural features of organisations and relate them to communication variables and processes. It's a reductionistic approach where communication is seen as contingent on some variables of an organisation's structure.

2. The *configurational* approach investigates the complexity of structures and the impact on and from communication. This holistic approach attempts to comprehend the impact of new information technologies and other factors on organisational design.

3. *New views* of structural dimensions consider structure primarily as a communicative phenomenon. This approach assumes communication to shape organisational structures.

The three streams are described below.

Dimensional approaches to organisation

This stream assumes that organisational structures determine communication processes to a greater extent than communication processes are thought to shape organisational characteristics (Krone et al. 1987).

Several models for organisational structures exist, which can be identified in a continuum from bureaucratic or mechanistic to networked or organic structures. Bureaucratic organisation structures are described as focused on efficiency, achieved through work specialization in a hierarchical relationship. This form of structure is suitable for relatively stable environments, where the communication with the environment is formal and structured, and mainly related to specific areas of specialization (Dixon 1996, Mintzberg 1982, Morgan 1996). Mechanistic or bureaucratic structures involve more control over the members of an organisation and generally less flexibility than organic structures. This is identified through the three dimensions of organisational properties: differentiation, centralization and formalization. Differentiation refers to the extent work is divided up into ever-smaller sets of tasks which can be rigidly distinguished from each other, as opposed to integration of diverse tasks into more meaningful work assignments for individuals in organic organisations. Centralization is the tendency in bureaucracies to grant decision making authority to the top of an organisation, as opposed to delegation based on competence or geographic responsibility. Formalization refers to the extent rules and procedures mandated for work are explicitly stated, usually in writing (McPhee & Poole 2000). The level of centralization, differentiation and formalization decreases from mechanistic to organic structures. At the same time communication frequency increases because of the increasing needs for feedback, error correction and synthesis of different points of view (Burns & Stalker 1994).

Burns and Stalker (1994) distinguished in their model between mechanistic and organic structures, where:

> *The distinction between organic and mechanistic is not a dichotomy; rather, these two forms represent the extreme points on a continuum. This means that there are intermediate stages and that organizations can oscillate between these forms as the rate of change varies* (Weick 1987, p.110).

Organic organisations put lesser emphasis on hierarchies, but more on expertise, co-operation and commitment to the firm. The higher level of co-operation requires an increase in communication (Burns & Stalker 1994).

Research by Huber & Daft (1987) showed that characteristics of the environment, such as information load, complexity and turbulence affect organisational communications. This is supported by Tushman's (1979a, 1979b) research on external communication in organisations with high levels of change in their environment. He showed that increases in environmental change requires the communicating individuals to increase their understanding of mutual information needs, while, at the same time, the number of resources in an organisation communicating with the environment decreases. High performing organisations show flexibility in adjusting their communication capabilities to the communication requirements of their environment. Galbraith and Lawler (1993) investigated the relationship between environmental uncertainty, information processing and organisation structure. In line with many other writers they concluded that dynamic organisations require more information processing because of horizontal and vertical information flows, which are needed to remain responsive to constant challenges from outside.

From the review of literature in the dimensional stream the following impact of organisation structure on communication frequency, contents and media is proposed:

- Communication occurs *more frequently in organic organisations* because of their need for increased capacity for feedback, error correction and synthesis of different points of view (e.g. Tushman & Nadler 1978, Burns & Stalker 1994, Galbraith & Lawler 1993).

- Mechanistic organisation structure and mechanistic communication contents are linked (McPhee & Poole 2000). Members of bureaucratic organisations are expected to have a clearer understanding of the specialized issue they are communicating. Communication content in mechanistic organisations is reduced to numbers or other measures (Burns & Stalker 1994). Given that, it is expected that the emphasis on quantitative measures, like quality data and earned value results, will be higher in bureaucratic structures.

- In organic organisation structures, when compared with mechanistic structures, more ambiguous and equivocal messages prevail due to the need for increased horizontal communication. While bureaucratic structures rely on written reports, organic structures require richer, more interactive communication media (Burns & Stalker 1994).

Organisation structures in projects are usually classified in a similar way from bureaucratic to organic (Andersen 2000). The applicability of the combined communication and organisation theories listed above for temporary project organisations is not yet researched.

Configurational Approaches to Organisation

This approach tries to understand organisations as a whole, without treating communication as a separate variable. Configurational approaches investigate the processes and communication flows within organisations to identify an overall structure. That allows to comprehend traditional structures, like bureaucracies, as well as newer or emerging ones, e.g. 'organisational networks' or 'virtual organisations'. A prominent representative of this approach is Mintzberg's (1982), who identified five different structures with a decreasing level of centralism and control, while at the same time an increasing level of communication. His most mechanistic structure, i.e. the machine structure, is similar to Burns and Stalker's (1994) mechanistic structure. Despite its prominence the Mintzberg model lacks empirical support. McPhee and Poole (2000, p. 513) report that Mintzberg's theory was only tested once. This test by Doty et al. (1993) showed that firms do not structure their organisations consistent with their contexts in terms of Mintzberg's typologies.

Morgan (1996) took a different approach by defining organisations in different metaphors. He argues

> *...that all theories of organization and management are based on implicit images or metaphors that lead us to see, understand, and manage organizations in distinctive yet partial ways* (p. 4).

He describes eight different metaphors starting also with a mechanistic metaphor by describing organisations as machines. One of the metaphors describes organisations as information processing brains with distributed data and communication structures, and increasing communication requirements.

Companies may also engage in organisation networks, which are characterized by a set of organisations connected by a set of relationships. The company is acting as a node in a network and the relationships are the links between the companies. The dimensions of links are content and strength (Warner 1996), where content is classified by communication content, exchange content, and normative content (Mitchell 1973). The interdependent relationships within the network require instant communication in all directions (Hastings 1995).

These views of organisation are challenged as being not comprehensive enough and overly simplified models of a complex structure (Donaldson 1996). From a postmodernist perspective it is argued that organisations are better understood by learning what they are not, thus learning not to fall victim of the seductive imagery of organizing (Kreiner 1992). However, there are no indications in this part of the literature that communication requirements with external organisations will be different than described by the models above. Generally speaking, tall and hierarchical organisation structures impede communication, whereas flat, organic structures facilitate communication and the emergence of communication networks (Loo 1995).

Another picture evolves by looking at organisations from a process perspective. This becomes increasingly important because of the benefits that companies recently achieved by redesigning their organisations around their core processes (Hammer & Stanton 1999). Garvin (1998) defines a process framework for the management of companies. As outlined in Table 2-4 it consists of the managerial processes for direction setting, negotiation and selling, as well as monitoring and control. These processes are mapped against three operational processes:

- Work processes, for accomplishing tasks such as product or service delivery and tasks that are necessary to run the business.

- Behavioural processes, as the sequences of steps used for accomplishing the cognitive and interpersonal aspects of work, including communication processes.

- Change processes, to grow individuals, groups and organisations.

This process based framework helps to identify roles and responsibilities that have not been defined before, together with its required communication needs. The framework reflects the different perspectives of buyer and seller organisation, where the buyer organisation's focus is on change processes, and the seller organisation focus is on work processes.

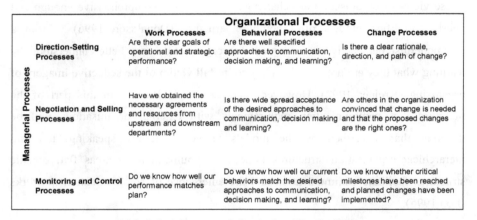

		Organizational Processes		
		Work Processes	Behavioral Processes	Change Processes
Managerial Processes	Direction-Setting Processes	Are there clear goals of operational and strategic performance?	Are there well specified approaches to communication, decision making, and learning?	Is there a clear rationale, direction, and path of change?
	Negotiation and Selling Processes	Have we obtained the necessary agreements and resources from upstream and downstream departments?	Is there wide spread acceptance of the desired approaches to communication, decision making and learning?	Are others in the organization convinced that change is needed and that the proposed changes are the right ones?
	Monitoring and Control Processes	Do we know how well our performance matches plan?	Do we know how well our current behaviors match the desired approaches to communication, decision making, and learning?	Do we know whether critical milestones have been reached and planned changes have been implemented?

Table 2-5: A Framework for Action (Garvin 1998)

Viewing organisations as processes allows to draw models of organisations as networks, where nodes represent the functional elements, and links represent their relationships, with the passing of knowledge, service or products (Turner 1997). This is visualized through organigraphs, a method of drawing organisational charts, which takes account of the process nature of a firm by introducing new components, such as hubs and webs to reflect the various ways people organize themselves at work. The distinction is drawn between chains, which reflect the traditional management of subsequent activities, the hubs, as coordination centres of activities, and webs as networked nodes with open ended communication and continuous movement of people and ideas (Mintzberg & Van der Heyden 1999).

Building on the information processing view of organisations in a networked structure Levitt et al. (1999) developed a simulation tool for project level information processing, communication and coordination. With a complex set of parameters it models the degree of incongruent goals between agents, as well as their information processing and communication behaviours. In terms of external communication processes the tool appears to be overly simplified. It assumes that every time a project manager receives a report from a project team member a message is sent to the project manager's supervisor, based on the supervisor's preference for micro-management and the degree of incongruent goals between supervisor and project manager. While that may be the case for company internal projects, it does not reflect the complex relationship between a seller organisation and its external customer.

The review of the *configurational* stream of organisation research showed that this stream is generally inward looking and does not provide new insights in inter-organisational communication requirements in buyer - seller relationships.

New Views to Organisation

This approach sees structure as a result of communication. Examples are the Formal Structural Communication Theory, which states that communication follows a prior meta-communication about structure. Examples are announcements about reporting relationships within organisations, which shape the communication between the individuals comprising the organisation (McPhee 1985, 1989, cited by McPhee &Poole 2000). Another perspective is provided through Taylor (1999) and the Text/Conversation Theory. Here communication is seen as a continuous repetition of communication circles where individuals represent their community (like project manager and sponsor represent their respective organisation) and communicate on their behalf through a translation of text (the message contents) to conversation (the transfer of the contents). Subsequent listening to speakers is a backward transformation from conversation to text, where the communication is merged with own opinions, which lead to a new round of text/conversation as described in the first step.

From the review of literature in *New Structural Dimensions* it can be concluded that the literature in this stream does not clarify the details of the communication processes *between* organisations, such as in IT delivery projects. No indication is given on the information content, frequency and media used in different organisational settings.

Organisational Support of Projects

However independent the project teams operate at the customer site they need a minimum level of support from their respective organisations to function successfully. Regularly held management reviews are the most common way for management to assess project progress and to give the project teams a forum to raise issues and discuss possible changes to project scope, time or budget. Especially in parallel team structures, with project teams in the buyer and seller organisation working jointly on a project, an explicit mechanism, in the form of a management or steering committee meeting, is needed to respond to recommendations raised by either of the teams (Galbraith & Lawler 1993). In networks of projects it is recommended to institutionalise this function through either the above mentioned steering committees or a project controller (Gareis 1992). The PRINCE 2 project management methodology (CCTA 2000) suggests that the Steering Committee, also called Project Board, should consist of representatives from the project's business management, users and suppliers. These members should have managerial authority because of the need for resource commitment (Cooper 2000). User representation is important, as shown by research on the measurement of end-user computing satisfaction, which showed that user involvement had a significant positive correlation with user satisfaction (Doll & Torkzadeh 1988).

Research on organisational support (Johns 1999) showed that project plans and formal management committees are frequently established, but management reviews are rarely held in practice. Furthermore, the extension of project requirements beyond the project team and into the functional organisation is lacking, and mechanisms for sharing and resolving resource issues are seldom in place. Line managers' performance evaluation is seldom tight to their degree of support of cross-functional project teams.

The sole communication through a supplier's project manager to the buyer's organisation has been criticized by Kerzner (1982) as being a bottleneck in communication and a creation of a buyer's perception that information is filtered before it is communicated. This does not take into account the environmental situation as investigated by Tushman (1979b) and Allen et al. (1980), who developed a contingency relationship between the centralization of communication and increase in environmental change.

The project sponsor's role has been described as being critical for the success of a project, due to the power and willingness to use the power to the benefit of the project. Sponsors can be found in various roles, such as the creative originator of the project's idea, as entrepreneur, senior manager, or even the project manager itself (Pinto & Slevin 1989). The sponsor should set the stakeholder expectations from the outset and closely monitor the project's progress for early identification of deviations from plan and launch of corrective actions. For that it is recommended to have frequent communication between the sponsor and the project manager (Wright 1997). This leads back to the original question which contents, frequency and media should be used for effective formal communication between project sponsor and manager.

2.5 Conclusions from the Literature Review

The project management literature recommends earned value as communication contents and a variety of other status and trend information, as well as a wide range of possible communication frequencies and media. Risk was identified as being influential on communication. Organisational communication theory indicates that the difference in buyer or seller perspective will lead to different communication requirements. Literature on organisational structure showed that organisations have a wide range of possible communication requirements, determined by their type of organisational structure. More research is required to identify the communication needs in different organisational structures and how they can be matched in projects where different organisation structures have to mutually satisfy their communication requirements. This follows Huber and Daft's (1987) recommendation for more research in how organisations should design their environment sensing and information processing system. How that is done is described in the next chapter.

CHAPTER THREE - RESEARCH MODEL

This chapter starts by presenting the model of the overall research and a discussion of the related variables. Subsequently a set of two research questions and six hypotheses are developed, guided by the literature review. The final section lists the theories underlying the research model and hypotheses.

3.1 Research Model

The underlying axiom of the research is that effectiveness in project sponsor – manager communication is achieved through a fit in communication requirements of one party and information processing capacity of the other party (see Figure 3-1). Similar axioms were used by Bensaou and Ventkatraman (1996), as well as Tushman 1979a) whose research showed the link between effectiveness in inter-organisational communications and improved organisational results.

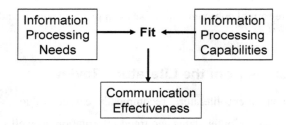

Figure 3-2: Information Processing Model

The research framework follows Pettigrew et al. (1992) and distinguishes context from process and contents. Situational and structural variables provide the context domain and communication variables define the contents and process domain. This approach is supported by Fichman and Goodman (1996) for buyer - seller studies. They distinguish between three levels of relationships, namely context, the dyadic relationship between buyer and supplier, and the individual. Their recommendation is for researchers to consider all three levels simultaneously to gain a fuller understanding of the dynamics of ties between buyer and seller. The dyadic nature of project sponsor-manager communication and the dependence of this communication on contextual factors supports the application of this model for this research. Figure 3-2 is a schema of the overall research model. The contextual differences of buyer and seller are assessed through three situational variables, which are organisation structure, relational norms and project risk. The influence of these situational variables on patterns of communication frequency, contents and media is assessed on the dyadic level of the Fichman and Goodman model. Third and last the congruency and effectiveness of project sponsor - manager communication patterns are assessed.

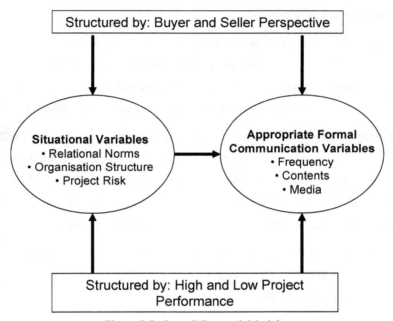

Figure 3-3: Overall Research Model

The underlying assumption that organisational properties determine communication processes (Krone et al. 1987) identifies the direction of impact as one from the organisational context onto the communication practices.

The results of each step are structured by buyer and seller perspective as well as high and low project performance (further discussed in chapter 4). That allows for assessment of information processing effectiveness as shown in Figure 3-1.

3.2 Research Questions and Hypotheses

The review of literature in project management, organisational communication and organisational structure theory did not provide an answer to the question how the different communication requirements of sponsors and managers are fulfilled to the satisfaction of both organisations. Three situational variables were identified to impact communication. These are a) the relational norms between buyer and seller, b) the organisation structures of the buying and selling firm, and c) the project's risk level. The impact of these variables on communication frequency, contents and media lead to the first research question:

> Q1. How do organisational structure, relational norms and project
> risk impact preferences for communication frequency,
> contents and media of project sponsors and managers in their
> formal communication during implementation of IT projects?

Differences in buyer and seller perspective towards a project were identified as impacting communication requirements. Effectiveness in communication was described as a congruency of communication requirements and capabilities of both sponsor and manager. Research question Q2 addresses the effectiveness of communication at the interface of the two independent organisations:

> Q2. How effective is the formal communication between project
> sponsors and project managers during IT project
> implementation?

In relation to research question Q2 organisational communication theory indicated different communication requirements, expressed as different communication preferences of project sponsor and manager. That leads to research hypothesis H1:

> H 1: There will be a significant difference between communication
> preferences of project sponsors from buyer firms and those of
> project managers from IT seller firms in terms of preferred
> communication frequency, contents and media.

Organisation structure was identified as being influential on the amount of communication, the media and contents used. The applicability of these findings from research in permanent organisations needs to be tested in temporary inter-organisational buyer - seller relationships, established for the implementation of IT projects. That leads to research hypotheses H2 to H4:

H 2: There will be a positive relationship between the extent of organic organisation structure and communication frequency. The more organic the organisation, the higher the frequency in communication.

H 3: There will be a negative relationship between the level of organic organisation structure and the use of lean media. Bureaucratic organisation structures will favour written reports, while organic structures favour more interactive media like verbal communication or face-to-face meetings.

H 4: There will be a negative relationship between the extent of organic organisation structure and the use of quantitative measures, like quality metrics and earned value numbers. Bureaucratic structures will favour quantitative data.

Project risk was identified in the Goals-Methods matrix as a function of unclearness of goals and unclearness of methods to achieve those goals. Media richness theory showed the link between unclear messages and the media used for communication. Research hypotheses H5 and H6 identify the link between project risk and communication media:

H 5: There will be a positive relationship between project goal equivocality and media richness; rich media (e.g. face-to-face meetings) will be selected for communications in projects with unclear goals, and lean media (i.e. written communication) in projects with clearly defined goals.

H 6: There will be a positive relationship between clearness of methodology and the use of written media for communications.

The aims of the research are to narrow a potential gap in communication between sponsor and manager and to provide a model for the industry to optimise communication effectiveness. That will allow to positively impact performance in project implementation through better communication between buyer and seller firm (Tushman 1979a).

3.2.1 Summary of Underlying Theories

The overall theoretical perspective is that of TCE and Agency Theory. The literature review identified the following theories as underlying the situational variables of:

- Relational norms: Heide & John's (1992) relational extension of TCE.

- Organisation structure: theories that describe a continuum from mechanistic or bureaucratic to organic or networked organisation structures, such as Burns & Stalker (1994), Morgan (1996) and Galbraith (1993). The one-dimensional nature of this continuum allows an assessment of all possible stages of organic organisation structures and is therefore equally applicable for permanent organisations of buyer firms, as for temporary project organisations of IT vendors. Burns and Stalker's (1994) model is especially recommended by McPhee & Poole (2000, p. 514) because of its appropriateness for testing consistency traits, such as the relationship between mechanistic organisation and mechanistic communication.

- Project risk: the Goals-Methods Matrix of project management risk theory (Turner & Cochrane 1993).

- Media choice: Media Richness Theory (Daft & Lengel 1986).

The relationships between research questions, constructs and hypotheses are outlined in Appendix A-1. Questionnaire items to measure the concepts of communication frequency, contents and media are based on the results of the project management literature review.

Theories underlying the structural variable 'Buyer – Seller Perspective' are those which identified differences in project perspectives due to an individual's role as manager or sponsor (Garvin 1998, Partington 1997, Turner & Keegan 2000).

The addition of a variable to categorize communication by project performance follows the recommendations of two focus groups, which were setup to validate the research model (further described in Chapter 4). The groups strongly recommended this additional variable to accommodate the differences in communication in high and low performing projects. The concept is based on research by Wateridge (1998), who developed a set of IT related success criteria that go beyond the narrow time, budget and specification view towards projects success and integrate stakeholder perceptions into the concept of success.

The methodology for the present study is described in the next Chapter.

CHAPTER FOUR – METHODOLOGY

The purpose of this chapter is threefold. First, to outline the reasoning for the methodological approach which fits the overall research objective outlined in Chapter 1 and research questions in Chapter 3. Second, to describe the research design and methodological approach taken. Third, describe the data collection process, the instrument used and the techniques for analysing the data.

This chapter is organized in three main sections. It starts with the underlying assumptions of the research, like purpose of the study, methodologies and underlying philosophy. This is followed by a section on quantitative research design, which comprises the development and refinement of the data gathering process and tool, followed by the sample and its demographics. The final section describes the qualitative methodology used. A short summary is provided at the end of each main section.

4.1 Purpose of this Research

This research has three purposes. Firstly, to answer the research questions stated in Chapter 3. This will narrow the knowledge gap identified by the research questions through testing the model of project sponsor – manager communication, which serves as the basis for improvements in communication effectiveness during IT project implementation. The research achieves this by identifying communicational 'best-fit' situations where communication requirements and capabilities from buyer and seller organisations match. This match will allow for communicating the 'right' message at the right time, which lowers misunderstandings, the costs for reworking, disappointments and communication efforts. It improves overall project profitability.

The second purpose of the research is to advance the existing body of knowledge in project management and organisational communication. Thirdly, all research on the functioning of organisations ultimately benefits society. This implies that improved understanding of communication will lead to some form of progress other than purely academic (Partington 1997). However, practitioners will incorporate results generated through academically accepted research methods only if the results are relevant to and interpretable for the practitioner community (Mohrman, et al. 2001). The relevance of this research for the practitioner community is addressed in the Introductory Chapter.

4.1.1 Research Methodologies

The methodology is the procedural framework within which the research is conducted. It describes the approach for operationalising the research process (Remenyi et al. 1998).

All research approaches have individual strengths and weaknesses. Therefore research designs and strategies can be offset by counterbalancing strengths and weaknesses from one another (Easterby-Smith et al. 1991). McGrath (1982) identifies four major research strategies (see Figure 4-1), which are accomplished through eight different research methods. McGrath notes that there is no single research method that achieves all of the three overarching research objectives of generalizability (A), precision in control and measurement (B), and existential realism (C). As can be seen from the positioning of the letters A, B, and C around the circle in 4-1, the three objectives are achieved through very different methodologies.

While laboratory experiments (B) yield the highest precision in measurement, the research results are flawed in generalizability and existential realism. Accordingly, when generalization is highest with sample surveys and formal theory (A), then precision is low and realism is low. The only way to mitigate the apparent weaknesses of any one methodology is through application of several methodologies to the same research problem (McGrath 1982).

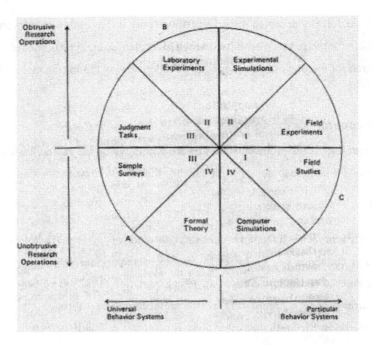

Figure 4-4: Research Strategies (Runkel and McGrath 1972)

This methodological pluralism is also essential for balancing inherent flaws in the reliability and validity (terms explained in section 4.4.4.2 and 4.4.4.3 respectively) of the measurement constructs of each of these methods, thus a multi-method approach enhances the validity of the research constructs (McGrath 1982, Remenyi et al. 1998), and allows for more confidence in the research results (Jick 1979). A combination of several methodologies and their results in the study of the same phenomenon allows for greater accuracy in the results and is known as triangulation (Jick 1979). Easterby-Smith et al. (1991) go further than pure methodological triangulation and list four different types of triangulation, with:

- Theory triangulation, i.e. borrowing models from one discipline and using them to explain phenomena in another discipline.

- Data triangulation involves data collected over different time frames or from different sources.

- Investigator triangulation refers to situations where different people collect data from the same situation.

- Methodological triangulation involves the combination of methodologies in the study of the same phenomenon (Jick 1979 citing Denzin 1978).

Jick (1979) distinguishes methodological triangulations in within-methods and between-methods. The former refers to the use of multiple scales for indices focused on the same construct in a questionnaire, which involves cross checking for internal consistency and reliability. Jick defines a continuum of methodological triangulations starting from simple within-method triangulations to more complex ones. The latter involves the use of complementary methodologies like quantitative and qualitative approaches which can capture a more complete, holistic and contextual portrayal of the phenomena under study. Silverman (1993) suggests that triangulation should start from a theoretical perspective and use methods and data that allow for structure and meaning within that perspective.

The theoretical framework of the present study is established through a quantitative study ("A" in 4-1) using a worldwide survey. A subsequent qualitative study ("C" in Figure 4-1) uses interviews to explore the communication practices of project sponsors and managers and to explain the results of the first study. Through that the research model is tested and subsequently validated. This approach led to a refinement of the model, confirmation of parts of it, and some additional findings. This methodological triangulation of quantitative results from a survey with qualitative results from interviews is frequently recommended by researchers (Jick 1979, Bartunek & Seo 2001, Möbius 2002). The *sequential mixed method design* applied in this study allows for thorough explanation of the assumptions behind each of the two phases by avoiding the difficulties arising from a simultaneous application of the two approaches (Tashakkori and Teddlie 1998).

The next section describes the philosophical implications of using quantitative and qualitative methodologies.

4.2 Research Philosophy

The different methodologies applied in this study are based on different philosophical perspectives, which need to be considered for the design of the research and the interpretation of the results. Easterby-Smith et al. (1991) give three reasons that underlay the importance of understanding philosophical issues. Firstly the clarifications of research design, i.e. the methods and the evidence to be collected for the research. Secondly, philosophical knowledge will help the researcher to recognize which research designs will work for a particular study. Thirdly, the knowledge of philosophy helps the researcher to identify or create designs outside the researcher's experience. This also includes the adaptation of designs in accordance with the constraints of different subject or knowledge structures.

Two central concepts of philosophy have to be considered to match research approach and underlying philosophy, these are ontology and epistemology.

4.2.1 Ontology

Ontology is the science or study of *being* and often used synonymously with Metaphysics, one of the oldest branches of philosophy. It analyses and systemizes all concepts that are not the exclusive property of any special science, like those of nature, space, time, history and society (Bunge 1996).

Most of the ontological choices are represented as a dichotomy of two extremes, often called positivism and phenomenology (Easterby-Smith et al. 1991, Bogdan & Taylor 1975, Bryman 1988), or realism and constructivism (Blaikie 1993). The polar extremes are generally:

- Positivism: the social world exists externally, is objective and its properties should be measured through objective methods, not inferred subjectively (Easterby-Smith et al. 1991).

- Phenomenology: reality is subjective and interpreted by members of a society (Blaikie 1993).

These two stances are widely debated as to their applicability in the social sciences. In Table 4-1 Easterby-Smith et al. (1991) map these two paradigms against the researcher's work, with a paradigm being a model or a very clear and typical example (Cambridge 2001).

	Positivist paradigm	Phenomenological paradigm
Basic beliefs:	The world is external and objective	The world is socially constructed and subjective
	Observer is independent	Observer is part of what is observed
	Science is value-free	Science is driven by human interest
Researcher should:	Focus on facts	Focus on meanings
	Look for causality and fundamental laws	Try to understand what is happening
	Reduce phenomena to simplest elements	Look at the totality of each situation
	Formulate hypotheses and then test them	Develop ideas through induction from data
Preferred methods include:	Operationalising concepts so that they can be measured	Using multiple methods to establish different views of phenomena
	Taking large samples	Small samples investigated in depth over time

Table 4-6: Key Features of Positivist and Phenomenological Paradigms (Easterby-Smith et al. 1991)

Positivistic research is based on established scientific methods valid for all forms of inquiry or domains of research. Positivists search for regularities and causal relationships through a process of reductionism, where the whole is further and further reduced into its constituent parts. Positivism is not related to any political, cultural, moral or ideological beliefs. Logic and mathematics provide its foundation and with it a universal language and formal basis for quantitative analysis (Hirschheim 1985). Positivistic research derives hypotheses from existing theories, often in form of postulated causal connections between entities, which are then submitted to empirical tests (Bryman 1988).

This reliance on existing theories is proposed by some philosophers as ensuring the required precision in defining the research (e.g. Bunge 1996), while it is criticized by opponents as preservation of older theories and not necessarily better theories (Feyerabend 1975).

Positivistic approaches are mainly based on observations and use the stages of literature review, hypotheses development, evidence collection, testing and analysis, as well as finally confirming and refining theory (Remenyi et al. 1998). Depending on the form of evidence collection and the research questions a quantitative or qualitative analysis will be used to establish the research results. Phenomenological research approaches are less strict in their starting point. The nature of the phenomena and the expected outcomes may also impact the decision on the nature of the evidence collection, i.e. whether quantitative or qualitative data are collected (Remenyi et al. 1998).

Phenomenologists (see Table 4-1) propose that only phenomena exist, i.e. a bundle of appearances for someone, and scientists should only study phenomena and the related human experience (Bunge 1996). Through the study of phenomena Phenomenologists try to understand and explain *why* people have different experiences and meanings (Easterby-Smith et al. 1991). With their specific methodologies they try to see the world as seen by the subjects they observe (Bogdan & Taylor 1975). Phenomenologists argue that the complexities of social science cannot be captured with positivistic methodologies. They recommend a more holistic view, which is opposed to the reductionist view of positivists. Symons (1996, p. 108) warns of a too strict polarization between the two paradigms by stating that:

> *The present day metaphysical stance of the phenomenologist is something of a reaction to the extremes of positivism. But, the extremes of phenomenology can lead to research where the validity is so questionable that it renders the work nugatory for all practical purposes.*

In between the two polar positions are a series of ontological stances that provide a mixed perspective. The popular realist paradigm focuses on structure and mechanisms of reality, which may or may not be observed (Symons 1996). Bashkar (1975), representing the transcendental realist, asserts that statements of laws are tendency statements, and these tendencies may be unexercised, exercised unrealized, or realized unperceived by men. Wicks and Freeman (1998) argue for a pragmatist ontology which rejects the positivists' sharp outline of categories, and the phenomenologists' 'illusionary' world. They argue that 'The world is out there, but not objective', and that any attempt to articulate situations becomes subjective. Thus reality can be experienced as in everyday life, but there is no truly objective account of a situation.

These theoretical concepts are only ideal types (Symons 1996) and when it comes to research these differences are not as distinct as outlined above. Easterby-Smith et al. (1991) show that some of the most well known studies either use mixed approaches by backing up quantitative results through qualitative studies or vice versa. They also found that researchers increasingly mix methods to some extent because it provides more perspectives on the phenomena being investigated.

This is also done in the present study, which starts from a positivist stance. Objective methods and techniques, such as a worldwide survey and quantitative analysis, are used to identify an objective 'common denominator' in formal communication of project sponsors and managers. These quantitative results are then backed up and complemented using results from a qualitative inquiry.

4.2.2 Epistemology

Epistemology comprises the concepts of knowledge, science, model and testability (Bunge 1996). It is closely linked with the ontological stance one takes. Due to the nature of their ontological difference positivists and phenomenologists try to answer slightly different questions. While positivists look for facts and causes to try to answer *What* and *How* questions, phenomenologists' attempt to explain human behaviour through questions on *Why* something happens. To that end the two approaches are complementary for the understanding of phenomena in communication studies (Miller 2002). The complementary questions and their associated analysis results together provide a more holistic understanding of project sponsor and manager communication and will therefore be applied in the present study.

To justify their findings many researchers rely on the scrutiny of the community of scholars to safeguard objectivity and growth of knowledge through publicly discussing and testing their research (Miller 2001). This provides for an in-depth assessment on a research's contribution to knowledge, which is at the heart of epistemology, where knowledge is seen as a development from a gestalt to an understood structure:

> *Knowledge arises in experience. It emerges from reflection. It develops through inference. It exhibits a distinctive structure* (Audi 1998, p. 214).

Through public scrutiny the researchers implicitly obey Popper's rule of falsification, i.e. a theory is validated not by testing it for being true, but by not being able to refute it (Popper cited by Silverman 1993).

For the present study the scrutiny of the academic and professional community was achieved through presentations of incremental research results at several research conferences and publications in refereed and acknowledged international journals, as summarized in Table 7-2 in the conclusions section.

The basic beliefs and researcher's focus were discussed above. A summary of the methodological and philosophical assumptions follow.

4.2.3 Summary of Underlying Assumptions

The field of project management is perceived as a relatively young academic discipline in the social sciences. Advancing the theory in project management through applied research will benefit the project management practitioners and scholars through increased understanding and practical usability of the results.

Chapter 1 has identified project sponsor – manager communication as an important factor for project success. However, the literature review in Chapter 2 showed:

- a lack of consistent recommendations on when to communicate, how often, and with which media, and

- a lack of theory about *How* project sponsors and managers communicate.

The present research intends to address these questions, and is based on the following assumptions:

- purposeful research will provide answers to the research questions, contribute to the advancement of the Body of Knowledge in Project Management, and advance organisational science through theories derived from applied and relevant research

- the researcher's underlying philosophical stance is that of positivism

---

- the starting point of the research is a set of hypotheses derived from the literature review, which define the framework for the inquiry in the communication practices of IT project sponsors and managers worldwide

- the degree of researcher involvement in the research process is minimized through use of survey techniques and structured interviews

- knowledge is gained though use of quantitative and qualitative methods, i.e. surveys and interviews, to triangulate and validate research findings and provide them to the community for test and public scrutiny.

The remainder of this chapter describes the steps to execute the research model.

4.3 Research Model Execution

The overall research model is described in Chapter 3. The model is executed through two steps described below. Step 1 assesses the impact of situational variables on communication variables at the level of individual variables and also as a set of variables. Constructs, which are used to measure the variables of the model, are necessarily hypothetical concepts and not directly observable events. They are abstractions used to explain apparent phenomena, whose existence must be inferred from observable actions or features (Morgeson & Hofmann 1999). Project Risk e.g. is not directly observable, but is assessed through two constructs consisting of a set of related questions, where one accounts for the level of clearness in project objectives and the other for the clearness in methods to achieve these objectives.

The two steps for executing the research model are as follows:

4.3.1   Step 1: Situational Factors as Antecedents of Communication Patterns

Step 1 examines the impact of the individual situational variables for relational norms, organisational structure, and project risk on project managers and sponsors preferences in communication frequency, contents and media for their formal communication with each other. This addresses research questions Q1 and tests hypotheses H2 to H6. The variables are based on prior research which identified organisation structure, and coordination mechanisms as the two dimensions effecting

---

information processing capacity in organisations (Tushman & Nadler 1978, Huber & Daft 1987). In accordance with the underlying assumption of causality, the situational variables are classified as independent variables and the communication preferences as dependent variables. A definition of the research variables is provided in Appendix A-2. Figure 4-2 below shows the path model of the relationships investigated.

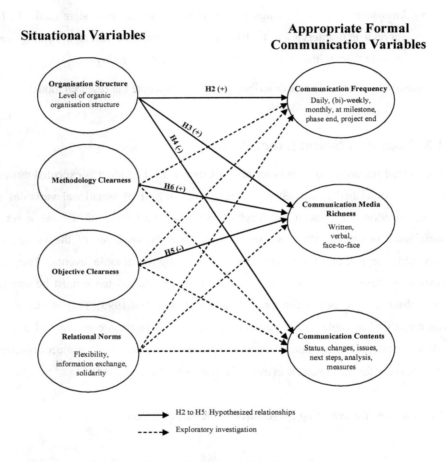

Figure 4-5: Research Model for Step 1: Antecedents

Solid lines, labelled H2 to H6, represent the hypotheses H2 to H6 listed in Chapter 3. H2 to H4 investigate the impact of organisation structure on the three dependent variables. H5 and H6 assesses the impact of methodology clearness on choice of written media, and objective clearness on choice of face-to-face media. The dotted lines show the possible impact of methodology and objective clearness, as well as relational norms, which are explored in this study. The results of the analysis are structured by buyer and seller perspective, as well as high and low performing projects.

The above model measures:

a) project managers and sponsors patterns in their preference for communications frequency, contents and media

b) relational norms, organisational structure, methodology and objective clearness as antecedents of these preferences.

Measures are taken independently by project manager and sponsor to allow for a subsequent gap analysis. Measures for bullet a) support the exploratory investigation, with items, measures and classifications derived from the literature review. Measures for bullet b) support the confirmatory part of the study, by assessing the impact of organisation structure and project risk on communication frequency, contents and media. It also supports the exploratory investigation on the impact of relational norms and project risk on communication patterns.

The above model allows assessment of the impact of the three situational variables on communication patterns. However, it only allows for predictions of changes in the pattern if one situational factor changes while all other are unchanged, i.e. *ceteris paribus*. Miller (2001) recommends that the assessment of multivariate relationships should match the complexity of the conceptual framework by assessing the entire system of relationships between and among variables. The impact of the entire set of situational factors on the entire set of communication patterns is assessed using the multivariate analysis technique Canonical Correlation Analysis, which takes into account the interrelationships among and between the situational and communication variables. This identifies prevalent communication patterns and allows for modelling the communication practices of project managers and sponsors.

4.3.2   Step 2: Effectiveness in Project Sponsor and Manager Communication

Step 2 assesses the effectiveness in project sponsor – manager communication by analyzing a possible gap between project sponsors and managers patterns identified in Step 1. The fit of communication expectations and capabilities is examined by assessing the level of congruency in sponsors and managers preference for communication frequency, contents and media (Figure 4-3). Effectiveness in communication is assessed through identification of differences in perceived level of project performance and how these differences relate to the choice of communication contents, frequency and media. This step addresses research question Q2 and hypothesis H1. It provides the answer to the question whether communication expectations from one party are met by the capabilities of the other party.

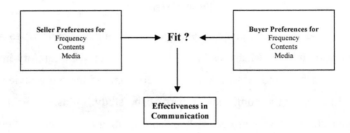

Figure 4-6: Research Model for Step 2: Congruency in Communication Requirements and Capabilities

4.4 Quantitative Research Design

The unit of analysis within this research is the formal communication between project sponsor and manager during IT project implementation. Focus is on congruency in choices of communication frequency, contents and media preferred independently by the two parties. The research investigates how these preferences are influenced by contextual factors, i.e. relational norms, organisation structure and project risk.

The research comprises confirmatory and exploratory parts. The former part tests the hypotheses stated above in the transient environment of IT projects, and the latter part identifies dominant communications patterns between project managers and sponsors, which are then assessed on their influence on communication effectiveness. The relationships between research questions, constructs and hypotheses are shown in Appendix A-1.

Time-wise the research is at the implementation stage of IT projects, which was identified by Hutinsky et al. (2001) as one of the two stages with highest communication complexity between buyer and seller firms in projects. The targeted respondents are project managers from IT seller firms and project sponsors from buyer firms in the implementation stage of an IT project. Implementation stage is the time after the contract between buyer and seller firm is signed, when work on the project deliverables has commenced, but before the operational use of the project deliverables.

A multi-site approach was chosen over a single site approach to accommodate the research model's requirements for a wide variety of organisational structures, relational norms, and project risks. This also accommodates the generalizability of the results across industries, geographies and cultures. Reservations of IT seller firms to disclose their projects, customers, and relationships with their customers to a researcher from a competitor firm (i.e. NCR) made it unlikely that a large enough sample could be achieved at a single site and within the timeframe of the study. Therefore, a multi-site approach was chosen.

Survey data from a large number of respondents were sought because of the large number of variables to be examined. To increase the validity of the results respondents were encouraged to answer the survey in pairs, i.e. project sponsors and mangers from the same project.

4.4.1 Focus Groups

Using focus groups is:

> ... a research approach for collecting evidence from a highly
> specialized group of individuals (Remenyi et al., 1998, p. 53).

Focus Groups usually consist of 4 to 12 members, who participate in moderated discussion to explore issues related to a specific topic (Bloor et al. 2001, Remenyi et al. 1998, Morgan 1993). A characteristic of focus groups is the explicit use of group interaction to derive data about a topic (Bloor et al. 2001). The purpose of focus groups is among others to test the feasibility of complex studies, add precision to research problems, to develop methodological techniques, or to test questionnaire items for readability, comprehension, wording, order and response variation (Frey & Fontana 1993, Edwards et al. 1996). Electronic communication in focus groups becomes increasingly popular (Adrianenssens & Cadman 1999). Research by Tse (1999) showed that electronic focus groups are more open in their interaction and experience greater participant satisfaction than traditional face-to-face groups. This is in addition to the possibility of engaging geographically dispersed members, such as scarce experts, together with low costs, members' timely synchronization across time-zones, individual availability, and avoidance of dominant behaviour of single members. Adrianenssens & Cadman (1999, p. 417) found that in electronic focus groups:

> *Responses are very thorough and considered. Respondents took care to explain their answers in great detail and used examples to illustrate certain points. The use of e-mail gives respondents time to compose their answers whereas real-time focus groups command an instantaneous response.*

These advantages are balanced by a lack of tacit information due to the written nature of the communication, and the difficulty of summarizing the findings due to the open-ended nature of the responses. For geographically dispersed focus groups Delphi techniques are recommended (Adriaenssens & Cadman 1999, Frey & Fontana 1993). This technique is based on multiple, anonymous inputs from individual group members. Ideas and suggestions are recorded by a central manager and then re-circulated to other members for their feedback (Mullins 1999c). In the original Delphi technique this process is continued until consensus is reached among the members. The focus groups within this study were setup for data gathering. Therefore the process was only repeated until the widest possible set of opinions was collected.

Two focus groups were set up. One group for IT seller firms, with nine high ranking project managers from Cap Gemini, Ericsson, HP, IBM, Intersys, NCR, and a freelance project manager. They represented eight different countries. Another group was set up for buyer firms, with five project sponsors from AT&T, Deutsche Telekom, NCR, and Telia. They represented three different countries. Using Delphi techniques five rounds of e-mail based questioning were used to assess and validate the research design in the order of validating research model, measuring constructs, questions, and wording. For each round the individual feedbacks of the participants were sorted and collected in a summary sheet (Stewart & Shamdasani 1998), which was subsequently sent to the participants for comments, together with further questions from the researcher. Important changes made as a result of these sessions were:

- Changes to questions on communication preferences: questions had to allow for *all* possible combinations of frequency, contents and media over the course of project implementation

- Harmonizing of definitions of terms: definitions had to accommodate differences from the various Project Management Bodies of Knowledge.

After completion of validation and questionnaire development a survey pre-pretest was done using the members of the focus groups. Results showed the need for a revision of the research model. The focus groups members expressed the need to put the research in a wider context by adding items for project risk and project performance, which were not part of the original model. The two groups validated the final research model, constructs and questionnaire.

4.4.2 Questionnaire Design

Wherever appropriate existing validated constructs and questions were used for the questionnaire. New constructs were developed following processes recommended by Churchill (1979, 1999) and by using existing research results in the subject area. Appendix A-3 shows the relationship between variables, questionnaire items, scales and authors. The individual questionnaire items were developed as follows:

4.4.2.1 Organisation Structure

The independent variable organisation structure was operationalized using Miles et al.'s (2000) set of seven question items on a seven point semantic differential scale. This set of questions is based on Khandwalla's (1977) questionnaire and frequently used to assess organisation structure for the Burns & Stalker (1994) model, e.g. by Miles et al. (2000) in their research on the relationship between small firm structure and environmental dynamism. This construct measures the project team's and buyer firm's level of organic organisation structure in form of an 'organicity' index, with

---

higher values indicating more organic organisation structures. The questions are listed in Appendix A-3 as items 68 to 74.

In a semantic differential scale the respondents judge on a scale that is anchored at its extreme points by words of opposite meanings, like e.g. good – bad. The number of scale points is usually between 5 and 11 (Edwards et al. 1996). For the present study the original seven point scale was used.

4.4.2.2   Relational Norms

The independent variable relational norms was operationalized through Heide & John's (1992) set of ten questions using a seven point Completely Inaccurate - Completely Accurate Likert scale, with higher values indicating higher efforts to maintain the relationship between the parties as a whole, and curtailing behaviour promoting the goals of the individual parties (Heide & John 1992). The questions are listed in Appendix A-3 as items 10 to 19. The sum of the ratings reflects the extent of relational oriented behaviour, i.e. the level of integrated relationship between buyer and seller firm.

The instrument's appropriateness for assessment of buyer-seller relationships has been frequently demonstrated, e.g. through Samouel's (1996) research on relational norms and TCE in the brewing industry.

4.4.2.3   Communication Frequency

The classification into frequency, contents and media builds on existing research models from communication theory (e.g. Rice & Shook 1990, Russ et al. 1990). Frequencies for written, verbal and personal communication were individually assessed using frequency items identified in the literature review, i.e. daily, weekly, bi-weekly, and monthly communications, as well as after milestone, project phase or end achievement. To complete the exhaustive list of options a question item for 'no communication' was added. The questions are listed in Appendix A-3, items 23 to 43. A seven point Strongly Disagree - Strongly Agree Likert scales was used for frequency and contents questions. On Likert scales respondents are asked to provide ratings that indicate how strongly they feel positively or negatively on an issue. A seven point scale was chosen to allow for consistent numbers of scale points across the survey and for being consistent with the already proven constructs for organisational structure and relational norms. Edwards et al. (1996) and Churchill (1999) recommend these scales as being popular and reliable. A mix of direction of the scoring statements, e.g. from a "Strongly Disagree - Strongly Agree" to "Strongly Agree – Strongly Disagree" to prevent respondents checking the same mark consistently, was not recommended by the focus groups on grounds of reducing the risk for accidentally checking wrong marks on the survey. A particularity of attitude scales like the one used here is the controversy whether it's an ordinal or interval scale. In accordance with Churchill (1999, p. 411) the prevailing posture in marketing was adapted and the scales interpreted as intervals.

The development of questions and scales followed Churchill's (1979) process of:

- Specifying the domain of construct: this was achieved through extensive literature research on communication in project management.

- Generating samples of items: items derived from the literature review were complemented by extreme values, like 'no communication' or 'other contents' to achieve an exhaustive list of possible communication frequencies and contents. As a representative sample of the project management population the two focus groups assessed the potential questionnaire items and provided input to the refinement of wording and grouping of items

- Collecting data: a pre-test of the questionnaire was performed with the focus groups to collect data and assess the validity of the construct.

Further steps in the process for measure development were applied in the final survey and are described in chapter 5.

4.4.2.4 Communication Contents

The construct identifies the preferred communication contents of sponsors and managers. Measurement scales for this construct were developed as outlined under Communication Frequency above. A seven point Strongly Disagree - Strongly Agree Likert scale was used. Contents preferences were individually assessed for written, verbal and face-to-face communication, using items identified in the literature review. These were status and achievements, measures and quality metrics, issues or open items, project changes, trends, next steps, other contents (see Appendix A-3, item 44 to 64).

4.4.2.5 Communication Media

The classification of media into written, verbal and face-to-face communication was adopted from Media Richness Theory (Daft & Lengel 1986). In accordance with prior studies by Rice & Shook (1990), and due to the present study's focus on formal communication only, the original six media groups were reduced to three by collapsing all written communication (fax and e-mail, personal written documentation, impersonal written documentation and numerical documents) into one category for written communication. Assessment was done on the perceived importance for each of the three media types, as shown in Appendix A-3, items 20-22.

This questionnaire design for communication frequency, contents and media allowed for all possible combinations of dyadic communication between project manager and sponsor, e.g. daily verbal updates about project status, and monthly written reports with status and quality measures, combined with face-to-face meetings at milestone achievement to assess trends and next steps.

4.4.2.6 Survey Instrument Refinement

Following recommendations from the focus groups items for project risk and project performance were added as structural variables. Both measures were seen as important by the focus group members because of the need to differentiate communication by its context, given through project risk levels and the state of project performance.

4.4.2.7 Project Risk

A construct was developed to measure and differentiate between risk levels in terms of objective clearness and methodology clearness. Questionnaire statements and items followed Turner & Cochrane's (1993) classification of risk into objective clearness and methodology clearness. The extent of clearness in definition, level of agreement between buyer and seller, and its extent of documentation was measured individually for goals and methods (Appendix A-3, items 4 to 9). A seven point Completely Inaccurate - Completely Accurate Likert scale for methodology risk and goal risk was developed as described in the Frequency of Communication paragraph, with higher scores indicating higher levels of clearness, thus lower risk.

4.4.2.8   *Project Performance*

Following the focus groups recommendations a control variable for project performance was added. The question items were derived from Wateridge's (1998) measures for success in IS/IT projects. Of the 10 criteria identified by Wateridge, five were deemed relevant for the study and answerable by sponsor and manager. Meeting of functionality, budget and timing objectives were combined into a single question. This together with meeting of user requirements and meeting the purpose of the project formed a three items construct to measure project performance and success. (Appendix A-3, item 65 to 67). As with the other questions, a seven point Strongly Disagree – Strongly Agree scale was selected, with higher ratings indicating higher performance of a project.

4.4.3   Survey Administration

Two different surveys were used, i.e. one for project managers and one for sponsors (Appendix A6 and A7). These differed only in the terms related to the respondent's individual perspective as sponsor or manager.

Churchill (1999, p. 331) recommends mail questionnaires (as opposed to telephone or face-to-face) for these type of structured-undisguised questionnaires. A special form of mailing, i.e. e-mail and computer based questionnaires is recommended by Booth-Kewley et al. (1993) if the survey lends itself to routine quantitative analysis and if the respondents had prior experience with computers. These conditions were given within the present study through the quantitative nature of the data gathered, the use of Likert scales throughout the survey and the expectation that project managers from

IT seller firms and their customers were experienced in using computers. Benefit of using electronic surveys are in the automation of survey data entry and associated higher accuracy of data, elimination of missing entries, elimination of out-of-range responses, and use of complex branching i.e. automatic skip over or branch to another question depending on the prior question's answer (Booth-Kewley et al. 1993). While automatic branching was used in earlier versions of the survey, a two survey approach was eventually chosen because of the difficulty in managing the complex network of 2 x 84 almost identical questions, and the need for discrete analysis of buyer and seller responses. These advantages were balanced by some drawbacks of computer based surveys, which are the high costs for equipment or survey providers, the lack of portability when compared with paper, as well as the chances for equipment failure and software problems (Booth-Kewley et al. 1993).

4.4.3.1 Sampling Error

Sample surveys are subject to four major sources of error and each of these errors must be addressed to achieve confidence in the results. These errors are (Dillman 2001):

- Coverage error: not all possible respondents have a nonzero chance to be included in the sample.

- Sampling error: the result of surveying only a sample and not the whole population.

- Measurement error: inaccurate responses stemming from poor question wording or interviewing, survey mode effects and/or some aspects of the respondent's behaviour.

- Non-response error: non-response of those who, if they had responded, would have provided different answers than those who did respond.

Dillman (2001) developed fourteen principles for the design of web surveys, which address the four types of errors listed above. The summary in Table 4-2 below lists these design principles and their relationship to sources of survey errors, as well as how these principles were implemented in the survey design for this study.

Design Principle	Error Types				Implementation in Survey
	Sampling	Coverage	Measurement	Non-response	
1. Introduce the web questionnaire with a welcome screen that is motivational, emphasizes the ease of responding, and instructs respondents on the action needed for proceeding to the next page				X	Welcome screen, followed by explanation and definition of terms. All instructions on actions were provided with the question asked
2. Provide a PIN number for limiting access only to people in the sample	X	X			A more rigorous way of identification was used by asking for respondents' role in projects.
3. Choose for the first question an item that is likely to be interesting to most respondents, easily answered, and fully visible on the first screen of the questionnaire				X	The first question after the identification dealt with the category of project (research, development, or service) the respondent is working on. That should be easy to answer.
4. Present each question in conventional format similar to that normally used on paper self-administered questionnaires			X		Layout was similar to paper based questionnaires
5. Restrain the use of colour so that figure/ground consistency and readability are maintained, navigational flow is unimpeded, and measurement properties of questions are maintained			X		One colour was used consistently for text, for background, and for a question grouping bar.
6. Avoid differences in the visual appearance of questions that results from different screen configurations, operating systems, browsers, partial screen displays, and wrap-around text.		X	X	X	Simple layout, suitable for computers with low resolutions was used and tested on computers with different browsers and operating systems.
7. Provide specific instructions on how to take each necessary computer action for responding to the questionnaire and other necessary instructions at the point where they are needed.				X	Instructions were provided with each set of questions, e.g. "Select one of the following ratings…"
8. Use drop-down boxes sparingly, consider the mode implications, and identify each with a "click here" instruction.			X		Drop-down boxes were not used to make survey handling as easy as possible
9. Do not require respondents to provide an answer to each question before being allowed to answer any subsequent ones.				X	The feature for enforcing an answer to each question was not used.
10. Provide skip directions in a way that encourages marking of answers and being able to click to the next applicable question.			X		The feature of skipping questions was not used.
11. Construct web questionnaire so they scroll from question to question unless order effects are a major concern, and/or telephone and web survey results are being combined.		X	X	X	Only scrolling from question to question was used, no skipping or other features.
12. When the number of answer choices exceeds the number that can be displayed in a single column on one screen, consider double banking with an appropriate grouping device to link them together			X		Number of choices always fitted in one row or one screen. All questions were visually grouped by colour bars.
13. Use graphical symbols or words that convey a sense of where the respondent is in the completion process, but avoid ones that require significant increases in computer memory		X		X	The scroll bar on the right-hand side of the browser indicated the level of completion. This was possible because scrolling, without skipping, was used.
14. Exercise restraint in the use of question structures that have known measurement problems on paper questionnaires, e.g. check-all-that-apply and open-ended questions.			X	X	Only widely used structures without measurement problems were used (7 point Likert scales)

Table 4-7: Web-survey Design Principles (Dillman 2001)

It shows that all principles were used. In case of principle 2 a more rigorous approach was implemented through the identification of respondent's role as internal or external project manager or sponsor in projects, and not just a PIN number as suggested. The approach to distribution of the survey to the targeted sample required a clearer identification than a PIN number.

An Internet based survey provider, Surveypro from Salt Lake City, USA (Surveypro 2001) was chosen as the central site for the survey. The questionnaire was developed online through the internet, using the Surveypro server system in USA. The editor tool provided immediate test possibilities, which were used to improve the survey layout. However, some of the editor functions appeared to be slow, e.g. the shifting of questions. A suitable layout for semantic differential scale questions, which requires a statement at both ends of a scale, was not available and had to be constructed manually through extensive trial and error work.

In summary, electronic mail in combination with an Internet based survey was used. Within these e-mails an introduction letter (Appendix A-5) presented the purpose of the survey to the prospective respondent and then provided two hyperlinks (web-links), one for project managers and one for sponsors. A mouse click on the respective hyperlink connected the respondent's computer via the Internet with the server system of the survey provider and displayed the chosen questionnaire on the respondent's computer screen.

4.4.3.2 Survey Pretest

The questionnaire was pretested using 68 project managers and sponsors from organisations represented in the focus groups. Twenty-three responses were achieved, of which 18 were from real projects (as opposed to generic answers), which was indicated as a requirement in the introductory letter, i.e. a valid response rate of 26%, was achieved. Of those 18 responses 11 were from seller firms, 8 from buyer firms. Four pairs of buyer – seller from the same project responded and one project sponsor – manager pair from a project internal to a company.

Participants in the pretest were not only asked to fill out the questionnaire, but also to feed back comments about time required for the survey, understandability of the questions, order of questions, and other comments. Their feedback indicated the need to reformat the questionnaire layout so that all answers of a question fitted on one screen. The duration for answering the survey was between 10 and 35 minutes, with a mode of 15-20 minutes. The responses from the pretest were not used for the final analysis, nor did the respondents from the pretest participate in the final survey.

At this stage no further attempt was made to purify the measures because of the small pre-test sample size of 18 responses and the associated low generalizability of analysis results. Purification of the measures was shifted to the analysis stage of the final sample, where a series of quantitative techniques were used to identify and subsequently drop inappropriate question items. The pre-test sample was used to gain familiarization with the quantitative techniques to be used at later stages.

4.4.3.3 Final Survey and Data Collection Process

Appendix A-4 shows the e-mail sent to the professional organisations targeted for questionnaire distribution. The introductory letter for the respondents is in Appendix A-5, and the seller and buyer questionnaires in Appendix A-6 and A-7 respectively.

The e-mail text explained the study background and the need to have pairs of respondents. The introduction letter for the respondents explained the objectives and purpose of the study, probable duration, links to the questionnaires, as well as identity, firm, contact address of the researcher, and confidentiality of the responses.

The overall design followed research results by Fahy (1998), as well as Jobber and O'Reilly (1998) to increase the survey's attractiveness through maximizing the value for the respondent through appreciation of respondents and offering of rewards. The questionnaire was designed to start with easy questions and then to increase complexity. Personal questions, like demographics, names and e-mail addresses were asked towards the end, when the respondents were more familiar with the questionnaire.

The questionnaire started with a definition of terms, like project manager, sponsor, formal communication, implementation stage of IT projects, and asked the respondent to answer the questionnaire with their current project in mind. The sequence of survey topics can be seen in Appendix A-3. An incentive was provided by offering to provide a summary of the result if the respondent was interested.

Answers from project managers and sponsors of the same project were sought to increase the validity of the research results. Therefore respondents were asked for their e-mail address and that of their counterpart, as well as the project name to synchronize the responses. Respondents who did not provide information about their counterpart were contacted by the researcher through e-mail within one week after their response. The e-mail explained the need for pairs of answers and asked them to forward the survey's introduction letter to their counterpart. Those respondents who provided the contact information about their counterparts but their counterpart did not respond within a week, were contacted by e-mail and asked for permission for the researcher to contact the counterpart to gather the required information.

4.4.4 Sampling Frame and Sample

The final sampling frame consisted of the members of the two largest professional project management organisations. Reason for that being:

- The study's focus on IT project implementation in buyer – seller relationships within business-to-business markets implied that only professional project managers and sponsors should be targeted.

- A certain level of professionalism in project management should be expected from the respondents. That includes professionally certified project managers and those engaged in professional organisations for the project management profession. The definition of project manager is blurred in practice. The pure title Project Manager doesn't say much about the extent a person performs project management tasks as defined in e.g. PMI's *'Guide to the Project Management Body of Knowledge'* (PMI 2000). The technical tasks of project managers in IT projects can outweigh project management tasks to a great extent, especially in smaller development or installation projects. Furthermore, some highly valued technical consultants are awarded the title Project Manager to justify higher salaries or recognition without the necessity of executing project management tasks. In summary the term project manager is inconsistently used in the industry (Turner & Müller 2003) and an attempt to target the professional project management population requires careful selection as to the individual's level of professionalism in project management.

- Attempts to target possible respondents through a top-down distribution of the questionnaire within their company proved to be unsuccessful. Firms like IBM and others referred to their policies which do not allow disclosure of customer related information like those asked in the survey. Others referred to the lack of resources, costs or the negative impact on productivity.

Through the exclusion of some parts of the wider project management population the sample turned into a judgment sample. However, given the inconsistencies in the use of the title Project Manager, it is assumed that this non-probability sample is more representative of project managers in buyer-seller projects in business-to-business markets than a simple random sample (Churchill 1999).

The sampling frame comprised two of the largest project management professional organisations, namely Project Management Institute (PMI) with approx. 80,000 members, and the International Association for Project Management (IPMA) with approx. 20,000 members. The number of IT project managers in both organisations and the possible overlap through individuals being member in both organisations is unknown. Closest estimate for number of IT project managers is the IT Special Interest Group in PMI, which comprises approximately 12,000 members, constituting 15% of the total members. The survey was also posted in the November and December 2001 issue of the online magazine PM World Today with approximately 3000 subscribers, and distributed within NCR Corporation using the e-mail subscriber list for project managers with approx. 600 subscribers. Using the 15% ratio of IT project managers from PMI the total sampling frame for IT project managers was approx. 16.000 project managers.

A series of constraints was given in the introductory letter to encourage responses only from project sponsors and managers

- from IT projects
- preferably from the same project
- from projects with buyer and seller organisations in business-to-business markets
- in the implementation stage of a project

which reduced the actual sampling frame to only those subjects possessing all these attributes.

The final survey took place from September 10, 2001 to January 2, 2002. The introduction letter with its web-link for the Internet based buyer and seller surveys was distributed by e-mail (Appendix A-4) to 267 PMI Chapter Presidents and Special Interest Groups, 30 Managers of IPMA country organisations, as well as the online project management magazine PM World Today. All recipients were asked to distribute the introduction letter (Appendix A-5) to their members. The time taken for web-posting and distribution of the survey was very different in the various organisations. Five PMI chapters and one IPMA organisation responded that they posted the survey on their web-site. The IS Special Interest Group within PMI (ISSIG) posted the survey during the month of November on their 'doctoral students' site. This web site is especially provided for doctoral students in IT and project management and continuously used for collecting research data through online surveys.

During the time of posting the survey on the Internet two major events happened, which impacted responses in the first few weeks:

- Terror attacks against the USA one day after the survey was launched. This caused a slow response from USA in the first few weeks, due to a general distraction from day-to-day business, which included e-mail and survey responses.

- Nimda Virus caused blocking of Internet access. The Nimda virus was the most serious virus attack within the Internet up until that day. Thousands of Internet servers were infected and shut-down for repair. Larger firms blocked all Internet access, e.g. at NCR Corporation all Internet access was blocked from September 19 to 25, 2001.

In light of these events, the originally planned eight weeks time window for answering the survey was extended to sixteen weeks, which at its end spanned the Christmas and New Years holiday season, i.e. a time with typically low business activity.

Respondents feedback in the early days of the survey on the Internet indicated that error messages from the questionnaire were not recognized by the respondents because they appeared too small on the screen, despite being displayed in red colour. The messages were caused by respondents trying to submit the survey without having answered all questions. The respondents felt that the survey could not be submitted due to technical problems with the Internet. Therefore the questionnaire feature which forced answers to all questions was switched off after the survey was approximately three days on the Internet. Two cases of unavailability of the server system were encountered. Even though the provider reacted quickly on e-mail notification about the server being down, the survey was not available for prospective respondents for several hours. Geographical instabilities of the Internet were encountered when no access was possible from California for several hours.

The timely distribution of answers is shown in Figure 4-4. Project managers from seller firms responded quickly after the survey was launched in week 1, and after it appeared on the web-site of the PMI ISSIG and the online magazine PM World Today, i.e. week 8. Buyer organisations showed a more normal distribution of responses.

The distributional approach through institutions and online magazine, and the constraints in respondents' profiles as listed above, reduced the sampling frame to an unknown size. The approach did not allow for calculating a conventional survey response rate. However, the provider of the Internet survey tool tracked a 'hit rate', which showed that 29% of those who accessed the survey also answered it.

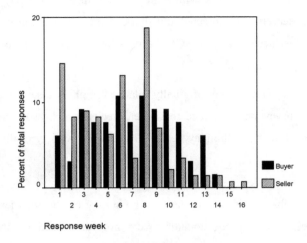

Figure 4-7: Buyer and Seller Responses over Time

The number of responses totalled to 209, of which 200 were used for analysis. Nine respondents were excluded from the analysis on the basis of being outliers from the normal distribution of the responses, which was measured by the individual response's impact on kurtosis and skewness of the variables, and visualized through boxplots. Kurtosis is a measure for the peakedness or flatness of a distribution, compared to a normal distribution. Positive values indicate relatively peaked, and negative values relatively flat distributions. Skewness measures the symmetry of a distribution. Positively skewed distributions show few large values and tail off to the right, and negative values show few small values and tail off to the left. Values outside the range of -1 to +1 indicate substantially skewed or peaked/flat distributions (Hair 1998). Table 4-3 shows the means, standard deviation, skewness and kurtosis of demographic and independent variables of the total sample and the sample with removed outliers. The nine outliers were significantly different from the total sample by having extreme low levels of relational norms, methodology clearness and objective clearness (significance $p < .000, .001, .000$ respectively), thus representing extremely risky projects with weak relationships between buyer and seller. These outliers were not deemed representative of the overall population and removed from the sample to prevent from distorting statistical tests.

Variable	Total Sample (n=209)				Outliers Removed (n=200)			
	Mean	Std. Dev.	Skewness	Kurtosis	Mean	Std. Dev.	Skewness	Kurtosis
Respondent's Age	42.34	8.22	0.18	-0.70	42.18	8.15	0.18	-0.69
Work Experience	20.27	8.88	0.25	-0.73	20.16	8.87	0.28	-0.70
Project Management Experience	10.40	6.63	0.95	0.62	10.26	6.47	0.97	0.78
Project Sponsor Experience	5.75	5.16	1.76	2.71	5.85	5.19	1.81	2.76
Methodology Clearness	4.98	1.37	-0.86	0.10	5.05	1.32	-0.89	0.24
Objective Clearness	5.29	1.27	-1.13	0.92	5.39	1.15	-1.02	0.64
Relational Norms	5.39	0.99	-1.28	2.51	5.45	0.90	-0.88	0.83
Organization Structure	4.57	1.04	-0.51	0.20	4.58	1.05	-0.53	0.23

Table 4-8: Differences between Included and Excluded Cases

Forty-three pairs of project sponsor and manager from the same project responded. However, only 38 pairs were left after removal of outliers, which constitutes 38% of the sample. The sample used for analysis consisted of 62 project sponsors and 138 project managers. Project types represented were 128 development projects, 66 technical service projects, and six research projects (64%, 33% and 3% respectively). Definitions of project types (see Appendix A-6) are based on Tushman (1979a) and were refined through the focus groups.

Respondents came from 34 countries, 47% of the respondents were from Europe, 34% from North America, and 19% from other regions. The average age of respondents was 42 years, with 20 years of business experience and 10 years of project management experience. Project Sponsors had in average 6 years of project sponsorship experience. Response bias analysis on the basis of early to late response comparison was not calculated due to the different dates the survey appeared in the media.

Missing data analysis showed that variables added for reasons of exhaustiveness of the questionnaire construct, such as 'No Communication' or 'Other Contents', had missing value levels between 6% and 11%. Variables for age, verbal weekly, and verbal monthly communication had missing values of 10%, 8% and 7% respectively. All other variables had missing values below 6%. No patterns were detected in missing data. Substitution of missing values with variable mean was chosen for the subsequent multivariate analysis because of the need to preserve the sample size and the general consistency in results (Hair et al. 1998).

Assessment of the respondents' roles showed that 167 were project sponsors and managers of IT projects in buyer-seller relationships, and 31 were from company internal projects, plus two missing responses. ANOVA technique (explained in chapter 5) was used to identify significant differences between responses from buyer-seller projects and company internal projects. No significant differences were found at a significance level of .05. A similar test was done at a later stage to identify significant differences between the two groups at the level of extracted communication factors. Again, no significant differences were found (see Appendix A-8). The responses from company internal projects were therefore kept within the sample. From a conceptual perspective this is supported by research from Turner and Keegan (2001), who identified similar governance structures in company internal projects and external projects.

4.4.4.1 Measurement Error

Measurements taken through constructs with several measurement variables for one construct variable are subject to several possible errors. These can influence the results of the multivariate analysis techniques applied to the survey data, and hence impact the results. According to Churchill (1999, p. 452) a measure X_0 consists of three components:

$$X_0 = X_T + X_S + X_R$$

where: X_0 = the observed measurement

X_T = the true score of what has been measured

X_S = the systemic error

X_R = the random error

The error in the measure is given by the sum of X_S and X_R. Systemic errors are constant errors caused by e.g. imprecisely calibrated measurement tools, whereas random errors are not constant and show the inconsistency of repeated or equivalent measures when the measurements are made on the responses from the same person (Churchill 1999, Hair et al. 1998).

4.4.4.2 Reliability

Measurement errors are addressed through assessment of a measure's reliability and validity. A measure can be reliable but may not necessarily be valid. However, a valid measure is often said to be reliable (Churchill 1999). Reliable measures are consistent in their values over several measures (Hair et al. 1998). Therefore the lower the measurement error X_R the more reliable the measure (Churchill 1999).

Reliability is established by either measuring the same individuals at two different points in time, or by calculating the internal consistency of the set of items which form the measurement scale. The latter approach was used in this survey. Internal consistency was measured by Cronbach Alpha (Cronbach 1951), which splits the sample in equivalent halves and then correlates the halves total scores. That is done for all possible half-splits of the sample and the average of the intercorrelations are calculated as the Cronbach Alpha measure. Its value varies between 0 and 1, with .70 being the lowest generally accepted level of internal consistency, which may decrease to .60 in exploratory research (Hair et al. 1998, p. 118). The Cronbach Alpha values for the multi-item constructs of this study are listed in Table 4-4. With all values greater than .70 acceptable levels of reliability were achieved. A Cronbach Alpha value of .80 for the construct Organisation Structure is similar to the results of a study by Miles et al. (2000), who reported a Cronbach Alpha value of .81.

Internal consistency measures for inter-item correlations and item-to-total correlations were acceptable. Inter-item correlations, which measure the consistency among the variables of a construct, exceeded .3 (Table 4-4), and item-to-total correlations, which measure the correlation of each item to the total scale score, reached or exceeded .5 (Hair 1998, p. 118). Appendix A-10 lists the details of the item-to-total correlations for the situational variables. The results indicate that the measuring instrument captured the characteristics of the hypothesized constructs.

Variable	Cronbach Alpha	Inter-item Correlation
Objective Clearness	.81	.60
Methodology Clearness	.86	.68
Relational Norms	.88	.43
Organization Structure	.80	.37
Project Performance	.75	.54

Table 4-9: Cronbach Alphas and Inter-item Correlations for Multi-item Constructs

Churchill (1979) recommends a factor analysis as a next step to refine the measures. This is described in the Data Analysis and Results chapter.

4.4.4.3 Validity

Validity is the extent a measure represents the concept under study. It shows how well the concept is defined by the measure, whereas reliability shows the consistency of the measure (Hair et al. 1998). It measures how accurately the survey instrument measures what it is supposed to measure (Churchill 1979).

Validity measures of interest for this study are content and construct validity. Content validity focuses on how adequately the measured characteristics are captured by the measure. Content validity is not directly measurable. It is partly a matter of individual judgment and therefore subjective. To achieve high levels of content validity it is important to focus on the process for development of measurement questions. Examination of literature is recommended to develop a wide set of possible measures and items, also including related items. The set of items can then be refined to produce the final measure (Churchill 1999). Within this study content validity was achieved through the literature review, which identified the items for the measures, the test and validation of the measures through two focus groups, and the use of complementary research methodologies.

Construct validity relates to the question of "What is the instrument in fact measuring?". It requires acceptable internal consistency levels, as given through the Cronbach Alpha levels reported above. This is a necessary, but not a sufficient condition for construct validity. The next step in establishing construct validity assesses whether the measure behaves as expected, i.e. "whether it confirms or denies the hypotheses predicted from the theory based on the construct" (Churchill 1999, p. 458). This is done in Chapter 5 and 7, where the analysis and results of the study, as well as the conclusions are described.

Construct validity also comprises the concepts of convergent and discriminant validity. For convergent validity to exist the results of several different methods of measuring the same trait or characteristic should be highly correlated (Churchill 1999). This cannot be done quantitatively within this study. However, the triangulation of the survey results with those of the interview indicates, though not quantitatively proven, a convergence of both. This is described at the end of Chapter 5. Discriminant validity exists when the measure does not correlate too highly with measures that it is supposed to differ from. If the measure's correlations are high the measure does not capture the isolated trait that it is supposed to measure (Churchill 1999). No evidence of discriminant validity was found in the literature for the existing constructs of organisation structure and relational norms. For the newly developed constructs this will be examined in the results section in Chapter 5.

4.4.5 Quantitative Analysis Techniques

The independent variables of organisation structure, relational norms and project risk are hypothesized to impact the communication of project managers and sponsors. The literature review in Chapter 2 outlined the underlying theories for these hypotheses and the existing recommendations from academics and practitioners on the frequency, contents and media for communication. The empirical investigation in communication of project managers and sponsors provided an exhaustive list of possible combinations of frequency, contents and media to project managers and sponsors, for them to score their preference in communication. Due to lack of prior studies in this area, the responses need to be analyzed to identify prevalent communication patterns. This is done by identifying underlying structures of the responses using factor analysis. This technique will reduce the number of variables to a set of factors, which reflect groupings of frequency and contents items belonging together in the respondents' perceptions. Research hypothesis H1 will be tested by assessing the significance of the difference in scores of buyers and sellers in the identified factors. The impact of the situational variables relational norms, organisation structure, and risk on the identified factors is assessed quantitatively using multiple regression analysis. This tests hypotheses H2 to H6 and provides the empirical results for the research model in step 1.

To account for possible interrelationships among the independent variables, as well as among the dependent variables Canonical Correlation Analysis is used. Here the correlation of the set of situational variables with the set of communication variables is assessed. It allows for modelling the communication of project sponsor and manager on several levels, i.e. the level of total sample, but also individually for buyers, sellers, high performing and low performing projects. The models derived from this step can be compared for their differences between communication practices in e.g. low and high performing projects.

Confirmatory Factor Analysis, such as Structured Equation Modelling, was not used because of the mainly exploratory nature of the research and response requirements of minimum 200 responses (Hair et al. 1999, p. 605). This was not given within the sub-samples, e.g. the sub-sample for low performing projects comprised only 78 responses. Finally ANOVA tests were used for comparing responses of project sponsors and managers on a question-by-questions level to identify details of the differences encountered through the regression analyses. Communication effectiveness was assessed through ANOVA techniques using the 38 dyadic pairs of project sponsors and managers to identify significant gaps in their respective perceived performance of their joint project. The impact of preferred communication contents, frequency or media on the identified gap was assessed using multiple regression analysis. That allowed for assessment of the fit between information processing needs and capacities of both parties. The quantitative techniques of ANOVA, t-test, factor analysis, multiple regression analysis, and canonical correlation analysis are described in the analysis and results chapter.

4.5 Qualitative Research Design

A series of interviews with subsequent qualitative analysis were held as part of the multi-method approach outlined in the beginning of this chapter. The interviews pursued exploratory and explanatory objectives, with the former seeking further evidence of the results from the quantitative study, and the latter seeking causes for the results found through the quantitative study. For that a set of three exploratory and seven explanatory open ended questions were used in semi structured interviews with pairs of project sponsors and managers from the same project. The interview instructions and questions are listed in Appendix A-9. After three interviews the results showed many similarities, despite differences in the projects geography, industry and performance. No further interviews were deemed necessary. The interviewees chosen were from IT projects at SparDa Bank, Germany; a major international apparel manufacturer in San Francisco, USA; and a Government Institution in the UK (both names not to be disclosed). Two of the projects were software development and systems delivery projects, and one a development project for IT concepts managed by a project management consultant external to the buying organisation. The three projects represent three different industries (manufacturing, finance, Government), three different countries (UK, Germany, USA), and three different risk levels, with one being a re-start of a failed project, another one being a project in recovery (230% over original schedule), and the third one being considered a successful project, albeit with reduction in project scope over the course of project execution. Access to two of the projects was by chance, through informal chats with former colleagues of the researcher. The third project was recommended by a member of the seller firm's management.

Each interview was handled as a case. The design of the qualitative research was guided by Yin's (1994) four design tests for construct, internal and external validity, and reliability. Construct validity was achieved through use of different sources of evidence, like the survey results and the open ended questions during the interviews. The measures were the phenomena identified through the quantitative analysis. Questions about the interviewees own communication behaviour provided the context in terms of project performance and buyer or seller perspective. Details are outlined in Chapter 5.

Internal validity was achieved through pattern matching techniques and subsequent explanation building. Time-series-analysis was performed on the study's content, i.e. the timely sequence of informal and formal communication events between project sponsors and managers. External validity and therefore generalization was aimed for through statistical generalization, i.e. from the quantitative study, and analytical generalization was done by relating the communication behaviour of the interviewees to the context of their projects in their companies. Reliability was achieved through use of protocols, i.e. semi structured interviews with pre-determined questions, tape recordings with transcriptions and validations, as well as a filing system for the interviews. The coding and classification of responses was done by two independent researchers to measure inter-coder reliability.

4.5.1   Qualitative Research Techniques

A standardized technique was sought to draw key features out of the data, while simultaneously allowing the richness of the material to remain for illustration purposes (Easterby-Smith et al. 1991). Case study techniques were used for the interview analysis. The nature of the data collected, i.e. relatively structured answers to pre-determined questions on patterns of communication, lend itself to cut-and-sort techniques using spreadsheets as analysis sheets (Easterby-Smith et al. 1991). Such techniques are suggested by Miles and Huberman (1994) to identify re-occurring subjects and terms for explanation and evidence of the context, causes and associated communication practices. Miles and Huberman's analytical process requires steps for data collection and iterative rounds of data reduction, data display and conclusions drawing and verifying.

Two of the interviews were held at the buyers facilities and the third in a meeting room at Stuttgart Airport. All interviews were tape-recorded, subsequently written-up and the write-ups validated by the interviewees. A first structure was introduced by copying the question responses in a spreadsheet. Project and subsequently project sponsor and manager response were ordered vertically, and questions asked horizontally. The response of each interviewee to each question was copied in the relevant intersection between the vertical (interviewee) and horizontal (question) dimension. In a next step the responses were grouped on a question by question basis

---

by common themes to identify the underlying commonalities in each question response. Responses to confirmatory questions were ordered by communication frequency, contents and media, i.e. the original structure of the study and questionnaire. The explanatory themes were consolidated in main categories identified through communalities in contents. The last step involved the reasoning behind the communication patterns.

Triangulation was done by assessing the results of the qualitative study against the quantitative study's results. For that the interviewees agreement with and reasoning for the results of the quantitative study was compared and conclusions drawn. Similarly were the exploratory results from the interviews assessed against evidence in the quantitative study. The details are outlined in Chapter 5.

4.6 Summary of Methodology Chapter

This chapter presented the philosophical background of the study as that of a positivist. Building on that a research design was developed which uses quantitative and qualitative methods to achieve triangulated results. The data collection processes were described and the survey sample presented. Outliers were removed from the sample leaving a sample size of 200 responses for the quantitative analysis. The process for interviews and qualitative analysis was described and the techniques for analysis were introduced. Their application is presented in the next chapter.

CHAPTER FIVE – DATA ANALYSIS AND RESULTS

The purpose of this chapter is to describe the research techniques in more detail, as well as to describe the results from the quantitative and qualitative analyses together with their triangulation. The underlying research model was described in Chapter 3 and the methodologies used were described in Chapter 4. The interpretation of the results from the various analyses in this chapter is provided in Chapter 6 and the overall conclusions from this study discussed in Chapter 7.

This chapter is organized in three main sections. It starts with the quantitative analysis of the worldwide inquiry in the communication practices of project sponsors and managers in IT projects. This is followed by a qualitative analysis of three interviews with pairs of project sponsors and managers from the same project. The third section triangulates and summarizes the findings from the quantitative and qualitative studies.

The central theme of this chapter is the overall results of the multi-method inquiry in communication practices of project sponsors and managers during IT project implementation. The chapter starts with a factor analysis on the total sample. This technique identifies the underlying structures as dimensions of communication, and then determines to what extent individual variables contribute to these dimensions. This is followed by a series of multivariate regression analyses to identify the impact of situational variables on project sponsor – manager communication preferences. These regressions are repeated on sub-samples for buyers and sellers, as well as low and high performing projects to identify the different impact of situational variables within different contexts, which allows for comparisons of communication practices in different situations. Canonical Correlation Analysis is used to identify and model communication patterns between project sponsors and managers. This is also done on the basis of total sample and sub-samples. Effectiveness of communication is assessed to identify areas where communication between sponsor and manager can be improved to the benefit of the project results.

All quantitative analyses were done using SPSS 10.0 on a Windows NT Computer.

5.1 Identification of Underlying Communication Structures

Factor analysis was used to identify the underlying structures of the frequency, contents and media preferences. In addition it was used to purify the measures by identifying variables that should be dropped from a conceptual and statistical perspective in order to improve the reliability and validity of measurement constructs (Churchill 1979, p. 69).

Factor analysis reduces the number of variables by summarizing the important information of the original variables in a new and smaller set of variables, which expresses the commonalities of the original set. Through that, it identifies structures of the interrelationships underlying the observed data (Churchill 1999, p. 840). It is an interdependence technique, which considers all variables and their relationships simultaneously (Hair et al. 1998, p. 91). The technique was used to explore the communication dimensions of the respondents. It showed which and how many variables were expected to form the communication patterns of project sponsors and managers. Factor scores (further explained on page 98) derived from this analysis were saved as variables that replaced the original, larger set of variables in subsequent multivariate analyses.

The variable coding used throughout the study is shown in Table 5-1. It shows that names for frequency and contents variables were constructed by starting with CO or FQ to identify them as contents or frequency variable respectively, followed by the media used, and subsequently the respective frequencies or contents names (Example is provided in Table 5-1, see also Appendix A-3).

Type	Variable			Coding
Demographic variables (in years):				
	Age of respondent			AGE
	Business experience			BUSEXP
	Project management experience			PMEXP
	Project sponsorship experience			PSEXP
Situational variables:				
	Organisation structure			ORGSTRUC
	Relational Norms			RELNOM
	Objective Clearness			OBJCLEAR
	Methodology clearness			METCLEAR
	Buyer – Seller perspective			BuySel (0 or 1 resp.)
	Low and high performing project			LoHiPerf (0 or 1 resp.)
Communication variables:				

	Variable Type	Media	Frequency / Contents
Example: FQWDAY =	FQ	W	DAY
	FQ = Frequency variable	W = written V = verbal P = personal	DAY = daily WEK = weekly 2WK = bi-weekly MON = monthly MIL = at milestone PHA = at project phase end NON = no communication
	CO = Contents variable	W = written V = verbal P = personal	STA = Status and recent achievements MEA = Quality and performance measures ISS = Issues CHA = Changes to the project TRE = Trends NXT = Next steps OTH = Other contents

Table 5-10: Variable Coding

5.1.1 Communication Frequency Factors

Two main types of factor analysis need to be distinguished. Confirmatory factor analysis confirms *a priori* hypothesized structures, and exploratory factor analysis searches for unknown underlying structures in the data. The latter was used in this study. The 9.5 to 1 ratio of observations-to-variables exceeded the minimum requirement of 5 to 1 (Hair et al. 1998, p. 99). Factor Analysis' underlying conceptual assumptions that data are metric and normally distributed were met.

Table 5-2 shows the means and standard deviations of the frequency variables. The non-communication variables for written, verbal and personal communication (FQWNON, FQVNON, FQPNON), showed extreme low preference scores with values between 1.20 and 1.36 ("Strongly Disagree" in the questionnaire), while all other variables showed preference scores between 2.57 and 4.90. These non-communication variables were originally added to the questionnaire to build an exhaustive list of options for respondents to choose from. The three variables were dropped from further analyses on conceptual and statistical grounds.

	N	Minimum	Maximum	Mean	Std. Deviation
Written daily communication	193	1	7	2.96	1.74
Written weekly communication	191	1	7	4.70	1.94
Written bi-weekly communication	190	1	7	3.78	1.90
Written monthly communication	192	1	7	3.26	2.12
Written communication at milestone achievement	191	1	7	3.10	2.18
Written communication at phase or project end	192	1	7	2.84	2.34
Verbal daily communication	195	1	7	4.35	1.90
Verbal weekly communication	193	1	7	4.90	1.88
Verbal bi-weekly communication	184	1	7	3.42	1.96
Verbal monthly communication	186	1	7	2.60	1.88
Verbal communication at milestone achievement	189	1	7	2.68	2.02
Verbal communication at phase or project end	190	1	7	2.57	2.11
Personal daily communication	189	1	7	3.11	1.83
Personal weekly communication	193	1	7	4.32	2.03
Personal bi-weekly communication	189	1	7	3.72	1.98
Personal monthly communication	191	1	7	3.22	2.07
Personal communication at milestone achievement	189	1	7	3.12	2.24
Personal communication at phase or project end	190	1	7	3.05	2.35
Valid N (listwise)	170				

Table 5-11: Means and Standard Deviations of Frequency Variables

Assessment of the appropriateness of the data for factor analysis was done by analysing:

Correlation Matrix

The original correlation matrix is shown in Appendix B-1. High correlations among the variables indicate that the variables can be grouped into underlying dimensions (Sharma 1996, p.116). Inspection of the correlation matrix revealed that 54 of the 153 correlations (35 percent) were at or above the .3 level. This suggests appropriateness for factoring (Hair et al. 1998, p. 99). Significant correlations at the .01 level were found for 85 of the 153 correlations (56 percent), which also qualifies the data for the next steps in factor analysis (Hair et al. 1998, page 212).

Anti-image Correlation Matrix

Partial correlations are the correlations between variables when the effects of other variables are taken into account, and the anti-image matrix is just the negative value of the partial correlation. Anti-image correlations should be small, to allow variables to be explained by the factors, and for factor analysis to be appropriate (Hair et al. 1998, p. 99). Appendix B-2 shows the anti-image correlation matrix of the original data. Inspection of this matrix showed that of all 153 correlations only those for verbal communication at milestone achievement (FQVMIL) and at project phase end (FQVPHA), as well as written communication at milestone and phase end (FQWMIL and FQWPHA) were correlated, with values of -.768 and -.644 respectively. The other 151 partial correlations were low. This indicates strength of the interrelationships among the variables and their appropriateness for factor analysis (Hair et al. 1998, p. 123; Sharma 1996, p. 116).

Kaiser-Meyer-Olkin (KMO) Test

KMO measures the adequacy of the whole sample, as well as its individual variables, for factor analysis. It is a measure of the homogeneity of variables (Sharma 1996, p. 116). This is measured through the Measure of Sampling Adequacy (MSA). Its values range from 0 to 1, with 1 being a perfect predictability of a variable by the other variables. MSA values of .80 or above are considered meritorious, .70 or above, middling, .60 or above, mediocre, .50 or above miserable, below .50 unacceptable (Hair et al. 1998, p. 99). The individual MSA values of the variables of the original set are shown in Appendix B-2. With the exception of one variable all variables exceeded MSA values of .60. An MSA of .504 for the variable Daily Personal Communication (FQPDAY) showed a correlation that was 'miserable' and just above the threshold of unacceptable. This variable was dropped from further analyses, because of its low the correlation with other variables. The factor analysis was re-run and all individual variables' MSA values were above .60 and therefore acceptable. For the overall sample Sharma (1996 p. 116) suggests MSA values above .80, with measures above .60 as being tolerable. An MSA value of .80 for the overall sample indicated appropriateness for factor analysis.

Extracting the Original Frequency Factors

In line with generally accepted practices a principle component analysis with Varimax rotation was performed, with minimum Eigenvalue of 1.0 for factor acceptance. Four frequency factors were extracted in the initial analysis. Factor loadings, Eigenvalues and Percent Variance Explained are listed in Table 5-3 below.

	Original 4 Factor Model			
	Factor 1	Factor 2	Factor 3	Factor 4
Eigenvalue	5.776	2.395	1.879	1.288
% Variance Explained	33.977	14.086	11.051	7.574
Variable/Item				
Frequency in Communication				
Written daily communication	-0.069	-0.098	**0.805**	-0.087
Written weekly communication	-0.082	-0.010	**0.537**	**0.499**
Written bi-weekly communication	-0.066	**0.692**	-0.302	0.297
Written monthly communication	0.371	**0.547**	**-0.409**	0.097
Written communication at milestone achievement	**0.844**	0.039	-0.293	0.073
Written communication at phase or project end	**0.858**	-0.004	-0.220	0.081
No formal written communication*				
Verbal daily communication	-0.075	-0.152	**0.569**	**0.418**
Verbal weekly communication	0.096	0.294	0.002	**0.646**
Verbal bi-weekly communication	0.216	**0.792**	-0.251	-0.042
Verbal monthly communication	**0.453**	**0.633**	-0.147	-0.253
Verbal communication at milestone achievement	**0.842**	0.212	-0.077	-0.107
Verbal communication at phase or project end	**0.852**	0.093	-0.082	-0.083
No formal Verbal communication*				
Personal daily communication**				
Personal weekly communication	-0.154	-0.095	0.030	**0.768**
Personal bi-weekly communication	-0.080	**0.623**	0.108	0.345
Personal monthly communication	0.276	**0.701**	0.209	-0.244
Personal communication at milestone achievement	**0.799**	0.207	0.153	-0.099
Personal communication at phase or project end	**0.825**	0.136	0.101	-0.112
No formal Personal communication*				

* Items not included because of low preference
** Items dropped because of low MSA

Table 5-12: Original Four Factor Frequency Model

Factor loadings at or above .40 were considered significant for a sample size of 200 (Hair et al. 1998, p. 112). The factors were difficult to interpret. Two of the factors also showed insufficient reliability with Coefficient Alpha values of .08 and .58. This was caused by a negative correlation associated with the variable for Written Monthly Communication (FQWMON).

A further factor analysis with three factors was performed for the frequency variables.

The three factor model led to better interpretability and reliability measures. It is shown in Table 5-4. As recommended by Churchill (1979, p. 68) Coefficient Alpha was calculated for each factor to purify the measures (as indicated in Chapter 4). The factor Continuous Communication showed a low Coefficient Alpha measure of .57. Following recommendations from Churchill (1979, p. 68) the Item-to-Total correlations of the individual items were inspected. The variable for verbal weekly communication (FQVWEK) showed a low Item-to-Total correlation of .18, which is below the recommended threshold of .50 (Hair et al. 1998, p. 118). The variable was dropped as recommended by Churchill (1979, p. 68) and the factor analysis re-run. This resulted in acceptable Coefficient Alpha measure of .60 for the factor, and an increase in explained variance from 58% to 61% for the whole model.

Appropriateness of the final data set was assessed as follows:

- Inspection of the correlation matrix (Appendix B-3) revealed a substantial number of correlations between variables at or above the .3 level, i.e. 57 of the 120 correlations (48 percent). This suggests appropriateness for factoring (Hair et al. 1998, p. 99).

- Significant correlations at the .01 level were found for 79 of the 120 correlations (66 percent), which also qualify the data for the next steps in factor analysis (Hair et al. 1998, page 212).

- The anti-image correlation matrix (Appendix B-4) showed generally low partial correlations, except for verbal communication at milestone and phase end (FQVMIL and FQVPHA) with a partial correlation of -.764, and written communication at milestone and phase end (FQWMIL and FQWPHA), with a partial correlation of -.631. The overall low level of partial correlations in the matrix makes it sufficient for factor analysis (Hair et al. 1998, p. 99 and 212).

- The KMO tests showed MSA values above .60 for all individual variables (Appendix B-4), and an overall sample MSA of .80. That suggests appropriateness of the data for factor analysis (Sharma 1996, p. 116).

Levels of Eigenvalue greater than 1 for each of the three factors and 61% of explained variance (see Table 5-4), supported the acceptance of the three factor model on a quantitative basis and interpretability of the factors, as given by the contributing variables, supported it qualitatively. The individual factor items, Eigenvalues, percent variance, loadings and variables are listed in Table 5-4 below, with the significant loadings in bold.

	Frequency Factors		
Final Factor Names:	Variable Interval Communication	Fixed Interval Communication	Continuous Communication
Eigenvalue	5.760	2.277	1.728
% Variance Explained	29.684	18.309	13.040
Variable/Item	Factor Loading		
Frequency in Communication			
Written daily communication	0.007	-0.273	**0.583**
Written weekly communication	-0.077	-0.014	**0.688**
Written bi-weekly communication	-0.087	**0.803**	-0.042
Written monthly communication	0.349	**0.641**	-0.243
Written communication at milestone achievement	**0.808**	0.121	-0.186
Written communication at phase or project end	**0.826**	0.074	-0.117
No formal written communication*			
Verbal daily communication	-0.060	-0.107	**0.766**
Verbal weekly communication**			
Verbal bi-weekly communication	0.229	**0.781**	-0.242
Verbal monthly communication	**0.485**	**0.570**	-0.273
Verbal communication at milestone achievement	**0.847**	0.196	-0.131
Verbal communication at phase or project end	**0.849**	0.090	-0.120
No formal Verbal communication*			
Personal daily communication**			
Personal weekly communication	-0.214	0.146	**0.563**
Personal bi-weekly communication	-0.070	**0.668**	0.309
Personal monthly communication	0.342	**0.549**	-0.011
Personal communication at milestone achievement	**0.821**	0.115	0.007
Personal communication at phase or project end	**0.841**	0.066	-0.027
No formal Personal communication*			

* Items not included because of low preference
** Items dropped because of low MSA or Alpha

Table 5-13: Final Frequency Factors and Loadings

Variable loadings in excess of .40 on a factor were the basis for naming the factors. The names and constituent variables of the factors are:

1. <u>Variable Interval Communication</u>, consisting of variables for written, verbal and personal communication at project milestone achievement and project phase end. It constitutes event driven communication, i.e. whenever notable progress is achieved in the project.

2. Fixed Interval Communication, consisting of variables for written, verbal and personal communication in bi-weekly or monthly intervals. This constitutes a calendar driven communication schedule.

3. Continuous communication, consisting of written daily and weekly communication, as well as verbal daily and personal weekly communication. This reflects a continuous communication between project sponsor and manager through daily e-mails and phone calls, combined with weekly written and personal updates.

Means and standard deviations for factors are listed in the summary statistic in Table 5-8. This table also shows that continuous communication is clearly the communication frequency with the highest mean, i.e. a mean of 4.04 and a standard deviation of .79 on a seven point scale. This is followed by fixed interval communication with mean score of 3.32 (sd = .44). Communication at variable intervals achieved the lowest preference with 2.83 (sd = .24). Verbal monthly communication loaded significantly high on the factors for fixed and variable interval communication, which marks the transition from highest frequency for variable intervals and lowest for fixed intervals. The factors for communication contents were extracted next.

5.1.2 Communication Contents Factors

A R-type exploratory factor analysis for communication contents was done similar to that for communication frequency. The sample size of 200 and the variables-to-observation ratio of 9.5 to 1 exceeded the minimum thresholds. The means and standard deviations are listed in Table 5-5. The mean values range from 3.83 to 6.42 with no outliers.

Assessing the data for their appropriateness for factor analysis led to the following results:

Correlation Matrix

The correlation matrix is shown in Appendix B-5. Inspection of the correlation matrix showed that 114 of the 210 correlations (54 percent) were significant at the .01 level, and 52 of the 210 correlations (25 percent) were at or above the .30 threshold. That suggests adequacy of the variable correlations for factor analysis (Hair et al. 1998, p. 99 and 121).

Anti-image Correlations

The Anti-image correlation matrix is shown in Appendix B-6. Its inspection showed no high partial correlations, with the exception of verbal other communication and personal other communication (COVOTH and COPOTH). These variables showed anti-image correlations of -.615. Overall, the partial correlations suggest appropriateness of the data for factor analysis (Hair et al. 1998, p. 212).

KMO

MSA values of individual variables were above .60 and therefore acceptable (Hair et al. 1998, p. 99). Overall sample MSA of .74 was tolerable (Sharma 1996, p. 116).

	N	Minimum	Maximum	Mean	Std. Deviation
Written contents: status and achievements	199	1	7	6.33	0.82
Written contents: measures and quality metrics	199	1	7	5.01	1.60
Written contents: issues or 'open items'	197	2	7	6.21	1.07
Written contents: project changes	199	2	7	6.42	0.92
Written contents: trends	197	1	7	4.56	1.48
Written contents: next steps	199	1	7	5.85	1.12
Written contents: other	179	1	7	4.49	1.38
Verbal contents: status and achievements	196	1	7	5.28	1.64
Verbal contents: measures and quality metrics	194	1	7	3.90	1.71
Verbal contents: issues or 'open items'	197	1	7	5.65	1.53
Verbal contents: project changes	198	1	7	5.42	1.78
Verbal contents: trends	196	1	7	3.83	1.70
Verbal contents: next steps	197	1	7	5.50	1.35
Verbal contents: other	179	1	7	4.57	1.46
Personal contents: status and achievements	196	1	7	5.62	1.38
Personal contents: measures and quality metrics	195	1	7	4.58	1.71
Personal contents: issues or 'open items'	196	1	7	5.78	1.29
Personal contents: project changes	196	1	7	5.90	1.37
Personal contents: trends	194	1	7	4.50	1.66
Personal contents: next steps	196	1	7	5.70	1.32
Personal contents: other	178	1	7	4.68	1.53
Valid N (listwise)	166				

Table 5-14: Communication Contents Variables

A principle component analysis with Varimax rotation was performed on the contents variables. A six factor model was initially extracted and is listed in Table 5-6. The mix of significant variables per factor was not interpretable. Some of the factors consisted of only three variables that loaded significantly on a factor, i.e. higher than .40 for a sample size of 200 (Hair et al. 1998, p. 112).

Original 6 Factor Model

	Factor 1	Factor 2	Factor 3	Factor 4	Factor 5	Factor 6
Eigenvalue	5.136	2.487	2.091	1.963	1.594	1.043
% Variance Explained	24.457	11.841	9.955	9.346	7.591	4.966
Variable/Item						
Contents in Communication						
Written contents: status and achievements	0.127	0.095	0.041	-0.035	**0.683**	0.108
Written contents: measures and quality metrics	-0.034	**0.613**	-0.186	0.144	**0.474**	-0.109
Written contents: issues or 'open items'	0.061	-0.040	0.175	0.182	**0.729**	0.050
Written contents: project changes	0.051	0.116	0.099	0.079	**0.751**	0.086
Written contents: trends	0.149	**0.672**	-0.185	0.084	0.367	0.202
Written contents: next steps	0.039	0.000	-0.027	0.086	0.346	**0.752**
Written contents: other	0.096	0.124	-0.171	**0.625**	0.208	0.157
Verbal contents: status and achievements	0.104	0.101	**0.764**	-0.122	0.096	-0.191
Verbal contents: measures and quality metrics	-0.068	0.747	**0.412**	0.121	-0.030	-0.034
Verbal contents: issues or 'open items'	0.133	-0.058	**0.782**	0.097	0.081	0.119
Verbal contents: project changes	0.057	0.094	**0.762**	-0.126	0.123	0.243
Verbal contents: trends	-0.013	**0.781**	0.233	0.165	-0.001	0.065
Verbal contents: next steps	0.140	0.083	**0.447**	0.191	-0.060	**0.687**
Verbal contents: other	-0.063	0.120	0.129	**0.877**	0.015	0.088
Personal contents: status and achievements	**0.828**	0.013	0.172	0.004	0.024	-0.132
Personal contents: measures and quality metrics	**0.586**	**0.595**	-0.070	-0.062	-0.006	0.000
Personal contents: issues or 'open items'	**0.723**	-0.037	0.082	0.242	0.247	0.066
Personal contents: project changes	**0.730**	0.104	0.229	-0.003	0.095	0.252
Personal contents: trends	**0.524**	**0.626**	-0.098	0.127	-0.017	-0.001
Personal contents: next steps	**0.632**	0.073	-0.087	0.337	0.039	**0.483**
Personal contents: other	0.320	0.149	-0.083	**0.822**	0.075	0.023

Table 5-15: Factor Loadings, Eigenvalues and % Variance of Original Contents Model

A five factor model showed similar difficulties. A four factor model showed interpretable factors loadings. This model explains 56% of the variance in the sample. The factor loadings, Eigenvalues and explained variance are listed in Table 5-7, with the factor loadings above .40 in bold. The results show that contents and media factors are intertwined and cannot be separated. Therefore they are treated as combined contents and media factors – labelled *contents factors* - for the remainder of the study.

| | Contents Factors | | | |
Final Factor Names:	Personal Review	Project Analysis	Written status report with possible follow-up	Verbal Update
Eigenvalue	5.136	2.487	2.091	1.963
% Variance Explained	15.396	13.999	13.812	12.392
Variable/Item	Factor Loading			
Contents in Communication				
Written contents: status and achievements	0.036	0.151	**0.489**	0.151
Written contents: measures and quality metrics	-0.078	**0.673**	0.356	-0.171
Written contents: issues or 'open items'	-0.004	0.044	**0.628**	0.212
Written contents: project changes	-0.027	0.186	**0.598**	0.177
Written contents: trends	0.156	**0.663**	0.364	-0.108
Written contents: next steps	0.137	-0.095	**0.611**	0.112
Written contents: other	0.217	0.139	**0.554**	-0.269
Verbal contents: status and achievements	0.025	0.154	-0.093	**0.740**
Verbal contents: measures and quality metrics	-0.029	**0.741**	0.027	0.353
Verbal contents: issues or 'open items'	0.150	-0.051	0.154	**0.747**
Verbal contents: project changes	0.053	0.069	0.115	**0.808**
Verbal contents: trends	0.047	**0.759**	0.109	0.194
Verbal contents: next steps	0.301	-0.034	0.350	**0.481**
Verbal contents: other	0.129	0.137	**0.548**	-0.093
Personal contents: status and achievements	**0.762**	0.060	-0.114	0.184
Personal contents: measures and quality metrics	**0.560**	**0.590**	-0.104	-0.016
Personal contents: issues or 'open items'	**0.711**	0.006	0.272	0.088
Personal contents: project changes	**0.727**	0.085	0.106	0.304
Personal contents: trends	**0.540**	**0.624**	0.000	-0.096
Personal contents: next steps	**0.750**	0.012	0.367	-0.059
Personal contents: other	**0.465**	0.186	**0.495**	-0.263

Table 5-16: Final Contents Factors and Loadings

The factors were named based on the variables that loaded in excess of .40 on a factor. The names and constituent variables of the factors are:

1. Personal review, consisting of all variables for personal communication. This shows that respondents associate personal meetings as detailed reviews of the project, where all aspects of project management are discussed.

2. Project analysis consists of variables for measures, quality metrics and trends using all media. It identifies project analysis as a standalone subject in project sponsor – manager communication. It is also linked to the personal meetings, as visualized by the variables for measures and trends in personal communication. These two variables have significant loadings in both factors. It shows the need to discuss project measures and trends at personal meetings, while the written and verbal communication of these data can be done outside the personal meetings.

3. Written status report with possible follow-up, consists of the variables for written communication of project achievements, issues, changes, next steps and other

items. The variables for verbal and personal communication on *other items* loaded also significantly on this factor. The factor shows the need for written status reports with above listed standard contents as recommended by the project management methodologies. It also shows the possibility to follow-up on other, non-standard items using richer media. The significant loading of the variable for personal communication of other items on factor one and three shows the intent to discuss non-standard items at personal reviews. The non-standard nature of the other items may make the respondents use media with higher transfer capabilities.

4. Verbal updates, consist of verbal communication variables for achievements, issues, changes, and next steps. It indicates a more informal, but timely communication about the project status and the short-term plans.

The means and standard deviations are listed in the summary statistic in Table 5-8. It shows that written status reports are the most preferred means of communication between project sponsor and manager, scored 5.51 on a seven point scale. Verbal updates scored second with 5.47. Personal communication follows closely with 5.2, while project analysis scored lowest, with a mean preference of 4.4.

The difference between the perceived importance of a media and the preference for it can be seen from the difference in scoring of the questions about media importance and the scoring of the contents/media factors. Written media scored highest both in importance and in preference, which identifies it as the media of choice for project sponsors and managers. Personal communication scored second in importance, but third in preferences, so it is least preferred but important for the project. Verbal communication was perceived least important, but more preferred than personal communication, indicating sponsor and manager's desire to use this medium for less important messages.

In summary, factor analysis was used to reduce the number of communications variables, i.e. the variables for communication frequency, contents and media. Three frequency and four contents factors were identified as the respondents' underlying dimensions in project sponsor – manager communication. The seven factors were saved in SPSS as Factor Scores and used in subsequent multivariate analyses as a replacement for the larger set of variables. Use of Varimax rotation ensured that the factors are orthogonal and therefore uncorrelated within the group of frequency factors, as well as within the group of contents factors (Hair et al 1998, p. 100). This allows for better interpretation of the upcoming results of the regression analyses, where the antecedents of the factors are assessed and a clear differentiation between the factors is required.

Further validation of the results was done through a series of advanced diagnostics to detect influential observations, which are observations with a disproportionate influence on the results of the regression analyses described in the next section. These diagnostics are described in the section about Regression Analysis.

In the next step the situational variables for project sponsor - manager communication were analysed.

5.2 The Project Situational Variables

The responses to the multi-item constructs for objective clearness, methodology clearness, relational norms, organizational structure and project performance (described in section 4.4 and listed in Appendix A-3) were each summated and averaged to obtain an overall rating per construct. A summary of the means, standard deviations, and related construct variables is provided in the summary statistics in Table 5-8. Coefficient Alpha values and Inter-item Correlations for the summated scales of the Situational Variables were assessed in Chapter 5 and are listed in Table 5-4.

Mean scores were taken for each of the two situational variables relational norms and organisation structure. This follows earlier studies, e.g. Heide & John (1992) for relational norms, and Miles et al. (2000) for organisational structure. Relational norms' mean score of 5.45 on a seven point scale with a neutral position at 4 indicates bi-lateral, mutual interest of buyer and seller in the wellbeing of the relationship within IT implementation projects.

Variable	Questionnaire Item(s) (from Appendix A-3)	Mean	Standard Deviation (SD)
Project Variables			
Respondents Role	1	N/A	N/A
Project Type	2, 3	N/A	N/A
Objective Clearness	4, 5, 6	5.39	(1.15)
Methodology Clearness	7, 8, 9	5.05	(1.32)
Relational Norms	10, 11, 12, 13, 14, 15, 16, 17, 18, 19	5.45	(0.90)
Organisation Structure	68, 69, 70, 71, 72, 73, 74	4.58	(1.05)
Project Performance	65, 66, 67	5.69	(0.96)
Communication Media			
Importance of Written Communication	20	6.34	(0.97)
Importance of Verbal Communication	21	6.19	(0.96)
Importance Personal Communication	22	6.21	(1.04)
Communication Frequency			
Variable Interval Communication	27, 28, 33, 34, 35, 41, 42	2.83	(0.24)
Fixed Interval Communication	25, 26, 32, 33, 39, 40	3.32	(0.44)
Continuous Communication	23, 24, 30, 38	4.04	(0.79)
Communication Contents			
Personal Review	58, 59, 60, 61, 62, 63, 64	5.23	(0.63)
Project Analysis	45, 48, 52, 55, 59, 62	4.40	(0.45)
Written Status	44, 46, 47, 49, 50, 57, 64	5.51	(0.91)
Verbal Update	51, 53, 54, 56	5.47	(0.16)
Demographic Variables			
Age	80	42.2	(8.15)
Years of work experience	81	20.2	(8.87)
Years of experience in proj. mgmt.	82	10.3	(6.47)
Years as sponsor	83	5.9	(5.19)

Table 5-17: Summary Statistics

Of the two risk constructs objective clearness scored 5.39 on the seven point scale and methodology clearness 5.05. The three questions on project performance were averaged for each respondent to a mean score of 5.69. Following the recommendations from the focus groups, this variable was used in the upcoming analyses to identify the communication differences in high and low performing projects. Therefore, the variable was converted from scale to nominal. To preserve the largest possible sample size this variable was not split in more than the two sub-categories high and low. The variable was split at the mean level. Projects with performance levels at or over 5.69 were classified as high performing projects, those lower than 5.69 as low performing projects. This split could have also been done at the median, i.e. 6.00, without a change in the classifications of responses in high and low projects.

The situational and structural variables for organisation structure, relational norms, objective clearness, methodology clearness, and project performance were used as independent variables, and the factor scores of the contents and frequency factors were used as dependent variables in subsequent multiple regression analyses. These regressions are described next.

5.3 Revised Research Model for Step 1

The results of the factor analysis showed that the original research model for Step 1 had to be changed. The intertwined nature of communication contents and media, as shown by the factor for communication contents, did not allow assessing the impact of the independent variables on both contents and media variables individually. The original research model for Step 1 (shown in Figure 4-2) was revised to reflect the combined content and media factor and the associated relationships for investigation. Figure 5-1 shows the revised model, with the hypothesised relationships, as well as those for empirical investigation.

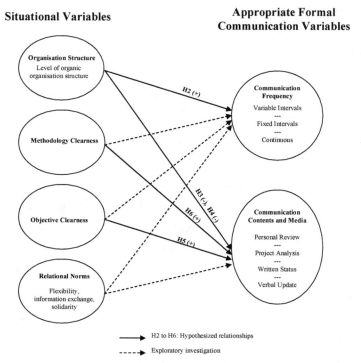

Figure 5-8: Revised Research Model for Step 1

5.4 Step 1: Situational Variables as Antecedents for Communication Patterns

The impact of situational and demographic variables on communication variables was assessed using multivariate regression analysis. This technique analyses the relationship between a dependent variable (also called criterion variable) and several independent variables (also called predictor variables). The objective is to predict the value of the dependent variable through the known values of the independent variables. An example for a general formula for regression is given by Churchill (1999):

$$Y = \alpha + \beta_1 X_1 + \beta_2 X_2 + \beta_3 X_3 + \varepsilon$$

where:

$Y =$ the value of the dependent variable, estimated from the regression equation

$\alpha =$ the intercept parameter or constant in multiple regression

$\beta_j =$ the partial regression coefficient, indicating the change in Y for every unit change in X_j controlling for the influence of the other independent variables

$X_j =$ the value of the independent variable ($j = 1, 2, 3 ...$)

$\varepsilon =$ the error associated with the prediction, also called residual

The mathematical technique to estimate values of α and β_j is called the method of least squares, which determines estimates of α and β_j values that allow prediction of Y with the minimum sum of squared errors of prediction (ε).

The goodness of fit of the data to the regression model is measured by the squared correlation of the actual and the predicted values, called the Coefficient of Determination (R^2), which takes on values between 0 an 1, with 0 indicating no predictive accuracy and 1 indicating perfect fit. Beta Coefficients are regression coefficients derived from standardized data. These standardized data are used to eliminate the influence of different units of measurement on the regression coefficients. Beta regression coefficients allow one to compare coefficients as to their relative impact on the dependent variable for a change of one standard deviation in either variable. Beta Coefficients, however, should only be used as a guide for variable importance when collinearity is minimal. Individual Beta Coefficients should only be interpreted in the context of the other variables in the equation, and they are only valid for the range of data used in calculating the equation (Hair et al. 1998, p.188).

Within the present study, the situational and demographic variables were categorized as independent variables. The factor scores of the factors for communication frequency and contents, as identified in the factor analysis, were classified as dependent variables. Multiple regression analysis was used to analyse the impact of work experience, project management experience, sponsor experience, organisation structure, relational norms, objective clearness, and methodology clearness on the frequency factors for continuous, fixed interval and variable interval communication, as well as the contents factors for personal review, project analysis, written status report, and verbal update (see Figure 4-2). Results were structured by buyer-seller perspective and high-low performing projects. Significance level for all regression models was set to the .1. This higher level than the usual .05 level was chosen because of the wide variety of influences on the responses, given by the large number of geographies, cultures, industries, project sizes and complexities, and the need to filter-out this 'noise' to arrive at a 'common denominator' for communication in IT projects.

Sample sizes for multiple regressions should be at minimum five observations per independent variable. However, 15 to 20 observations per independent variable are desired for results to be generalizable (Hair et al. 1998, p. 166). This minimum was exceeded in the current sample with a ratio of 33 observations per independent variable. Dummy variables, with values 0 and 1, for buyer and seller, as well as for low and high project performance were used to accommodate the perspectives and performance situations in project context. Underlying assumptions of multiple regression were tested through inspection of normal probability plots to assess the normal distribution of the dependent variables before running the regressions (see Appendix B-7), as well as scatterplots of the standardized residuals against their predicted values, and the histograms of the error term distributions after calculation of the regression models (see Appendix B-8). All tests showed acceptable results.

The backward elimination method with missing values replaced by mean was used to regress the impact of situational variables and demographic variables on the dependent variables. This method for selecting variables starts with all variables in the formula and then deletes all those independent variables not contributing significantly to the prediction of the dependent variable. In line with the set significance level of .1 for this study backward regression in SPSS by default *'removes a variable from the model if the observed significance level for its coefficient is greater than 0.10'* (Norusis 2000, p. 475). Four significant regression models were calculated, which were subject to several tests before acceptance. These are described below.

Multicollinearity can reduce the predictive power to the extent an independent variable is correlated with one or more of the other independent variables included in the model. To maximize prediction of dependent variables the independent variables should have low multicollinearity with other independent variables and high correlation with dependent variables. The former is identified by observing the correlation matrix for independent variables. Correlations above .90 indicate substantial collinearity between two variables (Hair et al. 1998, p. 191). The correlation matrix of the regression variables in Appendix B-9 shows only low correlations among the situational and communication variables. Low correlations were also expected and found among the communication frequency factors and the contents factors, because both groups of factors consist of factor scores, which are orthogonal. Among the demographic variables a high correlation (.910) was found between the variables for Age and Business Experience. Business experience was deemed a more important variable for the study. Therefore the variable Age was excluded from further analyses to prevent from incorrectly estimated regression coefficients caused by multicollinearity of the independent variables (Hair et al. 1998, p. 189).

Multicollinearity can be identified through the Variance Inflation Factor (VIF), which measures the extent to which each independent variable is explained by other independent variables. Acceptable levels of VIF are usually 10 or below (Hair 1998, p. 193 & 220). The VIF values found in the regression models of this study ranged from 1.0 to 1.439. The results showed no threat of multicollinearity.

Hair et al. (1998) recommend a series of advanced diagnostic tests to assess multicollinearity and identify influential observations together with their impact on the regression analysis. These tests should all be applied together and decisions on how to proceed with individual observations identified as being influential should be based on the results of *all* of the tests, not just a single one. Thus, observations should only be deleted if they are identified as influential observations in all or the majority of the following tests, and found unrepresentative of the sample (Hair et al. 1998, p. 235).

Assessing Multicollinearity

This is a two-part process. The first part identifies multicollinearity through a Condition Index, which represents the collinearity of combinations of variables in the data set. Threshold values above 15 to 30, with 30 being used most often, identify variables subject to part two examination. The second part identifies the proportion of variance for each regression coefficient attributable to each condition index. This process identifies a collinearity problem when a variable with a high condition index identified in part 1 accounts for a substantial proportion of variance in one or more regression coefficients, usually .90 or above. Thus, a Condition Index over 30 and a Variance over .90 identifies collinear variables (Hair et al. 1998, p. 220).

The maximum value for a Condition Index found in the regression models was 15. Being below the usual threshold level of 30 the second part of the assessment was omitted. No threat of multicollinearity existed.

Identifying Influential Observations

Hair et al. (1998, p. 221) suggest a four step process which supports the selection and accommodation of influential observations by identifying outliers, leverage points and influential observations. The process was applied to the four regression models. Observations identified in these tests were marked for an overall assessment at the end of the process.

Step 1: Examining Residuals

The deleted studentized residuals technique estimates the regression while omitting the particular observation and standardizes its residuals. All standardized residuals follow the t-distribution and can be assessed against a threshold of 2 standard deviations (Hair et al. 1998, p. 222). Studentized, standardized, and studentized deleted residuals greater than the threshold are outliers and were marked as potentially influential observations.

Step 2: Identifying Leverage Points from the Predictors

This identifies observations that are substantially different from the remaining observations in one or more observations of the independent variables. Mahalanobis Distance (D^2) does that by identifying the distance of an observation of an independent variable from the mean value of all the independent variables. Observations with larger differences may cause the estimation of one or more regression coefficients to be affected and 'leveraged' in their direction. Predictors with possible leverage are identified by finding Mahalanobis values that are two or three times the next lower values (Hair et al. 1998, p. 224). These predictor observations can be considered as potential outliers and were marked accordingly.

Hat values were used to identify independent variables with a disproportionate weight in determining its predicted dependent variable value. A threshold of 2p/n (p=number of independent variables plus one for the constant, n=sample Size) for *hat values* was used to identify and mark observations as possible leverage points (Hair et al. 1998, p. 224).

Step 3: Single-Case Diagnostics Identifying Influential Observations

These methods measure the influence of an observation by deleting it and subsequently observing the changes in the regression's residuals. Threshold values are calculated for four different measures, which are used to identify outliers.

DFBETA (Difference in Beta value) measures changes of a coefficient when a single observation is deleted. Threshold values to identify outliers were determined by calculating $\pm2\sqrt{n}$ and comparing the standardized values of DFBETA, called

SDFBETA with the results (Hair et al. 1998, p. 225). SDFBETA values outside the calculated values were marked as outlier observations.

The single most representative measure of influence is Cook's Distance (D_i). It gives an overall measure of the change in all the regression coefficients when a case is left out, and a measure of the observation's distance from the other observations. D_i values of 1.0 or greater indicate the need for investigation of the observation (Hair et al. 1998, p. 225). No observations with Cook's Distance at 1.0 or greater were found.

The degree to which an observation impacts the standard errors of the regression coefficients is measured by the covariance ratio or COVRATIO, which contrary to SDFBETA, considers all coefficients collectively. COVRATIO estimates the effect of the observation on the efficiency of the estimation process. The threshold is established by $1 \pm 3p/n$, where p is the number of independent variables and n the sample size. Values above the higher threshold make the estimation process more efficient, whereas those lower than the lower threshold detract from estimation efficiency. This identifies both positively influencing observations as well as negative ones (Hair et al. 1998, p. 225). Both were marked accordingly.

A complementary measure for identification of outlying residuals and leverage points of predictors is SDFFIT (Standardized Difference in Fit). It measures the degree the fitted values change when a case is deleted. Thresholds are calculated through $2\sqrt{((k+1)/(n-k-1))}$, where k is the number of independent variables. Observations with SDFFIT values beyond the threshold and identified in step 1 and 2 as outliers were considered outlier observations and marked accordingly (Hair et al. 1998, p. 225).

Step 4: Selecting and Accommodating Influential Observations
No single measure represents all dimensions of possible influence of an observation. Therefore the combination of all measures needs to be taken into account when deciding on a course of action with the outliers. Cases consistently identified by several diagnostics as outliers should be closely examined and if it is ascertained that a case is unrepresentative of the population it should deleted (Hair et al. 1998, p. 235). Observations identified through the techniques as potential outliers were assessed on

their impact on all or the majority of the measures (Appendix B-10). No observation was identified as an outlier in all measures. One observation was marked as outlier in more than 50% of the measures in one of the four regression models listed in Appendix B-10. The observation was retained in the sample because it was identified neither as a leverage point, nor as outlier through the Cook's Distance measure.

5.4.1 Regressions on Total Sample

A regression analysis on the level of total sample (buyers plus sellers) was performed to investigate the overall impact of the situational and demographic variables on communication preferences. Table 5-9 shows the minimum and maximum values of the variables, as well as their mean and standard deviation.

	N	Minimum	Maximum	Mean	Std. Deviation
Personal Reviews	200	-3.709	1.690	.000	1.000
Project Analysis	200	-3.450	2.116	.000	1.000
Written Status Report	200	-4.026	2.360	.000	1.000
Verbal Update	200	-3.835	1.579	.000	1.000
Variable Interval Communication	200	-1.543	2.406	.000	1.000
Fixed Interval Communication	200	-2.089	2.474	.000	1.000
Continuous Communication	200	-2.721	2.424	.000	1.000
Work Experience	189	5.000	42.000	20.156	8.873
Project Management Experience	189	.000	31.000	10.259	6.472
Sponsor Experience	48	1.000	22.000	5.854	5.190
Methodology Clearness	200	1.000	7.000	5.045	1.324
Objective Clearness	200	2.000	7.000	5.392	1.151
Low / High Performance	199	.000	1.000	.608	.489
Relational Norms	200	2.600	7.000	5.449	.900
Organisation Structure	199	1.571	7.000	4.578	1.047
Buyer / Seller	200	.000	1.000	.690	.464
Valid N (listwise)	48				

Table 5-18: Means and Standard Deviations of Independent and Dependent Variables

Each dependent variable was regressed against the set of all independent variables (i.e. combined situational, demographic, buyer-seller perspective, and high-low project performance). The results were assessed for both statistical and practical significance, where the former determines whether the results are attributable to chance, and the latter whether they are useful, i.e. substantial enough to warrant action (Hair et al. 1998, p.3).

Practical significance of the models was assessed by observing the effect size and statistical power of the models. Power is the probability that statistical significance will be found if it is present in the data. Power values are calculated based on effect size, the regression's significance level, and sample size. Conventional levels of power are .80 and above, so that existing phenomena can be statistically detected 80% of the time (Hair et al. 1998, p.11, Cohen 1988, p. 56). Effect size is *the estimate of the magnitude to which a phenomenon being studied exists in the population'* (Hair et al. 1998, p. 2). Larger effects are more likely to be found than smaller effects. Thus, other things being equal, larger effect sizes increase statistical power (Cohen 1998, p. 11). A classification of effect sizes in regression analyses in small, medium and low through use of the regression's R^2 values is given by Cohen (1988, p. 413), where:

Small effect size: $R^2 = .02$

Medium effect size: $R^2 = .13$

Large effect size: $R^2 = .26$

Small effect sizes are of a magnitude often found in relationships pursued in the 'soft' behavioural science (Cohen 1988, p. 79). Medium effect sizes are of a magnitude that *'would be perceptible to the naked eye of a reasonably sensitive observer'* (Cohen 1988, p. 80), and large effect sizes mark the *'practical upper limit of predictive effectiveness'* in the behavioural science (Cohen 1988, p. 81, citing Ghiselli 1964, p. 61).

Regression models with R^2 lower than .02 are considered trivial and of negligible practical use, and those with power values below .80 as ambiguous (Cohen 1988, p. 413 and 4). Regression models below these thresholds are reported in the following statistical analyses, but not considered in the interpretation and conclusions.

The regression analyses showed no significant model for the impact of years of experience in work, project management and as sponsor on communication preferences of the combined buyer and seller sample. Four statistically significant models (p<.1) were found for the situational variables' impact on communication preferences. These are listed in Table 5-10.

Dependent Variable: Continuous Communication		
Variable	B	Beta
Constant	.652	
Organisation Structure	-.120	-.126
Objective Clearness	-.172	-.198
Methodology Clearness	.164	.217
R^2 = .067	Sign. = .004	
Adj. R^2 = .052	Power = .937	
F = 4.656		

Dependent Variable: Project Analysis		
Variable	B	Beta
Constant	1.170	
Objective Clearness	-.161	-.185
Buyer - Seller Perspective	-.440	-.204
R^2 = .068	Sign. = .001	
Adj. R^2 = .058	Power = .963	
F = 7.151		

Dependent Variable: Personal Review		
Variable	B	Beta
Constant	.623	
Objective Clearness	-.116	-.133
R^2 = .018	Sign. = .060	
Adj. R^2 = .013	Power = .594	
F = 3.566		

Dependent Variable: Written Status Report		
Variable	B	Beta
Constant	-.527	
Organisation Structure	-.118	-.124
Objective Clearness	.198	.228
R^2 = .063	Sign. = .002	
Adj. R^2 = .054	Power = .949	
F = 6.656		

Table 5-19: Regression Models for Total Sample

The models for the dependent variables Continuous Communication, Project Analysis and Written Status Report showed effect sizes between small and medium, and power levels in excess of .90. They are therefore considered to be of practical significance. The model for Personal Review has a low power of .594 and its effect size is just below the threshold value of .02 for triviality. This model is therefore not considered to be of practical use.

The situational variables showed a significant impact on one of the communication frequency variables and two contents variables. Organic organisation structures reduce the preference for continuous formal communication and written reports. Low risks through clear objectives reduce continuous communication and analysis, while, at the same time, increase the use of written status reports. Low risk through clearness of methodology increases communication frequency. Relational norms have no impact on the basis of total sample. A significant difference exists between buyers and sellers in the preference for analysis data. As indicated by the negative sign, project sponsors from buyer organisations (coded 0) have a significantly higher preference for analysis data than project managers from seller firms (coded 1). The details of this difference will be assessed in Step 2.

Table 5-11 below summarizes the regressions on the total sample by showing the direction and significance of the individual relationships identified through the regressions above. The boxes contain the models with practical significance.

Independent Variables	Communication Frequency			Personal Review	Communication Contents		
	Variable Interval Communication	Fixed Interval Communication	Continuous Communication		Project Analysis	Written Status	Verbal Update
Demographic Variables							
Work Experience	0	0	0	0	0	0	0
Project Management Experience	0	0	0	0	0	0	0
Sponsor Experience	0	0	0	0	0	0	0
Situational Variables							
Relational Norms	0	0	0	0	0	0	0
Organization Structure	0	0	-*	0	0	-*	0
Objective Clearness	0	0	-**	-*	-***	+*****	0
Methodology Clearness	0	0	+****	0	0	0	0
Buyer - Seller Perspective	0	0	0	0	-****	0	0
Low - High Project Performance	0	0	0	0	0	0	0

Note: 0 = not significant   +/- = significant positive or negative correlation
* Significant at p < .10
**Significant at p < .05   ☐ = Model with practical significance
***Significant at p < .01
****Significant at p < .005
*****Significant at p < .001
n=200

Table 5-20: Summary of Regression Results on Total Sample

Results of the confirmatory research on the overall communication of project sponsor and manager are:

- Hypothesis 1: a significant difference between project sponsors and managers exists in their preference for analysis data about the project. Hypothesis 1 is supported.

- Hypothesis 2: organic organisation structures were found to reduce the preference for formal daily communication. Therefore, hypothesis 2 is not supported. The hypothesized increase in communication in organic organisation structures may be related to informal communication only, and therefore may not be relevant for this study.

- Hypothesis 3: the significant negative relationship found between organic organisation structures and written media supports hypothesis 3.

- Hypothesis 4: no significant correlation between bureaucratic structures and quantitative measures was found. Hypothesis 4 is not supported.

- Hypothesis 5: the correlation between clearness of objectives and use of lean media supports hypothesis 5.

- Hypothesis 6: no statistical evidence was found for a correlation between clearness of methodology and use of written media. Hypothesis 6 is not supported.

On the basis of total sample the media related theories tested through H3 and H5 were confirmed, albeit with only small to medium practical significance. Media choice is influenced by organisation structure and objective clearness. Communication effectiveness is hindered through a lack of fit between information processing needs and capabilities in the area of project analysis data.

To accommodate the sample's imbalance in the number of buyer and seller responses, as well as in high and low performing projects, further regression analyses were run individually for these four sub-samples. For each sub-sample the set of demographic variables and the set of situational variables were regressed independently against each dependent variable. This approach was used to keep the variable-to-observations ratio above the 15:1 suggestion from Hair et al. (1998, p. 166) for each regression model. This approach followed earlier studies that investigated the impact of external factors on communication, such as e.g. in Kettinger & Grover (1997).

5.4.2 Regressions by Buyer and Seller

At the next level of detail project sponsors and managers preferences were individually investigated on their impact through situational variables. The number of observations, means and standard deviations for the variables from the buyer and seller sample are listed in Table 5-12. Remarkable differences in mean values exist again in the sponsor's higher scores for project analysis.

Variables	Buyer Sample			Seller Sample		
	N	Mean	Std. Deviation	N	Mean	Std. Deviation
Demographic Variables						
Years of Work Experience	54	19.69	9.42	135	20.34	8.67
Years of Project Management Experience	54	10.29	7.44	135	10.25	6.07
Years as Sponsor	48	5.85	5.19	N/A		
Independent Variables						
Methodology Clearness	54	5.13	1.16	138	5.00	1.39
Objective Clearness	62	5.58	.99	138	5.31	1.21
Low / High Performance Project	61	.57	.50	138	.62	.49
Relational Norms	62	5.41	.88	138	5.47	.91
Organisation Structure	61	4.35	1.18	138	4.68	.97
Dependent Variables						
Personal Reviews	62	.00	.89	138	.00	1.05
Project Analysis	62	.27	.87	138	-.12	1.03
Written Status Report	62	-.05	1.00	138	.02	1.00
Verbal Update	62	-.06	1.00	138	.03	1.00
Variable Interval Communication	62	.12	1.10	138	-.05	.95
Fixed Interval Communication	62	.14	.99	138	-.06	1.00
Continuous Communication	62	.01	.97	138	.00	1.02

Table 5-21: Description of Buyer and Seller Sample

Backward regression analysis with missing values replaced by means was used for both samples to investigate the impact of demographic variables and situational variables on each dependent factor variable. Five statistically significant regression models were found in both buyer and seller samples.

5.4.2.1 Buyer Regressions

The regression models are listed Table 5-13. The proportions of variance explained by the regressions were between 3% and 15%. Four of five models showed a small effect size and low statistical power. For those models the sample size of 62 buyer responses was not sufficiently large to detect small effect sizes at power levels of .80 or above.

Only one regression showed a credible result, with a medium effect size and high statistical power. It shows that project sponsor communication is mainly influenced by demographic variables. Project management experience increases the preference for written status reports.

Regressions against Demographic Variables

Dependent Variable: Fixed Interval Communication		
Variable	B	Beta
Constant	.667	
Work Experience	-.027	-.239
R^2 = .057	Sign. = .061	
Adj. R^2 = .041	Power = .615	
F = 3.637		

Dependent Variable: Personal Review		
Variable	B	Beta
Constant	.437	
Work Experience	-.022	-.215
R^2 = .046	Sign. = .093	
Adj. R^2 = .030	Power = .525	
F = 2.917		

Dependent Variable: Written Status Report		
Variable	B	Beta
Constant	-.623	
Project Management Experience	.056	.387
R^2 = .149	Sign. = .002	
Adj. R^2 = .135	Power = .944	
F = 10.545		

Regressions against Situational Variables

Dependent Variable: Project Analysis		
Variable	B	Beta
Constant	-.901	
Relational Norms	.217	.220
R^2 = .049	Sign. = .085	
Adj. R^2 = .033	Power = .535	
F = 3.066		

Dependent Variable: Written Status Report		
Variable	B	Beta
Constant	-1.451	
Objective Clearness	.252	.250
R^2 = .062	Sign. = .051	
Adj. R^2 = .047	Power = .629	
F = 3.983		

Table 5-22: Regressions on Buyers

With power values between .53 and .63 and small effect sizes the other models were not deemed credible and of practical significance. They indicate the possibility that work experience is inversely related to preference for communication at fixed intervals and personal reviews. Also, that relational norms are positively correlated with the preference for project analysis. Objective clearness possibly correlates positively with the preference for written status reports, showing that lower risks possibly lead to a shift towards routine status reports. Organisation structure and methodology clearness showed no impact on the sponsor's communication.

Results of the confirmatory analysis are:

- Hypothesis 1 for buyers: not relevant

- Hypotheses 2 to 4 for buyers: no correlation was found between organisation structure and communication frequency, media choice and quantitative contents. Hypotheses 2 to 4 are therefore not supported. The existing theories underlying the hypotheses may not be applicable for formal communication between project sponsors and managers in IT buyer-seller projects.

- Hypothesis 5 for buyers: the correlation between clearness of objectives and written status reports is not clearly supported. The regression model showed a low practical significance. Hypothesis 5 is therefore not supported.

- Hypothesis 6 for buyers: no correlation between methodology clearness and choice for written media was found. Hypothesis 6 is not supported.

The results show that project sponsor communication preferences are driven by past experiences. It indicates a communication style of buyers based on perceptions or 'gut feelings' rather than a structured, analytic assessment of the supplier's performance in a project.

5.4.2.2 Seller Regressions

A similar regression analysis was done for the seller sample. No significant correlation between demographic variables and communication preferences were found. Five significant models showing the impact of situational variables on communication were found. These are listed in Table 5-14.

The model for Continuous Communication showed medium effect size and high statistical power. The models for Project analysis and Written Status Reports had small effect sizes at acceptable power levels. The two models for Personal Review and Variable Interval communication showed only small effect sizes and low statistical power and were therefore not considered to be of practical significance.

Dependent Variable: Variable Interval Communication		
Variable	B	Beta
Constant	.635	
Objective Clearness	-.129	-.165
R^2 = .027	Sign. = .053	
Adj. R^2 = .020	Power = .616	
F = 3.796		

Dependent Variable: Personal Reviews		
Variable	B	Beta
Constant	.826	
Objective Clearness	-.156	-.180
R^2 = .032	Sign. = .035	
Adj. R^2 = .025	Power = .684	
F = 4.551		

Dependent Variable: Continuous Communication		
Variable	B	Beta
Constant	1.048	
Organisation Structure	-.169	-.161
Objective Clearness	-.249	-.296
Methodology Clearness	.213	.291
R^2 = .128	Sign. = .000	
Adj. R^2 = .108	Power = .986	
F = 6.552		

Dependent Variable: Project Analysis		
Variable	B	Beta
Constant	.959	
Objective Clearness	-.204	-.238
R^2 = .057	Sign. = .005	
Adj. R^2 = .050	Power = .886	
F = 8.197		

Dependent Variable: Written Status Reports		
Variable	B	Beta
Constant	-.928	
Objective Clearness	.179	.216
R^2 = .047	Sign. = .011	
Adj. R^2 = .040	Power = .821	
F = 6.648		

Table 5-23: Regressions on Sellers

Relational norms have no impact on communication preferences. Organic organisation structures reduce the preference for continuous communication, while methodology clearness increases the preference for it. Objective clearness impacts five of the seven factors for communication, is significant within all identified models, and therefore clearly the most influential situational variable on project managers communication preferences.

The results of the confirmatory analysis are:

- Hypothesis 1 for sellers: not applicable

- Hypothesis 2 for sellers: organic organisation structure is negatively correlated with communication frequency. Hypothesis 2 is not supported. The hypothesized increase in communication frequency may not be related to formal communications of project managers.

- Hypotheses 3 and 4 for sellers: no correlation was found between organisation structure and media choice or quantitative communication contents. Hypotheses 3 and 4 are not supported.

- Hypothesis 5 for sellers: Clearness of goals increases the preference for written status reports and therefore lean media. Unclear goals increase communication frequency and detailed analysis. Hypothesis 5 is supported.

- Hypothesis 6 for sellers: no correlation was found between methodology clearness and use of written media. Hypothesis 6 is not supported.

Table 5-15 summarizes the buyer and seller regression analyses and shows the differences in significance of impact. Project managers' communication preferences are project related, i.e. they are mainly driven by project risk, whereas project sponsors communication is mainly impacted by demographic variables.

Independent Variables	Communication Frequency						Communication Contents							
	Variable Interval Communication		Fixed Interval Communication		Continuous Communication		Personal Review		Project Analysis		Written Status		Verbal Update	
	Buyer	Seller	Buyer	Seller	Buyer	Seller	Buyer	Seller	Buyer	Seller	Buyer	Seller	Buyer	Seller
Demographic Variables														
Work Experience	0	0	-*	0	0	0	-*	0	0	0	0	0	0	0
Project Management Experience	0	0	0	0	0	0	0	0	0	0	+****	0	0	0
Project Sponsor Experience	0	n/a	0	n/a	0	n/a	0	n/a	0	n/a	0	n/a	0	n/a
Situational Variables														
Relational Norms	0	0	0	0	0	0	0	0	+*	0	0	0	0	0
Organization Structure	0	0	0	0	0	-**	0	0	0	0	0	0	0	0
Objective Clearness	0	-*	0	0	0	-****	0	-**	0	-****	+*	+**	0	0
Methodology Clearness	0	0	0	0	0	+****	0	0	0	0	0	0	0	0
Low - High Performing Project	0	0	0	0	0	+****	0	0	0	0	0	0	0	0

Note: 0 = not significant   +/- = significant positive or negative correlation
* Significant at p < .10
**Significant at p < .05   ☐ = Model with practical significance
***Significant at p < .01
****Significant at p < .005
*****Significant at p < .001
Buyer: n = 62
Seller: n = 138

Table 5-24: Summary of Buyer and Seller Regressions

The results show that a difference in the drivers for formal project related communication between project sponsors and managers exists. Project sponsors communication is impacted by their individual prior experience and the relationship between the parties, therefore driven by a high level of subjectivity. It is context driven through the broader organisational perspective of the project sponsor

(Partington 1997), and therefore in need of objective, preferably quantitative data about project status and progress. Contrary to that is the project managers' communication driven by project risk, especially clearness of project objectives. Their communication is project driven and reflects the delivery-contract focused perspective of the project manager. The parties' different drivers for communication, i.e. project context versus project focus, results in different expectations as shown by the significant difference in preference for analysis data. Project sponsors look for objective, quantitative data about project progress, while project managers report qualitatively the status on recent achievements.

5.4.3 Regressions by High and Low Performing Projects

The purpose of this analysis is to identify antecedents for communication in high performing projects and those in low performing projects. Identified differences in antecedents will provide insight into the more ideal communication practices, such as in high performing projects, and comparing them with those projects of lower performance. The confirmatory analysis, using Hypotheses H1 to H6, shows to what extent communication in low and high performing projects conforms to communication practices in permanent organisations. The exploratory analysis shows the impact of situational variables in different contexts, such as good or bad performance of a project.

The number of observations, means and standard deviations are shown in Table 5-16, which reveals a higher preference for personal reviews, verbal updates and project analysis in low performing projects.

Variables	Low Performing Projects			High Performing Projects		
	N	Mean	Std. Deviation	N	Mean	Std. Deviation
Demographic Variables						
Year of Work Experience	71	20.13	9.61	117	20.13	8.47
Years of Project Management Experience	71	9.99	6.95	117	10.48	6.18
Years as Sponsor	19	6.68	6.11	29	5.31	4.52
Independent Variables						
Methodology Clearness	78	4.70	1.40	121	5.26	1.23
Objective Clearness	78	4.97	1.29	121	5.66	.97
Relational Norms	78	5.25	.95	121	5.59	.84
Organisation Structure	78	4.53	1.06	120	4.62	1.04
Dependent Variables						
Personal Reviews	78	.03	.97	121	-.02	1.03
Project Analysis	78	.05	.93	121	-.05	1.04
Written Status Report	78	-.10	1.07	121	.07	.96
Verbal Update	78	.03	.85	121	-.03	1.09
Variable Interval Communication	78	-.04	.96	121	.03	1.03
Fixed Interval Communication	78	-.02	.99	121	.02	1.01
Continuous Communication	78	-.06	1.03	121	.03	.98

Table 5-25: Description of Low and High Performing Projects Samples

Analysis of Variance (ANOVA) was used to statistically assess the significance of differences in mean values between high and low performing projects. ANOVA compares the variability of a variable within its sample, e.g. in low performing projects, with the variability of a variable in the other sample, e.g. between high and low performing sample (Hair 1998). The results of ANOVA show whether the two means are significantly different.

Table 5-17 shows that significant differences (at .05 level) exist between low and high performing projects in clearness of methodology, clearness of objectives and relational norms. High performing projects score significantly higher on these measures, thus bear lower risks and better buyer –seller relationships.

		Sum of Squares	df	Mean Square	F	Sig.
Years of Work Experience	Between Groups	1.445E-03	1	1.445E-03	.000	.997
	Within Groups	14776.056	186	79.441		
	Total	14776.057	187			
Years of Project Management Experience	Between Groups	10.607	1	10.607	.253	.616
	Within Groups	7811.212	186	41.996		
	Total	7821.819	187			
Years as Sponsor	Between Groups	21.667	1	21.667	.801	.375
	Within Groups	1244.312	46	27.050		
	Total	1265.979	47			
Methodology Clearness	Between Groups	15.065	1	15.065	8.895	.003
	Within Groups	333.668	197	1.694		
	Total	348.734	198			
Objective Clearness	Between Groups	22.371	1	22.371	18.282	.000
	Within Groups	241.056	197	1.224		
	Total	263.427	198			
Relational Norms	Between Groups	5.388	1	5.388	6.848	.010
	Within Groups	155.010	197	.787		
	Total	160.398	198			
Organisation Structure	Between Groups	.370	1	.370	.335	.563
	Within Groups	216.100	196	1.103		
	Total	216.470	197			
Personal Reviews	Between Groups	.121	1	.121	.120	.729
	Within Groups	198.711	197	1.009		
	Total	198.832	198			
Project Analysis	Between Groups	.464	1	.464	.469	.494
	Within Groups	195.193	197	.991		
	Total	195.657	198			
Written Status Report	Between Groups	1.416	1	1.416	1.414	.236
	Within Groups	197.361	197	1.002		
	Total	198.777	198			
Verbal Update	Between Groups	.150	1	.150	.150	.699
	Within Groups	197.797	197	1.004		
	Total	197.948	198			
Variable Interval Communication	Between Groups	.214	1	.214	.213	.645
	Within Groups	198.284	197	1.007		
	Total	198.498	198			
Fixed Interval Communication	Between Groups	6.226E-02	1	6.226E-02	.062	.804
	Within Groups	198.169	197	1.006		
	Total	198.232	198			
Continuous Communication	Between Groups	.420	1	.420	.417	.519
	Within Groups	198.064	197	1.005		
	Total	198.483	198			

Table 5-26: ANOVA between Low and High Performing Projects

The investigation in the impact of situational variables on the communication of project sponsors and managers in low and high performing projects was done similar to the regression analysis for buyers and sellers described above.

5.4.3.1 Regressions on Low Performing Projects

No correlation between demographic variables and dependent variables were found. Four models for impact of situational variables on communication preferences were found. They are shown in Table 5-18. Only one model shows practical significance through an effect size between small and medium together with a statistical power above the minimum level of .80. The model shows that bureaucratic organisation structures increase the preference for project analysis. The other regression models show effect sizes close to the lower threshold of triviality, and low statistical power. They are not considered to be of practical use.

Dependent Variable: Fixed Interval Communication		
Variable	B	Beta
Constant	-.651	
Methodology Clearness	.135	.190
R^2 = .036	Sign. = .095	
Adj. R^2 = .024	Power = .513	
F = 2.861		

Dependent Variable: Personal Reviews		
Variable	B	Beta
Constant	.961	
Objective Clearness	-.187	-.250
R^2 = .063	Sign. = .027	
Adj. R^2 = .050	Power = .722	
F = 5.079		

Dependent Variable: Continuous Communication		
Variable	B	Beta
Constant	.855	
Objective Clearness	-.184	-.230
R^2 = .053	Sign. = .043	
Adj. R^2 = .040	Power = .654	
F = 4.242		

Dependent Variable: Project Analysis		
Variable	B	Beta
Constant	1.351	
Organisation Structure	-.287	-.328
R^2 = .107	Sign. = .003	
Adj. R^2 = .096	Power = .912	
F = 9.140		

Table 5-27: Regressions on Low Performing Projects

The confirmatory results are:

- Hypothesis 1 for low performing projects: no significant differences were found in buyer - seller communication preferences. Hypothesis 1 is not supported.

- Hypotheses 2 and 3 for low performing projects: no significant correlation between organisation structure and communication frequency and media were found. Hypothesis 2 and 3 are not supported.

- Hypothesis 4 for low performing projects: the negative correlation between organic organisation structure and preference for project analysis supports hypothesis 4. Bureaucratic organisation structures prefer quantitative, analytical contents.

- Hypothesis 5 for low performing projects: the regression model showing clearer objectives being correlated with less preference for personal reviews is not considered to be of practical use. Hypothesis 5 is therefore not supported.

- Hypothesis 6 for low performing projects: no significant correlation between methodology clearness and preference for written reports was found. Hypothesis 6 is not supported.

The results emphasize the preference for analysis in low performing projects, done in order to understand the reasons for the low performance and to develop ways for improvement. This preference is stronger in organisations with bureaucratic structures when compared with those of organic structures.

5.4.3.2 Regressions on High Performing Projects

Similar regression analyses were done for high performing projects. Seven significant models were found, one of which was based on demographic variables and six on situational variables (Table 5-19). Four of the seven models show practical significance through effect sizes around the medium level and statistical power in excess of .90. These are those for Variable Interval Communication, Continuous Communication, Project Analysis, and Written Status Reports. The empirical results of these models show that increasing relational norms lead to a reduction in both continuous and variable communication (with a tenuous indication that higher relational norms stabilize communication at fixed intervals). Clearer objectives lead to less project analysis and communication at variable intervals, as well as more use of written status reports. Bureaucratic organisation structures and methodology clearness both increase the preference for continuous communication and use of written status reports. Differences between buyer and seller are in the buyer's significantly higher preference for communication at variable intervals and analysis data.

Dependent Variable: Variable Interval Communication		
Variable	B	Beta
Constant	-.137	
Project Management Experience	-.028	-.167
Sponsor Experience	.087	.185
R^2 = .042	Sign. = .078	
Adj. R^2 = .026	Power = .396	
F = 2.601		

Dependent Variable: Variable Interval Communication		
Variable	B	Beta
Constant	2.753	
Relational Norms	-.205	-.167
Objective Clearness	-.223	-.209
Buyer - Seller Perspective	-.443	-.195
R^2 = .122	Sign. = .002	
Adj. R^2 = .100	Power = .964	
F = 5.426		

Dependent Variable: Fixed Interval Communication		
Variable	B	Beta
Constant	-.061	
Relational Norms	.267	.222
Organization Structure	-.151	-.155
Methodology Clearness	-.136	-.165
R^2 = .064	Sign. = .051	
Adj. R^2 = .040	Power = .749	
F = 2.674		

Dependent Variable: Continuous Communication		
Variable	B	Beta
Constant	.644	
Relational Norms	-.203	-.174
Organization Structure	-.202	-.214
Methodology Clearness	.277	.347
R^2 = .143	Sign. = .000	
Adj. R^2 = .121	Power = .984	
F = 6.495		

Dependent Variable: Personal Reviews		
Variable	B	Beta
Constant	-.721	
Organisation Structure	.152	.153
R^2 = .023	Sign. = .094	
Adj. R^2 = .015	Power = .521	
F = 2.857		

Dependent Variable: Project Analysis		
Variable	B	Beta
Constant	1.618	
Objective Clearness	-.218	-.204
Buyer - Seller Perspective	-.609	-.268
R^2 = .092	Sign. = .003	
Adj. R^2 = .077	Power = .929	
F = 5.994		

Dependent Variable: Written Status Report		
Variable	B	Beta
Constant	-1.059	
Organisation Structure	-.130	-.150
Objective Clearness	.180	.180
Methodology Clearness	.138	.177
R^2 = .109	Sign. = .004	
Adj. R^2 = .086	Power = .937	
F = 4.785		

Table 5-28: Regressions on High Performing Projects

Results from the confirmatory analysis are:

- Hypothesis 1 for high performing projects: significant differences are in the sponsors' higher preference for communication at variable intervals and for analysis data. Hypothesis 1 is supported.

- Hypothesis 2 for high performing projects: organic organisation structure reduces the preference for frequent formal communication. Hypothesis 2 is not supported.

- Hypothesis 3 for high performing projects: bureaucratic structures increase the use of written reports. Hypothesis 3 is supported.

- Hypothesis 4 for high performing projects: no correlation was found between bureaucratic organisation structures and preference for quantitative measures. Hypothesis 4 is not supported.

- Hypothesis 5 for high performing projects: lean media like written reports are preferred in projects with clear objectives. Hypothesis 5 is supported.

- Hypothesis 6 for high performing projects: clearness of methodology is positively correlated with preference for written status reports. Therefore hypothesis 6 is supported.

Table 5-20 summarizes the results. Communication in high performing projects corresponds to a larger extent with existing communication theories than communication in low performing projects. It indicates presence of structures similar to those in permanent organisations. Low performing organisations seem to lack these structures, but focus on quantitative measures and leaner media instead.

Independent Variables	Communication Frequency								Communication Contents					
	Variable Interval Communication		Fixed Interval Communication		Continuous Communication		Personal Review		Project Analysis		Written Status		Verbal Update	
Project performance	Low	High	Low	High	Low	High	Low	High	Low	High	Low	High	Low	High
Demographic Variables														
Work Experience	0	0	0	0	0	0	0	0	0	0	0	0	0	0
Project Management Experience	0	-*	0	0	0	0	0	0	0	0	0	0	0	0
Sponsor Experience	0	+*	0	0	0	0	0	0	0	0	0	0	0	0
Project Variables														
Relational Norms	0	-*	0	+**	0	-*	0	0	0	0	0	0	0	0
Organization Structure	0	0	0	-*	0	-**	0	+*	-****	0	0	-*	0	0
Objective Clearness	0	-**	0	0	-**	0	-**	0	0	-**	0	+**	0	0
Methodology Clearness	0	0	+*	-*	0	+*****	0	0	0	0	0	+*	0	0
Buyer - Seller Perspective	0	-**	0	0	0	0	0	0	0	-****	0	0	0	0

Note: 0 = not significant
* Significant at p < .10
** Significant at p < .05
*** Significant at p < .01
**** Significant at p < .005
***** Significant at p < .001

+/- = significant positive or negative correlation
n-low = 78, n-high = 122

☐ = Model with practical significance

Table 5-29: Summary of Regressions on High and Low Performing Projects

A comparison of the results with practical significance in high and low performing projects shows that communication in low performing project is mainly driven by the desire for analysis, whereas high performing projects are driven by all independent variables. Differences between buyer and seller perspectives are only identified in high performing projects. This indicates a generally higher engagement level in high performing projects. Project sponsors in these projects do not give-up their control over the project too easily. Even though the project is performing well, they retain their interest in analysis data and trend information.

5.4.4 Summary of Regression Analyses

The regression analyses showed different impacts of situational variables on communication preferences. The first analysis on the overall project sponsor – manager communication identified the common denominator within the two parties' communication preferences. Subsequent analyses showed the antecedents for these communication preferences in different scenarios, like for project managers, project sponsors, as well as for low and high performing projects. The results showed that communication preferences differ by scenario, caused by differences in magnitude of impact that individual antecedents have in different scenarios. The interpretation of the individual results is described in Chapter 6.

The former analyses identified the individual independent variable's impact on individual dependent variables. The following section analyses the simultaneous impact of all independent variables on all dependent variables.

5.5 Modelling Project Sponsor – Manager Communication

A model of sponsor – manager communication was developed using canonical correlation analysis (CCA). This multivariate statistical technique analyses the association between two sets of variables. In the present study one set, also called variate, was the set of situational variables and the other variate the communication factors. CCA identifies the optimum structure that maximizes the relationship between the two variates (Hair et al. 1998). It is particularly useful in revealing overall relationships prevailing among sets of variables, and is especially valuable when there is no *a priori* knowledge about these relationships (Lambert & Durand 1975). So CCA is appropriate for identifying prevalent patterns in project sponsor - manager communication.

CCA's requirements of at least 10 observations per variable (Hair et al. 1998) were met through the observation-to-variable ratio of 18 to 1. Requirements for linearity of the data were fulfilled as outlined in the section on regression analysis.

Similar to factor analysis CCA extracts factors where the first factor accounts for the maximum amount of variance one factor explains in the other factor, and subsequent factors maximize variance not used by prior factors. Unlike factor analysis, CCA focuses on the relationship between variates. The first pair of canonical variates has the highest intercorrelations possible between the two sets. The second pair of variates accounts for the maximum relationship of variates not accounted for in the first pairs etc. These factors (pairs) are orthogonal and therefore independent from each other.

The strength in the relationship between a pair of variates is measured as the canonical correlation. Its squared value represents the amount of variance in one variate explained by the other variate. According to Hair et al. (1998), canonical functions should only be interpreted when three conditions are satisfied. These are:

- a minimum significance level of .05 as in most other studies

- a magnitude of the canonical relationship. Even though no clearly established threshold exists it is recommended using the guidelines for factor loadings from factor analysis because canonical correlations also refer to variance explained in canonical variates

- a redundancy index of practical relevance, which measures the average amount of the dependent variables variance accounted for by the independent variate. The latter index is analogous to R^2 in multiple regression and its value is similar (Hair et al. 1998).

The associations are measured as loadings of canonical variates. Loadings are chosen in this study over canonical weights as basis for interpretation because the canonical variates are regarded as factors, whose loadings reveal the relationship between the factors and the observed variables (Fornell 1978), which allows interpretation of the meaning of the factors (Sharma 1996). The point at which loading values are considered to be nontrivial ranged in past studies from .28 to .45 with .30 being used most often (Lambert & Durand 1975). The usual level of .30 was applied in this study.

5.5.1 Canonical Correlation Model for Total Sample

A significant one-dimensional canonical correlation model was found on the level of total sample (see Table 5-21). With a significance of .005 and factor loading values over .30 it satisfied two of the three conditions listed above. Its practical significance is relatively low with a Redundancy Index of .018, which shows that only approximately 2 percent of the variance in the dependent factor is explained by the variance in the independent variate. Practical applications of the model need to take this limitation into account. Even though the predictive power is low, the analysis was continued to assess the difference between communication in all projects with that in low and high performing projects.

The model shows significant positive loadings of three variables, which identifies an association between relational norms and objective clearness as independent variables and written reports as dependent variable, all in one factor. Methodology Clearness and fixed interval communication have similar loadings, but are just below the threshold value of .3. It also shows significant negative loadings of three dependent variables, which reveal the association of continuous communication, personal review and project analysis within a second factor. Using the data from Table 5-21 the model is shown in Figure 5-2, following Luthans et al. (1988).

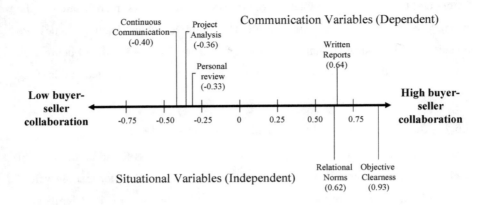

Figure 5-9: Canonical Correlation Model for Buyer - Seller Communication

The figure shows the two factors at opposite ends of a continuum. High relational norms and clear objectives indicate a strong collaboration between project sponsor and manager. Their mutual communication can be reduced to written reports. On the other end, the association of frequent communication, need for analysis and personal reviews indicates a 'problem' scenario in which communication frequency and detail is increased in order to improve the understanding of the status of the project, potentially caused by a lack of collaboration at earlier stages in the project. Collaboration in this context is defined by Cooper (2000, citing Mattessich and Monsey 1992):

> *... collaboration refers to a more durable and pervasive relationship where people and resources, previously separated by organisational and reporting relationships, are pooled and products shared.*

As shown in Figure 5-2, highly collaborative projects share those attributes through their mutual interest in the relationship and their improved understanding of the project objectives. Low collaborative projects lack these attributes and try to overcome the lack of collaboration through increased communication.

5.5.2 Canonical Correlation Model for High Performing Projects

To identify possible differences in communication patterns between high and low performing projects a CCA was done with these sub-samples. A significant two-dimensional model was found for successful projects (details in Table 5-21).

However, the redundancy index .058 shows a low proportion of shared variance that can be explained by the canonical functions, which indicates low predictive power of the model (Hair 1998, Sharma 1996). Practical applications should take this limitation into account.

	Total Sample	High Performing Projects only	
	Dimension: Level of Collaboration between Buyer and Seller	Dimension 1: Level of Collaboration between Buyer and Seller	Dimension 2: Level of Structuredness
Multivariate Test Statistics			
Statistic			
Wilk's	0.766	0.565	0.722
Chi-Square	51.092	64.530	36.795
Degress of Freedom	28.000	28.000	18.000
Significance	0.005	0.000	0.006
Canonical Correlation	0.367	0.467	0.428
Canonical R2	0.135	0.218	0.183
Redundancy Index	0.018	0.030	0.028
Canonical structure correlations (loadings) between variables and their respective canonical variate			
Situational Variables (independent)			
Relational Norms	**0.62**	**0.77**	0.15
Organization Structure	-0.04	-0.01	**-0.75**
Objective Clearness	**0.93**	**0.73**	0.24
Methodology Clearness	0.25	0.03	**0.62**
Communication Factors (dependent)			
Variable Interval Communications	-0.19	**-0.59**	0.06
Fixed Interval Communications	0.26	**0.46**	0.12
Continuous Communications	**-0.40**	**-0.38**	**0.80**
Personal Review	**-0.33**	-0.13	-0.21
Project Analysis	**-0.36**	-0.21	0.09
Written Report	**0.64**	**0.45**	**0.60**
Verbal Update	-0.10	0.07	0.00

Table 5-30: Canonical Correlations for Total Sample and High Performance Projects

The first dimension is highly significant (.000), with a canonical correlation of .467 the independent factor explains about 22% of the variance in the dependent factor, i.e. Canonical R^2. The dimension is similar to the collaboration dimension extracted on the level of total sample by associating relational norms, objective clearness, fixed interval communication and written reports as one factor. The second dimension has a canonical correlation of .428, which is a Canonical R^2 of .183. It associates methodology clearness, continuous communication and written reports as positively loaded variables and organic organisation structure as negatively loaded variable. Through that, it identified a structural dimension, with methodology clearness at one extreme and organic organisation structures at the other. The relationship between the situational variables (in square boxes) and the communication preferences (in circles) is conceptually displayed in two dimensions (see Figure 5-3). The horizontal axis shows the level of collaboration and the vertical axis the level of operational structure.

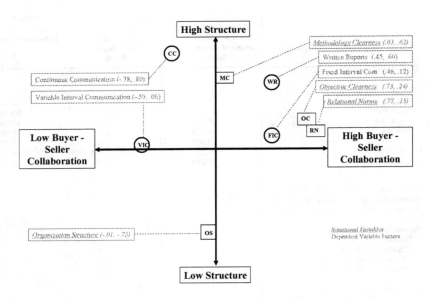

Figure 5-10: Canonical Correlation Model for High Performing Projects

The two dimensional model identifies communication between project manager and sponsor in high performing projects as a function of the level of collaboration between the parties and the extent of operational control in project execution, with the latter being the extent of methodology clearness and organisational structure, i.e. the process through which efficiency in task and project execution is achieved (Gunnarsson et al. 2000).

The model is redrawn in Figure 5-4. Here the dotted line arrows show the relationships, directions of relationships, and significance of correlations between independent and dependent variables, as taken from the regressions for the sub-sample of high performing projects (Table 5-20). The model shows that increasing levels of structure increase communication frequency and stabilize contents at written reports. That is shown through the positive relationships between methodology clearness (MC) and continuous communication (CC) and written reports (WR), as well as the negative relationship of organic organisation structure with CC and WR. In the collaboration dimension increasing levels of relational norms (RN) stabilize written reports (WR) and also fixed interval communication (FIC). Objective Clearness (OC) has a reducing effect on extremes in frequencies, i.e. CC and variable interval communication (VIC).

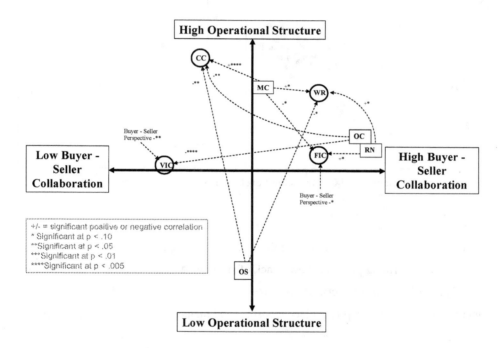

Figure 5-11: Relationships of Variables in the Canonical Correlation Model for High Performing Projects

No significant canonical correlation model was found for low performing projects, buyers or sellers.

Differences in collaboration and structure between low and high performing projects are shown in Figure 5-5. Here the structure and collaboration levels of the top 10% and lowest 10% of projects in terms of performance are plotted. To display the model on a two-dimensional scale the measure for organic organisation structure was inversed into a measure for mechanistic organisation structure. High performing projects show a minimum structure level of 3.3 and a minimum collaboration level of 4.5 on a 7 point scale. The clustering of the results shows that high performing projects balance structure and collaboration at the highest levels of collaboration and medium to high levels of structure.

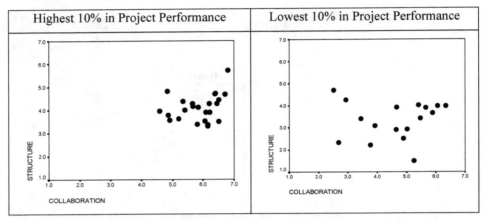

Figure 5-12: Structure and Collaboration Levels of Top and Bottom 10% in Performance

The 10% of projects with the lowest performance ratings did not exceed structure levels of approx. 4.0 – 4.5 and their collaboration levels appear randomly distributed. Thus, low performing projects show a lack of structure and lower collaboration levels as high performing projects. It indicates lower communication intensity, which increases the risk of a gap in project sponsor's and manager's performance perception of these project.

5.5.3   Summary of Canonical Correlation Analyses

The canonical correlation models for communication in IT project delivery show the level of collaboration as the common denominator in project sponsor – manager communication. High levels of collaboration are associated with good relationships, clear objectives and 'routine' written reports. High performing projects show an additional dimension which identifies organisation structure and methodological clearness as a structure dimension in these projects. Plotting the top and bottom 10%

of project performers in this model indicates homogenous levels of structure and collaboration in top performing projects, but lack of structure and collaboration in low performing projects. Further interpretation of the results is described in Chapter 6.

5.6 Step 2: Differences in Communication Patterns of Project Managers and Sponsors

The former analysis focused on the impact of situational variables on the communication preferences. This allowed for model building of communication in IT project implementation. Project sponsors showed significantly higher preference for analysis data across all projects, and significantly higher preference for variable interval communication in high performing projects. The next section will investigate the details of these differences by analysing them on a question-by-question basis. This will reveal the specific media and contents required to achieve a fit in communication expectations and capabilities of project sponsors and managers.

5.6.1   Analysis of Sponsor – Manager Differences

In paragraph 4.3.1 a significant difference between project sponsors and managers preferences for analysis data was detected. The 95% confidence interval in Figure 5-6 shows graphically the differences between project sponsor (coded 0) and manager (coded 1) responses and reveals that no overlap exists in the majority of cases.

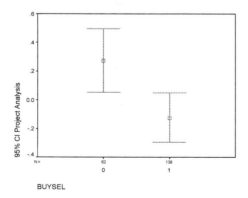

Figure 5-13: 95% Confidence Interval of Buyer and Seller Preference for Project Analysis

ANOVA techniques were used to assess the differences on the level of individual questionnaire item. Table 5-22 shows the results at a significance level of .1.

Variable	Questionnaire Item (Appendix A-3)	Buyer Mean (SD)	Seller Mean (SD)	Significance of Difference (p)
Communication Frequency				
Variable Interval Communication		*0.12 (1.10)*	*-0.05 (0.95)*	
Written communication at milestone achievement	27	3.34 (2.29)	2.99 (2.13)	
Written communication at phase or project end	28	2.87 (2.49)	2.83 (2.27)	
Verbal monthly communication	33	**3.12 (2.24)**	**2.36 (1.64)**	.010
Verbal communication at milestone achievement	34	**3.08 (2.18)**	**2.50 (1.92)**	.065
Verbal communication at phase or project end	35	**2.98 (2.30)**	**2.38 (1.99)**	.069
Personal communication at milestone achievement	41	3.34 (2.31)	3.02 (2.21)	
Personal communication at phase or project end	42	3.22 (2.44)	2.97 (2.31)	
Fixed Interval Communication		*0.14 (0.99)*	*-0.06 (1.00)*	
Written bi-weekly communication	25	3.95 (1.75)	3.70 (1.97)	
Written monthly communication	26	3.51 (2.11)	3.15 (2.12)	
Verbal bi-weekly communication	32	**3.80 (2.06)**	**3.25 (1.89)**	.077
Verbal monthly communication	33	**3.12 (2.24)**	**2.36 (1.64)**	.010
Personal bi-weekly communication	39	3.95 (2.01)	3.62 (1.97)	
Personal monthly communication	40	2.98 (2.04)	3.33 (2.08)	
Continuous Communication		*0.01 (0.97)*	*0.00 (1.02)*	
Written daily communication	23	2.83 (1.66)	3.02 (1.77)	
Written weekly communication	24	4.71 (1.92)	4.70 (1.96)	
Verbal daily communication	30	4.49 (1.76)	4.28 (1.96)	
Personal weekly communication	38	4.26 (2.01)	4.34 (2.04)	
Communication Contents				
Personal Review		0.00 (0.89)	0.00 (1.05)	
Personal contents: status and achievements	58	5.53 (1.43)	5.66 (1.36)	
Personal contents: measures and quality metrics	59	4.73 (1.73)	4.52 (1.71)	
Personal contents: issues or 'open items'	60	5.80 (1.07)	5.76 (1.38)	
Personal contents: project changes	61	5.88 (1.20)	5.91 (1.43)	
Personal contents: trends	62	4.78 (1.49)	4.38 (1.73)	
Personal contents: next steps	63	5.85 (1.03)	5.64 (1.42)	
Personal contents: other	64	4.74 (1.40)	4.66 (1.59)	
Project Analysis		*0.27 (0.87)*	*-0.12 (1.03)*	.009
Written contents: measures and quality metrics	45	**5.30 (1.43)**	**4.88 (1.66)**	.095
Written contents: trends	48	4.78 (1.34)	4.46 (1.53)	
Verbal contents: measures and quality metrics	52	**4.32 (1.79)**	**3.71 (1.64)**	.021
Verbal contents: trends	55	**4.38 (1.57)**	**3.59 (1.70)**	.002
Personal contents: measures and quality metrics	59	4.73 (1.73)	4.52 (1.71)	
Personal contents: trends	62	4.78 (1.49)	4.38 (1.73)	
Written Status		*-0.05 (1.00)*	*0.02 (1.00)*	
Written contents: status and achievements	44	6.26 (0.75)	6.36 (0.84)	
Written contents: issues or 'open items'	46	6.22 (1.19)	6.20 (1.02)	
Written contents: project changes	47	6.28 (1.11)	6.48 (0.81)	
Written contents: next steps	49	5.75 (1.18)	5.89 (1.10)	
Written contents: other	50	4.44 (1.33)	4.50 (1.40)	
Verbal contents: other	57	4.75 (1.36)	4.49 (1.50)	
Personal contents: other	64	4.74 (1.40)	4.66 (1.59)	
Verbal Update		*-0.06 (1.00)*	*0.03 (1.00)*	
Verbal contents: status and achievements	51	5.15 (1.77)	5.33 (1.59)	
Verbal contents: issues or 'open items'	53	5.57 (1.72)	5.68 (1.44)	
Verbal contents: project changes	54	5.34 (1.74)	5.46 (1.80)	
Verbal contents: next steps	56	5.57 (1.33)	5.47 (1.36)	

Table 5-31: Differences between Buyer and Seller by Questionnaire Item

Project sponsors show higher interest in forward looking information, such as trends, whereas project managers are more interested in providing information about status and recent achievements. Verbal communication is perceived by project sponsors as equally important as communication through other media. They also prefer to include analysis data about quality measures and trends in verbal communication. This perception is not shared by project managers, who scored verbal communication and analysis data lower in importance compared to other communication contents. This reveals a gap in the effectiveness of project sponsor – manager communication. Contents wise the expectations of sponsors are not fulfilled by the project managers through a lack of analysis data in verbal and written communication.

5.6.2 Analysis of Sponsor - Manager Communication Effectiveness

The subset of 38 pairs of project sponsors and mangers from the same project were used to analyse the effectiveness of dyadic communication. An indicator of communication effectiveness was established by calculating the gap in project sponsors and managers perceived performance of their joint project. Underlying assumption was that this gap should be small or zero in highly effective communication and wider in ineffective communication. Gaps in sponsor and manager preference scores for each communication factor were also calculated to identify the direction and magnitude of incongruence of the two parties' communication preferences. The gap in perceived performance was then regressed against the gaps in communication preferences to identify communication factors that have a narrowing or widening effect on the gap in perceived performance. These factors have positive or negative impact on communication effectiveness. The method follows Brown and Swartz's (1989) gap analysis of professional services quality.

The 38 pairs of respondents came from 16 different countries, of which 53% were from Europe, 25% from North America, and 13% from other countries. The average age of respondents was 42 years, with 20 years working experience, 10 years project management experience, and the project sponsors had in average 5 years of sponsorship experience. An ANOVA analysis of differences between the sample of 38 dyadic pairs and the larger sample showed a significant difference in the level of organic organisation structure. Paired respondents scored higher in organic structure then the overall sample. The sample description and ANOVA results are listed in Appendix B-11 and B-12 respectively.

The performance rating per respondent was calculated by taking the average rating of the three performance questions. The Gap between project sponsor's and manager's perceived project performance was calculated on a pair-by-pair basis by subtracting the manager's performance rating from the sponsor's performance rating. The mean performance gap in low performing projects was +1.0, which showed a higher perceived performance on the side of the project sponsors than on the side of project managers. The mean performance gap in high performing projects was -0.8, which showed a lower performance perception of sponsors compared to managers in these projects (see Table 5-23). ANOVA analysis between the groups of high and low performing projects showed a significant difference in perceived performance gap (F = 19.576, p < .000). The mean gap in perceived performance is smaller in high performing projects than in low performing projects.

	Low performing projects	High performing projects	Total
N	17	21	38
Mean	1,000	-0.81	0
Std. Deviation	1,404	1.118	1.536

Table 5-32: Perceived Performance Gap in Low and High Performing Projects

The summed gap scores for each factor (listed in Appendix B-13) were entered as independent variables in a regression analysis. The gap in perceived performance was entered as dependent variable (normality and heteroscedasticity test in Appendix B-14). A stepwise regression, as previously done by Swartz and Brown, was not performed due to Hair et al's (1998, p. 166) recommendation on minimum 50 observations per independent variable in a stepwise regression. Backward regression was used instead. The result is shown in Table 5-24.

Dependent Variable: Difference in Performance		
Variable	B	Beta
Constant	-.010	
Fixed Interval Communication	-.046	-.306
Personal Review	-.065	-.376
Written Status Reports	.149	.504
R^2 = .260	Sign. = .016	
Adj. R^2 = .195	Power = .710	
F = 3.981		

Table 5-33: Regression Model for Perceived Performance Gap

The model shows a large effect size with a small statistical power. Due to its large effect size the model is considered to be of practical significance. It identifies a strong impact of written communication on widening the difference in performance perceptions in projects. Personal meetings and communication at fixed intervals have a narrowing impact on the gap in perceived performance. The results show that communication effectiveness increases through personal meetings at regular intervals, while written reports have an adverse effect on communication effectiveness.

5.6.3 Summary of Differences and Effectiveness

The two analyses revealed a lack in congruency of project sponsor and manager communication, caused by an unequal perception of importance of verbal communication and use of analytic data in formal communication about the project. The results clearly show that written reports are a source for communication ineffectiveness due to their widening effect on the gap in project sponsors and managers perceived performance of the project. Personal communication showed a narrowing effect on that gap and therefore a beneficial contribution to effectiveness in communication.

5.7 Qualitative Analysis

The qualitative analysis followed Miles & Huberman's (1994) iterative process of data collection, data reduction and display, followed by conclusion drawing. As recommended by Silverman (1993) a standardized set of questions was used for all interviews (see Appendix A-9) to ensure a reliable research instrument. The interviewee-validated write-ups from the interviews were used as input for both an explanatory and exploratory analysis. The former seeking answers to the phenomena identified in the quantitative study, i.e.

- *Why* do project sponsors have a significantly higher preference for

  - Verbal media, like phone calls and voice mails?

  - Trend data, quality measures and earned value results?

  - Forward looking information like trends and issues, as opposite to backward looking information on status and recent achievements?

- Why are bi-weekly or monthly written reports preferred in high performing projects and not in low performing projects?

The exploratory analysis was setup to identify the context of specific communication patterns and the common reasons underlying the choices of these patterns. Cross-case techniques were used in both analyses to identify common variables among the cases. The pairs of project sponsor and manager came from the following projects.

SparDa Bank, Germany

The project was about the extension of an existing marketing IT system from a data-mart solution to a data-warehouse solution. Through that, the IT system was migrated from a departmental system to an enterprise wide marketing system. The project failed in its first attempt and was stopped. The current project is about the restart of the failed project and the implementation of a first data warehouse for a limited set of users (4), which can later be extended to the targeted number of users (35). The project was delivered within the planned schedule. Minor reworks are ongoing after the finish date to finalize the concepts for systems operations.

Communication practices within the project were based on frequent, at least weekly, informal communication between sponsor and manager using phone calls or e-mails to discuss open issues and to ensure that the project sponsor 'knows what's going on there'. Anticipated risks or possible escalations were first discussed informally. A formal monthly written status report was used to communicate issues, risks and schedule deviations to the project sponsor, as well as to the buyer and seller firm's management and the project team.

Apparel Designer and Manufacturer, San Francisco, USA

The objectives of this project were threefold, first the enterprise logical data model for an existing IT data warehouse, second a data warehouse architecture, and third a data warehouse infrastructure. All goals were achieved. Not all deliverables are currently being used, but all participants perceive the project as a success. The communication practices at the beginning of the project were a weekly status report, outlining the tasks that were achieved for the week, the tasks that were due for the following week, and any issues that required resolution. This practice was overruled at a later stage in the project through a new internal policy within the buyer firm, which required a comprehensive monthly report to the firm's management, backed up by a monthly status review meeting for all projects. The weekly status report was abandoned. Informal communication through face-to-face meetings or e-mail was frequent, especially when issues had to be clarified.

Government Institution, UK

The project objective was the development and implementation of a new spare-parts system, which integrated data from several existing systems in order to have all related information in one computer system. The endeavour was started as a six month project, but encountered severe problems during the development stage. The seller firm's project manager was replaced after about six month in the project. By the time of the interview, the project had about 230% time overrun and was about six weeks from the newly planned finish date. The new project manager and the sponsor stated the need for strict control structures, e.g. change control and contract management, to avoid the delays experienced in the early stages of the project.

Communication between project sponsor and manager was formally on a bi-weekly basis using face-to-face meetings, which were also attended by other members of management. Informal communication was on a weekly basis through meetings of buyer and seller project managers, followed by a written protocol of the meeting.

The analyses of the three cases aimed for identification of similarities in interview answers, explained through fact-sheet variables external to the interview (Silverman 1993, p. 104, citing Baker 1984). For that, the answers were entered in a spreadsheet, sorted by firm, interviewee and question. Subsequently the overall patterns for each question were identified. This step was also performed by an independent second researcher. The inter-coder reliability between the two results was calculated using Miles and Huberman's (1994) formula

$$\text{Reliability} = \frac{\text{Number of agreements}}{\text{Total number of agreements + disagreements}}$$

Inter-coder reliability of 77% was achieved, indicating a sufficient level of agreement between the two researchers (Miles and Huberman 1994). The explanatory results are summarized in the following.

5.7.1 Explanatory Results

Project sponsors, when asked why they prefer verbal communication significantly higher than project managers, responded that they use this media for reassurance of the formal information they get through written status reports. It is seen as a quick and easy way to get up-to-date information about the project in order to quickly resolve possible issues. Verbal information is perceived as being supplementary to the formal communication, e.g. as the Sponsor from the UK Government Institution stated:

> It's reassurance. Verbal reassurance is easy to achieve.... I might like the opportunity to be able to do that, but I will be more reassured if it was done in a formal environment. ... I would rather have a considered answer. So I think there's a place for both.

The statement reflects agency theory. The principle (sponsor) has to be confident that the agent (project manager) is telling the truth about the project and tries to find that out through verbal communication. Assuming that it is less easy to embellish verbal communication than written communication the principal finds verbal communication more reliable.

Two of the project managers were surprised that project sponsors in average rank verbal communication that high. Their perspective was related to the contractual buyer-seller situation, for which they need to deliver a well thought through written and auditable track record of project achievements.

Project sponsors higher preferences for quantitative data, like quality metrics, earned value numbers and trends, was perceived by all interviewees as being caused by the need for project sponsors to present evidence of project progress to higher management in the buyer organisation. This reflects agency theory again, but this time between the project sponsor and higher management. Upper managers assume that quantitative data is easier to believe than qualitative statements about project progress.

Project managers, however, do not use these quantitative data for the management of their projects. They perceive the calculation of these metrics as a waste of time, e.g. as one project manager puts it:

> In my opinion, it is perceived, certainly by myself and probably by a lot of project managers, as essentially unproductive time in terms of achieving the project deliverables.

Shared opinions were found on the question why project sponsors are more interested in forward looking information, like next steps, issues, trends, and project managers more in reporting backward looking information, like recent achievements and general status. Here the project sponsor's wider view of the project, the integration of the project in the overall organisation and the associated need for 'looking ahead' to mitigate risks were acknowledged. Whereas project managers, with their constraint perspectives on the contracted deliverables and the mitigation of any risks associated with these deliverables, were interested in providing a track record of successful project achievements, like the project manager of the UK Government project stated:

> ... sometimes the project manager may or may not know what the bigger picture is. They are very much focused on delivery of a piece work.

Why only successful projects show a pattern of bi-weekly or monthly written status reports, and unsuccessful projects don't, was explained by three categories of reasons. First, all respondents stated that this frequency is a good balance between formal overhead and the risk of missing deviations from plan as early in the project as possible. Second, it was perceived as a structural attribute of a project, enforcing discipline and showing liability in project execution, as e.g. the project manager of the apparel manufacturer stated:

> *Because it forces a certain amount of project management discipline on all of the participants in the project.*

Third, the distribution of formal, auditable reports to higher levels of management was perceived as a requirement for good project management.

In summary, the responses to the explanatory questions indicate that sponsor and manager both are aware of most of the differences in perspective and respect the other party's view towards communication contents, frequency and media. One apparent difference not known by project managers is their customers' expectation for frequent verbal project updates in addition to the bi-weekly or monthly written reports. Clarification of this need to the project manager community would increase the fit between expectations and capabilities and therefore increase communication effectiveness. A summary of the findings is provided in Appendix B-15.

5.7.2   Exploratory Results

The exploratory analysis identified communication practices and their context in the interviewee's projects. Observing the spreadsheet entries showed the following model.

> Sponsors and managers communicate informally daily or at least weekly, discussing project issues, changes, status and upcoming events. These meetings are face-to-face and supported through e-mails in case of the need for documentation of issues.

> Semi-formal communication takes place at weekly status meetings, covering issues, achievements and next week's tasks. Protocols are used to document these meetings. The information from these

meetings becomes the input to a formal bi-weekly or monthly written report, covering issues, risks, time, cost, progress to plan and people issues. These reports are distributed widely and used as input for project review meetings with upper management.

This reveals a three-stage model which starts at an informal level through frequent face-to-face communication. A semi-formal step of weekly meetings with written protocols constitute the transition from informal to formal communication, which then becomes a formal written report to management and other stakeholders.

Identification of underlying reasons for this communication model was done by cutting and sorting the responses into groups of reasons. A summary is provided in Appendix B-16. Three grouping variables were identified by observing the responses to the exploratory questions. The variables were subsequently tested for negative evidence, but none was found. The groupings are:

- **Trust building**

    Trust, as a result of frequent collaboration between sponsor and manager, was the term most often used to describe the aspect of highest importance in the sponsor – manager relationship. The project sponsor of SparDa Bank in Germany stated:

    ...aus meiner Sicht das Wichtigste ist Vertrauen.

    [... from my perspective trust is important]

    This group of responses appeared in informal communication only.

    Hartman (2000, p. 96) defines trust in project management as a complex construct with different 'flavours' of trust. The most important ones are integrity (personal and professional trust), competence (trust in technical capability), and leadership (following the leader will result in a positive outcome).

- **Surprise avoidance**

    A major aspect in communication was to ensure the avoidance of sudden surprises in projects. In informal communication this was achieved through a 'feeling of what's going on at the other side", while formal communication required balancing of efforts for formal reports with the needs for continuous status updates.

- **Control enhancement**

  Frequent informal communication is perceived to enhance the control over the project, like the sponsor of the apparel manufacturer stated:

  > *[weekly communication] gives me more control over the project, when it comes to meeting deadlines, meeting deliverables. Otherwise... when problems happen, it will become a disaster, it will be dragged on along with the project.*

  Enhanced controllability is markedly evident in formal communication, e.g. the need for written documentation was expressed by the project manager of the UK Government project as:

  > *... a lot of things were just said and weren't put on paper, they weren't documented. There wasn't that bit of control that goes with a project. So, I think, you come across problems...*

  Further evidence was in upper management's interest in project status classifications, such as red, yellow, and green, together with face-to-face meetings setup to review the details of project status and progress.

As indicated by the number of statements in Appendix B-16, a shift from informal to formal communication is accompanied by a shift from trust building activities (through informal communication), to enhanced controllability (through formal communication). Surprise avoidance is a reoccurring theme in both informal and formal communication. This is schematically displayed in Figure 5-7. While the amount of trust decreases, the amount of control increases when communication migrates from informal to formal modes of communication.

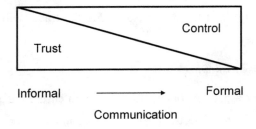

Figure 5-14: Trust to Control Shift during Migration from Informal to Formal Communication

5.7.3   Summary of Qualitative Analysis

Sponsors and managers are aware of their different perspectives towards their project and respect the other's position in their communication expectations. Effectiveness in communication can be improved through project managers awareness of project sponsors expectations about frequent verbal updates and need for objective data about project status, such as quality metrics, trends and earned value results. Sponsors and managers communication migrates from frequent informal face-to-face interactions, via weekly meetings, to formal monthly reports for upper management. The underlying communalities for this communication model are in the need for trust building through informal communication, joint work on avoidance of surprises through informal and formal communication, as well as enhanced controllability achieved through formal reports on project issues, results and the classification of projects by their overall status.

5.8 Triangulation of Qualitative and Quantitative Results

Interviewees' statements supported the results of the quantitative study by showing that project sponsor and manager gradually build trust through collaboration on an informal basis. Collaboration was one of the two dimensions in the quantitative model described above and comprises objective clearness and relational norms. Both are necessary preconditions to establishing a trustful relationship (Bell et al. 2002). The second category of statements also supported the quantitative study. Interviewees repeatedly expressed the need for rigorous control and avoidance of surprises. Project sponsors and managers in projects that were off the plan at one time stated the need for increased control, as well as awareness within the project team that certain control structures are in place. These results from the qualitative study triangulate the quantitative model for communication in successful projects. Both studies show that the level of collaboration between buyer and seller and the degree of structure determine the communication between the project sponsor and manager, and that the level of structure in execution constitutes a necessary precondition for successful projects. Table 5-25 shows a mapping of the results:

| | | Results from the Quantitative Study | |
		Collaboration	Structure in Execution
Results from the Qualitative Study	Trust Building	X	
	Surprise Avoidance	X	X
	Enhanced Controllability		X

Table 5-34: Mapping of Qualitative and Quantitative Study Results

Table 5-25 explains the relation between the *How* questions in the quantitative study, and the *Why* questions in the qualitative study. Collaboration (the how) is done to achieve trust and avoid surprises (the why). Similarly, structure in execution prevails in successful projects (the how) to avoid surprises and enhance controllability during project implementation (the why).

The above shows that trust building and collaboration are interlinked. Avoidance of surprises is achieved through collaboration, but also serves the objective of risk minimization through structure in execution. Enhanced controllability interlinks with structure in execution as both aim for clearness in tasks, methods, roles and accomplishments.

5.9 Summary of Data Analysis and Results Chapter

The results from this chapter identified different antecedents for communication preferences, depending on buyer or seller perspective, or performance level in projects. Project sponsors communication is mainly driven by their past experience, whereas project managers are driven by the risk level of the project. The hypotheses tested showed that high performing projects reveal communication structures similar to those in permanent organisations, while communication structures in low performing projects differ markedly from those in high performing projects. A model for sponsor-manager communication identified written status reports at fix intervals as the means of communication in highly collaborative projects and frequent communication with detailed analysis as practice in low collaboration projects. High performing projects showed a structural dimension in addition to the collaborational dimension identified in all projects. Detailed analysis of the differences between sponsor and manager communication revealed that managers put low priority on verbal media, whereas sponsors rate this media equally important to other media. Effectiveness in communication was shown to be positively impacted by personal communication and meetings, but negatively impacted through the use of written status reports.

Qualitative analysis of three pairs of project sponsor and manager showed that they communicate frequently and informally to establish a level of trust, and then work jointly to avoid surprises. To the extent that their communication is shared with other individuals or upper management, their communication becomes more formal and with that more focused on controllability of the project.

Explanatory analysis of the interviews showed that sponsors and managers acknowledge their different perspectives in a project and the associated differences in communication preferences. However, a lack of knowledge exists on the side of project managers about the sponsors needs for frequent verbal updates. Eliminating this gap would increase communication effectiveness.

A triangulation of the results from the quantitative and qualitative study confirmed both results. The dimensions of collaboration and structure, identified through the quantitative study as the *How* project sponsors and managers communicate was corroborated by the dimension of trust building, surprise avoidance, and controllability enhancement as the dimensions for *Why* they communicate the way they do.

The next chapter will provide the interpretation of the findings.

CHAPTER SIX – INTERPRETATION

The purpose of this chapter is to summarize the results from the Data Analysis Chapter, interpret the findings and subsequently answer the research questions.

6.1 Summary of Exploratory Results

6.1.1 Communication Frequency and Contents

Project sponsors and managers distinguish between three communication frequencies, each preferred in a specific situation. These are:

- Continuous communication, i.e. daily or at least weekly communication, is the most preferred frequency across all projects. For project managers, high performing projects, and the combined project manager - sponsor sample the preference for this frequency increases with the clearness of the methodology used, the unclearness in the project's objectives, and the extent of bureaucratic organisation structures.

- Fixed interval communication, i.e. at bi-weekly or monthly intervals, is the preferred communication frequency in projects with clear objectives and good buyer - seller relationships. It is the typical frequency for written status reports in high performing projects.

- Variable interval communication, i.e. at milestone or project phase achievement, is especially preferred by project sponsors in high performing projects. It is an attempt to reduce communication efforts in well running projects. However, this preference is not shared by project managers, who aim for higher communication frequencies.

Communication contents and media selection are intertwined and distinguished by project sponsors and managers in:

- Personal review, i.e. face-to-face communication covering all possible contents. No strong evidence was found on the specific drivers or situations for this preference. However, it is indicated that personal reviews are associated with projects of low buyer-seller collaboration and with unclear objectives.

- Project analysis, i.e. communication of quantitative measures, metrics and trends using all media. It is significantly more preferred by project sponsors than by project managers. With the exception of low performing projects the preference for this contents is continuously related to the extent project objectives are unclear. In low performing projects it is correlated to the extent of bureaucratic organisation structures.

- Written status reports with possible follow-up, i.e. reports covering information about achievements, issues, changes, next steps and other items, with the possibility to follow-up verbally or face-to-face on other items. It is the preferred media and contents in projects with clear objectives and good buyer-seller relationships. It is also preferred in bureaucratic organisation structures, as well as in high performing projects with high methodology clearness.

- Verbal update, i.e. an informal but timely update about achievements, issues, changes, and next steps. No antecedent or specific situation was found that fosters preferences for this communication.

Significant differences between project sponsors and managers are in the sponsors' higher preference for analytic data, verbal communication, and variable interval communication in high performing projects.

6.1.2 Differences in Antecedents in Different Scenarios

Overall project sponsor – manager communication is driven by project risk. Clearer objectives lead to reduction in both communication frequency and media richness. Clearness of methodology increases communication frequency.

A differentiated picture emerges by looking at the antecedents in the four sub-samples. Figure 6-1 shows the final path models of the sub-samples for project managers and sponsors. The arrows indicate the antecedents with both statistical and practical significance. Project manager communication preferences are driven by project related factors, mainly the risk level of the project. Sponsors' communication preferences are determined by demographic factors, i.e. prior experience in project management. For project managers the antecedents influence preferences for both communication frequency and contents, whereas antecedents for sponsors' preferences influence communication contents only. This reflects the project managers' closeness and identification with their projects, and the sponsors distance and 'gut feeling' that underlies their steering of projects.

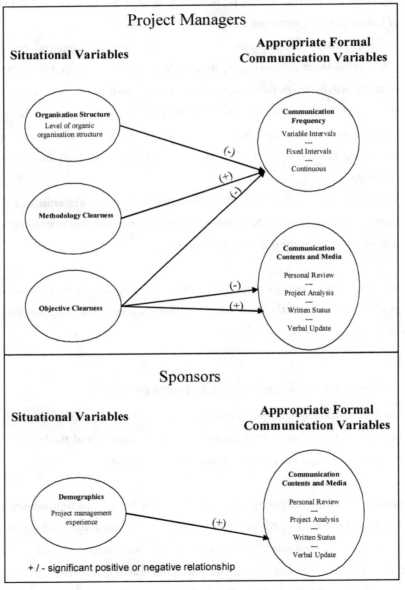

Figure 6-15: Antecedents for Project Manager and Sponsor Communication

Individual analysis of high and low performing projects (Figure 6-2) identified for the former projects communication structures similar to those in permanent organisations, as indicated through the hypotheses described below.

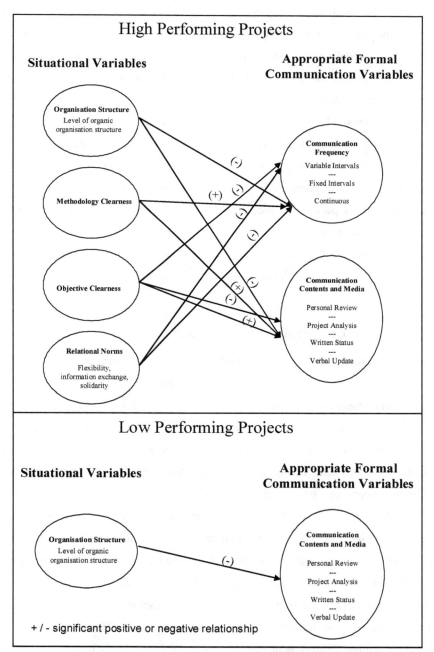

Figure 6-16: Antecedents in High and Low Performing Projects

Communication in high performing projects is determined by a balance of relational norms, organisational structure and risk. Increasingly integrated buyer - seller relationships stabilize communication frequency at fixed intervals, while lower risk and more bureaucratic structures lead to preferences for written status reports. Antecedents in low performing projects are not as balanced. Here organisation structure is the only antecedent detected, showing that more bureaucratic structures lead to preferences for detailed project analysis. Communication in these projects focuses on the identification of reasons for the low performance through detailed project analyses. The disappearance of relational norms as antecedent for communication is a potential indicator for mixed levels of integrated relationships between sponsor and manger. This is also shown in Figure 5-5 with decreasing collaboration in low performing projects. In a similar way risk diminishes as an antecedent in low performing projects, because organizational forces, i.e. structures, take precedence in determining the need for examination of the project and the associated reporting of analysis data in order to solve the project's problems, or at least predict the further development of the project in terms of its performance.

6.2 Summary of Confirmatory Results

The confirmatory part tested the hypotheses in three different settings, i.e. for the combined sample of sponsor and manager responses, individually at the level of sponsor and manager, and individually at the level of high and low performing projects. The results are listed in Table 6-1 and show that hypothesis 5 is supported in three of the five settings. The two settings not supporting hypothesis 5 show statistically significant, but practically insignificant models. Through that Media Richness Theory can be considered applicable for IT project settings, albeit with partially low practical use. Hypothesis 2 is not supported in any of the settings. The hypothesized increase in communication caused by organic organisation structures is not evident within formal communication between sponsor and manager. It might only be evident in informal communication. This questions the validity of Khandwalla's (1977) construct for measuring organisation structure in research that distinguishes between formal and informal communication. That should be assessed in further studies. Discriminant validity was given in the newly developed constructs through their orthogonal structure as factor scores and the associated low correlation between factors.

Low performing projects, when compared to high performing ones, show no difference between sponsor and manager preferences for communication. Similarly, only these projects confirm hypothesis 4, i.e. bureaucratic organisation structures lead to quantitative measures. High performing projects, in turn, are the only projects to confirm that clearness of methodology leads to preference for written media, i.e. hypothesis 6.

Hypothesis	Sponsors and Managers Combined	Project Sponsors	Project Managers	High Performing Projects	Low Performing Projects
H1	Y	N/A	N/A	Y	N
H2	N	N	N	N	N
H3	Y	N	N	Y	N
H4	N	N	N	N	Y
H5	Y	N	Y	Y	N
H6	N	N	N	Y	N

Note:
H1 - H6: Hypotheses
Y = hypothesis accepted
N = hypothesis rejected
N/A = not applicable

Table 6-35: Summary of Tested Hypotheses

6.2.1 Hypotheses

The results of the confirmatory study support the exploratory results stated above by showing differences between sponsors and managers and between high and low performing projects. In accordance with the study's overall theme the confirmatory results are related to the total sample. Confirmatory results at the level of sponsor, project manager, low or high performing projects are only mentioned to identify the contribution of each of these sub-samples to the overall sample's support or not-support of a hypothesis in order to identify the context in which the stated hypotheses are applicable.

Hypothesis 1:

Differences between sponsor and manager communication preferences were found on the basis of total sample and for high performing projects. Hypothesis 1 is supported. It confirms the empirical finding that a 'healthy scepticism' on the side of project sponsors is an attribute of high performing projects. Low performing projects showed no evidence for this level of criticality and interest in project progress.

Hypothesis 2:

Hypothesis 2 is not supported at any level of analysis. The hypothesized impact of organic organisation structure on communication frequency is not evident in formal communication between project sponsors and managers. Being indifferent to formal and informal communications the validity of the measurement construct may be questionable. However, the same construct was used for hypotheses 3 and 4, with hypothesis 3 being supported on the total sample. Therefore it is more likely that organic organisation structure increases frequency in informal communication, but not in formal communication. This should be subject to further research.

Hypothesis 3:

The impact of bureaucratic organisation structure on choice of lean media is evident at the level of total sample and for the sub-sample of high performing projects. Hypothesis 3 is supported. It indicates similarities between communication in permanent organisations (where the theory was originally developed) and high performing projects. These similarities are also found with other hypotheses.

Hypothesis 4:

The hypothesized positive relationship between the extent of bureaucratic organisation structure and the use of quantitative measures, like quality metrics and earned value numbers, is not supported. Its impact was not evident at the level of total sample, only for low performing projects. This complements the exploratory findings for low performing projects, where lack of relational norms and high project risks are compensated through increased bureaucratic structures with mainly quantitative communication contents and personal reviews.

Hypothesis 5:

The hypothesized positive relationship between project goal equivocality and media richness was evident at the level of total sample and two sub-samples. Hypothesis 5 is supported. Rich media is selected for communication in projects with unclear goals, and lean media for projects with clearly defined goals. The results indicate the appropriateness of Media Richness Theory in buyer-seller IT projects and validates the measurement construct.

Hypothesis 6:

The hypothesized positive relationship between clearness of methodology and the use of written media for communications was expected to appear on the sub-sample of project managers, because of the project manager's responsibility for methodology use. Surprisingly the hypothesis was only supported in high performing projects, i.e. a combination of project sponsor and manager responses. This complements the canonical correlation model for communication in high performing projects, which identified a dimension of structure in project execution which is only evident in these projects. It also indicates that the impact of methodology is not constraint to project managers communication, and also applicable to project sponsors. It corroborates the exploratory findings that sponsors in high performing projects show higher interest and involvement in mutual communication.

The sum of confirmatory findings show a degree of isomorphic communication practices in high performing projects and permanent organisations. Four of the six hypotheses were supported for this sub-sample. The two hypotheses not supported (H2 and H4) proposed impact of organisational structure on communication frequency and contents. This failure of support is indicative of an orientation on the side of project sponsor and manager towards project objectives, as opposed to organisational objectives. This indicates why these projects perform better and why their sponsors are more involved in the communication with their suppliers.

6.3 A Model for Antecedents in Project Sponsor - Manager Communication

Situational variables that influence the choice of project sponsors and managers for communication frequency, contents and media are project risk and organisation structure. Figure 6-3 shows the results in form of the final model for communication antecedents, based the research model in Figure 4-2 and the results from Table 5-11. It shows the impact of the situational variables on the communication variables.

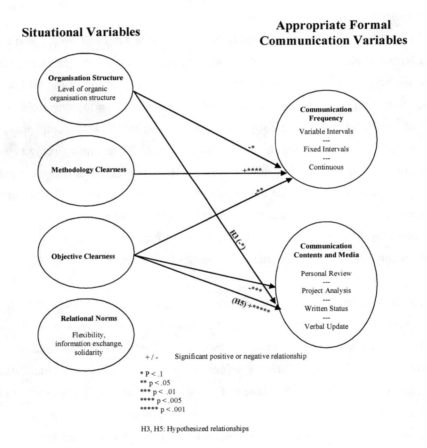

Figure 6-17: Antecedents for Formal Communication between Project Sponsor and Manager

Organic organisation structures reduce the preference for frequent formal communication and written reports. Methodology clearness increases communication frequency. Finally, objective clearness has a decreasing effect on communication frequency and project analysis, while it increases the preference for written reports.

The situational variable relational norms has no impact on the communication preferences of sponsors and managers.

6.4 A Model for Project Sponsor – Manager Communication during IT Project Implementation

The results in form of the models derived from the Canonical Correlation Analysis are not very strong and could be perceived as lacking practical relevance. However, the models confirm results from other current research and should therefore be considered at least of theoretical relevance. The models indicate that formal communication in IT projects can be classified along a continuum of increasing collaboration of project sponsor and manager. Low levels of collaboration are associated with personal and frequent communication to analyse the state of the project. High levels of collaboration are associated with clear objectives, high relational norms and written communication. This resembles current research results by Turner (2003), which showed the need for project sponsor and manager to collaborate, because:

> The Project does not take place through transactions between the players, but by their working together as one.

Taking a contracting perspective Turner (2003) recommends using contract types which allow buyer and seller to develop appropriate collaborative relationships. This approach allows for the transformation of the different perspectives of buyer and seller into a 'cooperative system', as described by Levitt and March (1995, cited by Turner 2003), with the terms collaborative and cooperative used synonymously:

> The problem of organizing [is] seen as one of transforming a conflict (political) system into a cooperative (rational) one. A conflict system is one in which individuals have objectives that are not jointly consistent. It organizes through exchanges and other interactions between strategic actors. A cooperative system is one in which individuals act rationally in the name of a common objective.

This explains the association of relational norms, clear objectives and lean media as outlined in the buyer - seller communication model in Figure 5-2. A collaborative (or cooperative) project sponsor - manager relationship integrates the need to 'work together as one' with a clear understanding of the project's outcome, which together reduces the communication to 'routine' written status reports at bi-weekly or monthly intervals. In terms of Agency Theory this combination of relational norms and shared understanding of project objectives provides a comfort level for the sponsor that allows a reduction in efforts to control the agent (through communication) to a minimum, monthly-routine level.

The present study also shows that projects with performance levels at or above average show a second dimension for communication, which is the degree of operational structure, given by the level of methodology clearness and organisational structure. This finding is supported by the many maturity models which claim better project results through structured project management methodologies, which provide a repeatable process and clearly defined roles of the individuals in the process. An example is the Capability Maturity Model for Software (CMM) from Carnegie Mellon University's Software Engineering Institute (SEI), which identifies the need for clear organizational structures and use of methodologies for successful software development (SEI 1993, p. 4):

> As a software organization gains in software process maturity, it institutionalizes its software process via policies, standards, and organizational structures. Institutionalization entails building an infrastructure and a corporate culture that supports the methods, practices, and procedures of the business so that they endure after those who originally defined them have gone.

The present study shows that high performing projects not only achieve highest levels of collaboration (as explained above), but also medium to high levels of structure, both of them unachieved by low performing projects. The choice of communication frequency, contents and media in those high performing projects is a balance between the level of collaboration and structure. Figure 6-4 shows the associated model. High performing projects balance structure and collaboration at equilibrium of written communication at fixed intervals. Deviations from this equilibrium, e.g. with higher communication frequencies, indicate higher levels of structure with lower levels of collaboration in a project. Less frequent communication indicates lower levels of collaboration. Use of richer media (verbal or face-to-face) indicates low levels in both structure in execution and collaboration between buyer and seller.

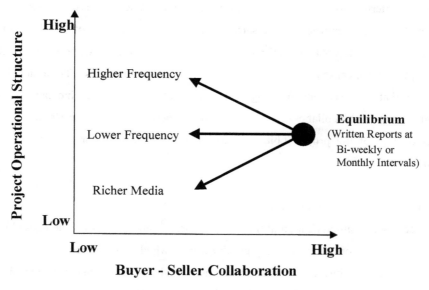

Figure 6-18: Structure - Collaboration Model

The model identifies possible imbalances between structure and collaboration in projects by relating communication frequency and media mix of any IT project to that of high performing IT projects. The identified imbalances indicate a potential risk to the project and can be further investigated through the constituent parts of one or both of the structure – collaboration dimensions, e.g. by using the related questions from the questionnaire.

Taking the UK Government project described in Chapter 5 as an example, the model shows that high communication frequency is an indicator for higher structure levels and lower collaboration levels than in high performing projects. In this case a new project manager was brought in to recover the project from its low performing situation and deliver what was contracted. The new project manager increased the internal structure by insisting on the usage of change management processes and written reports, weekly meetings with the project manager of the buyer organisation with meeting minutes reported to the sponsor. Weekly, later bi-weekly meetings were held with the sponsor resulting in a status report which was distributed to the management of buyer and seller organisation. Using the model (Figure 6-4) as a tool it shows that the increasing frequencies for written communication are indicative of the higher internal structures within the project, i.e. increasing organisational structure and methodology clearness. At the same time it shows a decrease of collaboration, given through the lower relational norms, caused by the buyer's disappointment with the project, which caused the buyer to ask for a new project manager. The model also indicates that a subsequent lowering of communication frequencies indicates a re-establishment of the collaboration, initiated by the new project manager's increased understanding of the project objectives and the emergence of common relational norms.

Lower communication frequencies indicate lower collaboration levels. This happens in projects with communication at milestone or phase end only. It can be caused by relatively simple or repetitive project objectives, which do not require a strong interaction between buyer and seller; or by one or both parties not being interested in a more integrated relationship, such as in sales of general purpose technology (Williamson 1985). Projects with these communication intervals are perceived as low risk, as evidenced in this study by the sponsors' preference for this communication frequency in high performing projects (which was not shared by the project managers). This communication frequency allows reducing the costs for communication to a minimum. However, it also bears the greatest risk of not reacting to upcoming issues or required changes in a timely manner, causing additional costs or other plan deviations to occur.

Formal sponsor - manager communication based on richer media is indicative of lowest levels of collaboration and structure (Figure 6-4). The survey's projects with lowest performance levels rank here (see Figure 5-5). These projects suffer from low internal structures (unclear methodology and resources roles) and low collaboration (unclear objectives and low relational norms). The problems in these projects are severe and richer communication media is required to address them. These media are chosen for having interactions with immediate feedback and transfer of multiple cues to address issues in detail and to observe the communication partners' reactions and behaviour. With an increase in performance the communication practices in these projects shift back towards equilibrium.

The two models for formal buyer-seller communication described above show that increased communication frequency does not compensate for low collaboration. They underscore the importance of good relational norms and clear determination of project objectives, and identify a minimum level of operational structure as a requirement for projects to be successful.

6.5 A Model for Project Sponsor and Manager Communication Effectiveness

The research results show large differences in communication effectiveness in high and low performing projects. Project sponsors in low performing projects have a higher perception of project status than their project managers. At the same time the project managers are more interested in personal communication and providing status reports than the project sponsors. That indicates low interest on the side of the sponsors and an illusion about the project status.

The opposite happens in high performing projects. Here sponsors have a lower perception, and higher interest in personal communication and status reports than project managers. This indicates higher interest and involvement on the side of the sponsors, combined with a healthy scepticism about the performance of the project.

The choice of media also impacts the communication effectiveness. Use of written status reports increases the gap in project sponsor's and manager's perception about the status of their joint project. This shows that written status reports have a negative impact on communication effectiveness. Personal meetings decrease this gap and therefore improve communication effectiveness. The findings link back to Nonaka and Takeuchi (1995) who describe knowledge (in this case the knowledge about the status of a project) as consisting of two elements. First the tacit knowledge in the minds of the people, and second the explicit knowledge in form of documents accessible by other people. They state that ambiguity in contents and redundancy in communication channels, like in personal communication, are necessary pre-conditions for transfer of tacit knowledge into explicit knowledge between communication partners. It creates a 'common cognitive ground' through interaction, and 'while members of the organization share overlapping information, they can *sense what others are struggling to articulate'* (Nonaka & Takeuchi 1995, p. 14). This increases effectiveness. With the constraints of lean media, like written status reports, the transfer of tacit knowledge about project status into explicit knowledge by the project manager, and the reverse transfer by the sponsor, are unlikely to be effective.

6.6 A Model for Migration from Informal to Formal Communication

Formal communication between project sponsors and managers during IT project implementation derives from informal communication. As shown in Figure 6-5, informal, frequent communication on a personal basis is used for mutual updates and avoidance of sudden surprises on either side. This personal interaction builds up mutual trust in the buyer – seller relationship. The migration to formal communication is not clear cut. On the way from informal to formal the communication between the parties passes a semi-formal grey-zone, where some issues are documented through use of meeting-minutes and e-mails at weekly or bi-weekly intervals, while other topics are only discussed verbally. This communication becomes the input for a formal, bi-weekly or monthly written report, which is then shared with upper management and other stakeholders. Along the migration from informal to formal, the purpose of the communication changes from trust building in informal communications to control enhancement in formal communication. The latter comprises information on project metrics and auditable information about project status and progress. The need for avoidance of surprises pervades all communication and can be seen as the core of communication between project sponsor and manager.

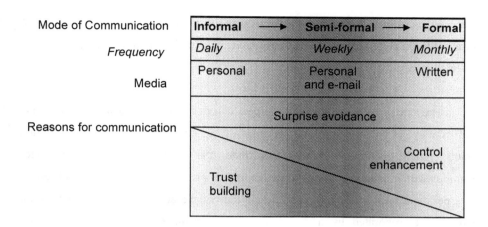

Mode of Communication	Informal → Semi-formal → Formal		
Frequency	Daily	Weekly	Monthly
Media	Personal	Personal and e-mail	Written
Reasons for communication	Surprise avoidance		
	Trust building		Control enhancement

Figure 6-19: Model for Migration from Informal to Formal Communication

Given the research results and models outlined in this chapter it is now possible to answer the two research questions stated in Chapter 3.

6.7 Answer to Research Question 1

The first research question was:

Q3. How do organisational structure, relational norms and project risk impact preferences for communication frequency, contents and media of project sponsors and managers in their formal communication during implementation of IT projects?

Organisational structure, relational norms and project risk impact the communication preferences of IT project sponsors and managers depending on the situational context.

Increasingly bureaucratic structures lead to higher communication frequencies and preference for written status reports. This was found on the most general level, i.e. basis of combined buyer and seller responses, as well as in high performing projects. The same increase in communication frequency was also found for project managers (not sponsors). In the context of low performing projects more bureaucratic structures increase the preference for project analysis. Medium levels of bureaucratic structures, integrated with methodology use, were identified as an attribute of high performing projects. These results indicate that bureaucratic structures support control and frequent reporting during the normal course of projects. If project performance thresholds are compromised then control increases and the communication preference shifts to measures, analysis and trends.

Relational norms were not found to impact communication frequencies or contents individually. In combination with clearness of objectives and preference for written status reports relational norms constitute the project sponsor - manager communication pattern in highly collaborative projects. The extent of objective clearness and high relational norms define the collaborative buyer-seller dimension, which is corroborated by a dimension of project internal structure, defined by organisation structure and methodology clearness, within high performing projects. The extent of collaboration and structure determines the preferences for communication frequency and media, with an equilibrium of written status reports at fixed intervals for high performing projects. Deviations from this equilibrium are indicative of lower levels in either collaboration, structure, or both.

The impact of risk on project sponsor - manager communication depends on the type of risk. Low risk through clear methodology leads to preference for continuous communication, and in high performing projects also to a preference for written status reports. Objective clearness, the second dimension of risk, is clearly most influential on the communication preferences. Lower risks through clearer objectives reduce the preference for continuous communication and project analysis, while, the preference for written status reports increases. Exceptions form these findings are project sponsors, whose communication preferences are less impacted by project risk than those of project managers, as well as low performing projects. Clearer objectives in low performing projects lead to a reduction in preference for project analysis.

6.8 Answer to Research Question 2

The question stated in Chapter 3 was:

> Q4. How effective is the formal communication between project sponsors and project managers during IT project implementation?

Effectiveness was first assessed on the level of congruency in project sponsors and managers choice in communication frequency, contents and media. Followed by assessment of the congruency in perceived project performance of sponsor and manager of the same project, as well as the impact of the choice of frequency, contents and media on the gap in perceived performance.

Assessment number one showed an overlap in frequency, contents and media in the majority of choices. However, project sponsors, when compared with project managers, showed a higher preference for verbal communication and analytic contents, as well as communication at variable intervals in high performing projects. Efficiency improvement in communication requires project managers to provide more forward looking and analytical data of the project, in addition to the statements about achievements and current status. This information can then be used by sponsors during their interaction with their management. Project managers need to be aware that their customers rely on several communication channels simultaneously, which includes not only face-to-face and written media, but also verbal communication.

Assessment number two showed that effectiveness of dyadic communication of project sponsor and manager is higher in high performing projects, where project sponsors keep a steady level of involvement and control over the project and its progress. The choice of media also influences effectiveness. Personal communication was found to increase effectiveness, whereas written status reports with qualitative statements about recent achievements decrease effectiveness in the dyadic project sponsor - manager communication.

Conclusions of the findings and the recommendations for the industry are described in the next chapter.

CHAPTER SEVEN – CONCLUSIONS

The purpose of this chapter is to discuss and conclude on the findings from the analysis and interpretation chapters. This is followed by a set of recommendations for improvement of project results through better project sponsor - manager communication. Finally the strength and limitations of the research are discussed and recommendations for future research are provided.

7.1 Conclusions

The research showed the communication preferences of project sponsors and managers during IT project implementation, and identified the sponsors information requirements beyond what project managers typically provide to them. Specific information requirements of project managers were not found.

Communication preferences of project sponsors and managers are influenced by different factors. The personal characteristic or competence that determines the communication preferences of project sponsors is their number of years with project management experience. Contents-wise sponsors prefer quantitative project analysis data and forward looking information like trends and issues over that of project managers. Analytic data, such as quality metrics or earned value results, are preferred because they are perceived more credible than qualitative statements in status reports about recent achievements. Sponsors are aiming for timeliness of the information they receive. Their preferences for verbal media, as a means to confirm data from written reports, are higher than the preferences of project managers for this media. This links to O'Reilly et al.'s (1987) findings that managers receiving information judge the validity of the information based on the credibility of the source. It also resembles agency theory where the principal has to make sure that the product is delivered at the right time and that it will work for its intended purpose. But the sponsor cannot perfectly monitor the agent or acquire the information available to the agent. Therefore the sponsor asks for forward looking and qualitative information to lower the risk.

While sponsors and managers start from different perspectives and are driven by different influential factors their expectation for communication frequency, contents and media largely overlaps. Project managers' communication is driven by project risk, where communication frequency is balanced through clearness of objectives and clearness of methodology. Written media is increasingly used when objectives are clearer. This differs from the project sponsors' higher interest in multi-channel access to latest project data through verbal updates in addition to written reports. It is contrary to the project managers opinion that project status needs to be formal and auditable and therefore in written manner only. This finding is supported through prior research by Carlson and Davis (1998), as well as Trevino et al. (2000), which showed that lower level (project) managers are more 'other' oriented when choosing media. They select media based on the perceived attitude of the receiver towards the media, as well as the relationship they have with the recipient. Those managers higher up in the organisation, such as project sponsors, select media based on ease of access and are therefore more 'self' oriented in media selection.

Effectiveness in sponsor – manager communication can be improved through awareness about these additional communication expectations of project sponsors and the provision of the expected communication contents and media through project managers. A higher reliance on personal meetings than on written status reports also improves their communication effectiveness.

Project sponsor - manager communication in high and low performing projects differs widely. High performing projects show higher levels of communication effectiveness, impact of methodology on communication practices, as well as higher levels of buyer-seller collaboration and structure in project implementation. Harris and Dibben (1999) also identified these higher levels of structure in their research on the development of trust and co-operation in business relationships as necessary in short term relationships between supervisors and subordinates (such as sponsors and managers in projects) not only to initiate objectively proper behaviour, but to be able to attune the behaviour to the more subjective requirements of the situation. They state that in dyads of shorter duration the socialization among supervisor and subordinate positively impacts subordinate performance. In summary they state (p. 386):

In a technical environment, close communication and a collaborative spirit between supervisors and subordinates are important to the individual and organization.

High performing projects also display a steady difference in project sponsors and managers' communication expectations, caused by the project sponsors sceptical stance towards project performance. This constructive conflict between sponsor and manager indicates a high interest on the side of the buyer organisation and a reluctance to give up control over the project progress despite its high performance status. It links back to prior research on communication in Critical Social Theory, especially the *Theory of Communicative Action* (Habermas 1987), which showed that, depending on a person's orientation to other individuals, message receivers can question the appropriateness of contents and therefore the validity of a message by not accepting it at face value. These message recipients go beyond achieving a mutual understanding with the message sender by '*critical reflection, that is, assessing one or more validity claims pertaining to what the speaker or writer expressed'* (Ngwenyama and Lee 1997, p. 156). Depending on the sender's social action of either being instrumental, communicative, discursive or strategic the message recipient engages in assessing the validity as outlined in Table 7-1 (Habermas 1987, table adopted from Ngwenyama and Lee 1997). Senders engaged in instrumental social action merely treat their message recipient as an organisational resource and not as another social actor. Validity claims from these senders are assessed for appropriateness of the stated action, efficiency and effectives. Those engaged in communicative social action try to achieve or maintain mutual understanding among those involved in a coordinated organisational situation. These actors assess statements for their completeness, truthfulness, clarity and possibly appropriateness for the situation. Senders in discursive action try to achieve or restore agreement for joint action or issue handling. Their messages are assessed for clarity and appropriateness, and possibly also for truthfulness and sincerity. Finally, messages from strategic actors, who try to influence the behaviour of other actors, are assessed against appropriateness of the action and possibly sincerity, efficiency and effectiveness.

Social Action Types	Validity Claims						
	Completeness	Truthfulness	Sincerity	Clarity, Comprehensibility	Contextuality, Appropriateness	Efficiency	Effectiveness
Instrumental Action					Does Apply	Does Apply	Does Apply
Communicative Action	Does Apply	Does Apply		Does Apply	Can Apply		
Discursive Action		Can Apply	Can Apply	Does Apply	Does Apply		
Strategic Action			Can Apply		Does Apply	Can Apply	Can Apply

Table 7-36: Types of Social Action and Applicable Validity Claims (Ngwenyama & Lee 1997)

Even though the social actions and validity claims were not measured or evident in the results of the present study the overall results for high performing projects indicate a critical reflective stance of project sponsors towards the communication from the project manager.

Communication in low performing projects lack almost all attributes of their high performing counterparts. As the only sub-sample the low performing projects showed a correlation between bureaucratic organisation structures and preference for project analysis. Their communication contents focuses mainly on analysis and review. When compared with high performance projects the communication in these projects is ineffective, shown by a significantly larger gap in sponsor and manager's perceived project performance. Collaboration in these projects is missing, as shown by significantly lower levels of relational norms, objective and methodology clearness. With generally higher performance perceptions on the side of the sponsor (compared with the seller firm's project manager) these buyer firms appear to have an 'illusionary' attitude towards the status of their projects.

Frequent informal communication and trust was mentioned as an important attribute of successful project sponsor – manager interaction. This is supported by prior research which defined trust as confidence in another's behaviour, and identified trust building as an ongoing process where increasing levels of trust are gradually developed over time through interaction between buyer and seller firms (Bell et al. 2002).

In summary, IT project managers' typical practices for communication with their customers are not wrong, but incomplete. Project managers' communication is driven by project risk, whereas their sponsors' communication is driven by past experiences. However, most of the sponsors' expectations in communications frequency are met by the practices of project managers. Efficiency in communication can be improved by project managers providing more forward looking and analytical data of the project, which can be used by sponsors in their interaction with their management. Project managers need to be aware that their customers rely on several communication channels, which includes not only face-to-face and written media, but also verbal communication. The effectiveness of their dyadic communication is positively influenced by personal communication and negatively by written reports about recent achievements.

The implications of the findings for communication theory are discussed in the following section.

7.2 Theoretical Implications

The results outlined in Chapter 6 and their relationship to the *Theory of Communicative Action* (Habermas 1987) as shown in the section above suggest a model of formal communication of project sponsors and managers during IT project implementation. The model consists of a hierarchy of five layers that build upon each other in the sequence of:

- Motivation for communication
- Interpretation of project situation and context
- Understanding the meaning of communication contents
- Frequency and media selection
- Message transfer

Senders (or creators) of information process these layers from top to bottom, while receivers do that from bottom to top. The sender and receiver communication flow through the layers is shown in Figure 7-1 and described in the following.

7.2.1 Message Sender

Motivation

A prerequisite for communication to occur is a relationship between a project manager and sponsor, as given through their joint project. The motivation for communication is either externally triggered through existing communication schedules or expressed expectations by one communicator (i.e. a project sponsor or manager), alternatively it is internally triggered by the perception one communicator has about the information needs of the other party (as outlined in section 2.3).

Interpretation of Project Situation and Context

Driven by the desire to avoid surprises during project implementation trust has been build up between the parties on an informal basis in earlier stages of their interactions. Formal communication is initiated to provide an official means for project communication, which potentially serves a wider distribution, like e.g. the management of sponsor or project manager in their respective organisations. To accommodate the wider audience's lack of insight in the project the formal communication between sponsor and manager shifts gradually away from *trust* building (in informal communication) towards a *control* contents (in formal communication). Through that formal communication becomes a migration from prior informal communication, which provides objective information to those who are not regularly involved in the project (section 6.6). Communication content is determined by the level of risk, especially by clearness of objectives and organisational requirements for communication, which are influenced by the organisation's structure (section 6.3). In the context of high performing projects this is a written status report covering recent achievements, issues, project changes, next steps, and other items as they appear. In the context of low performing projects contents is focused on project analysis in order to understand the reasons for low performance, constrain plan deviations, or recover from the current situation (section 6.1.2).

Understanding the Meaning of Communication Contents

Project sponsors and managers depend on a common language and a shared understanding of the situational context in order to enact meaning from each other's communication (Ngwenyamy & Lee 1997). For that the message derived from the former layer is set in a social context by using one of two different paradigms. Depending on the sender's perception of the receiver as being

- *Instrumental*, i.e. just another organisational resource, easily to manipulate. This could result in an order or equivalent communication.
- *Strategic*, i.e. another organisational actor, capable of intelligent counteraction. This results in more covert actions and perhaps 'political' phrasings.

In case the communicators have to establish agreement or mutual understanding, the sender engages in *discursive* action, which entails a discussion and subsequent agreement for a joint course of action. The phrasing of these messages is subsequently refined in order to make sure the receiver understands its meaning. This is the *communicative action* required to achieve mutual understanding in communication contents (Habermas 1987, Ngwenyamy & Lee 1997).

Frequency and Media Selection

At this layer the frequency with which messages are transferred, i.e. formal communication occurs, is determined depending on the project situation in terms of buyer - seller collaboration and structure in execution. As outlined in section 6.4, high performing projects typically use written reports in bi-weekly or monthly intervals, while projects in recovery or with less complex objectives use higher or lower communication frequencies respectively. In projects with very low levels of both structure and collaboration project manager and sponsor might use richer media than written reports for their formal communication.

Message Transfer

At this layer the message is transferred through telephone, mail, electronic mail or other means from sender to receiver. This might includes further coding and recoding, as in the case of email and other electronic communication channels (section 2.2).

7.2.2 Message Receiver

Receivers process messages in the opposite direction, i.e. from message transfer layer, through frequency selection, understanding and interpretation, up to motivation.

Message Transfer

At this level the message is received through the communication media selected by the sender.

Frequency and Media Selection

Through the perceived level of structure and collaboration in the project the receiver assesses the appropriateness of communication frequency and media. This results in the determination of the speed of a possible response based on the project situation, as well as a satisfaction level for frequency and media in communication.

Understanding the Meaning of Communication Contents

As outlined in section 7.1 the received message is assessed on its validity. Based on the perceived social action of the sender (instrumental, strategic, discursive, or communicational) the message contents is assessed for its validity in terms of completeness, truthfulness, sincerity, clarity, contextuality, efficiency and effectiveness (Table 7-1). Based on the results of the assessment the message is either accepted or rejected (Habermas 1987). Rejection at the communication level means a message was not understood, which leads to further clarification and discursive communication. Rejection at the instrumental or strategic social action level requires a re-phrasing that allows the sender to address the validity claims rejected by the receiver, or a switch between instrumental and strategic phrasing of the message.

Interpretation of Project Situation and Context

Messages at this layer add to the receiver's perception about the status of the project. These perceptions are influenced by the receiver's revised understanding of clearness of objectives and organisational expectations, which, in turn, may trigger further communicative actions based on the revised understanding of the project situation. It is at this layer where e.g. the sponsor determines the level of comfort with the information provided by the project manager and may engage in further actions if the expected comfort level is not achieved.

Motivation

Based on the comfort level achieved through the communication the receiver may engages in a revision of the externally agreed communication schedule, or the internal perception about appropriate communication frequencies and contents in the project.

Figure 7-1 shows the five communication layers, the message flow from creation by the sender to interpretation and reaction by the receiver.

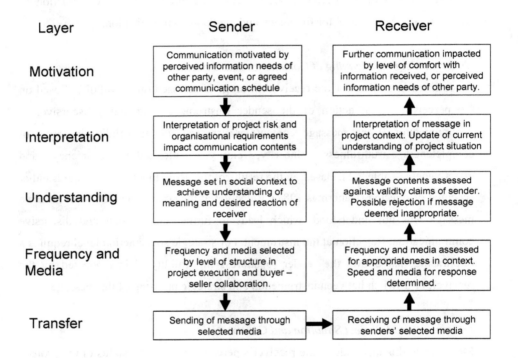

Figure 7-20: Project Manager - Sponsor Communication Model

The research took the perspective of Transaction Cost Economics and Agency Theory. The results resemble agency theory's problem of information asymmetry between principal and agent, i.e. project sponsor and manager. Their information asymmetry, together with their differences in objectives, causes monitoring costs (agency costs) on the side of the principal, which prevents firms from maximizing their profits (Laffont & Martimort 2002). The aim of the research was to identify ways to lower this information asymmetry through increased communication effectiveness, which allows for higher profits. The importance of this is outlined by Jensen (2000, p.108):

> *All firms will incur agency costs; competitive pressure will be felt only by firms with higher agency costs than their competitors.*

Based on the present study's results a series of recommendations for lowering of agency costs was developed and is provided in the next section.

7.3 Managerial Implications

The research results should be used to develop strategies to prevent gaps in project sponsor and manager communication. Preventive actions like these lower agency costs and increase confidence in the outcomes of a project. Using the layers from the theoretical model described above a series of recommendations are outlined in the following and subsequently summarized.

Project managers should ensure that their project's sponsors are comfortable with the level of detail and frequency of the information provided to them. Insufficient information can cause personal involvement of the sponsor in the project. By trying to understand the project situation the sponsor potentially engages in micro-management of the project, which undermines the project manager's authority and confuses the project team. To avoid this, project managers should regularly inquire on their sponsors' satisfaction with the formal communication. Project sponsors and managers should both voice their information requirements and agree on communication practices to satisfy their mutual information needs. This leads to efficient communication between the parties, i.e. a major contributing factor for project success. A communication schedule, outlining contents, frequency and media for formal communication should therefore be agreed at the outset of a project and adjusted to the project's situation when necessary.

Project sponsors and managers build-up mutual trust through informal communication. However, formal communication, i.e. the official reference for project status which is potentially distributed to a wider audience, should be based on more objective information. Project managers should therefore supply sponsors with objective, quantitative information about the project, e.g. about trends, quality

---

metrics, earned value results, so that sponsors can present them to their management. Sponsors often seek re-assurance of the contents and their understanding of formal written reports through phone calls, which give them quick timely updates of the project situation. These should be pro-actively scheduled by project managers so that both parties are prepared, have the required data at hand, and the time that is needed for the call is reserved in their calendars. In their interaction the two parties need to be aware that their communication is driven by different factors and that project managers communicate in relation to project risk, whereas sponsors do that in relation to their past experiences. Misunderstandings should be avoided by clearly outlining and possibly discussing the background and underlying assumptions of the information the parties provide to each other, as well as the reasons of the questions they ask during formal communication. This is necessary in order to ensure a shared understanding of the project situation together with its context.

Communication content is formulated in a social context, i.e. different wordings are chosen depending on the sender's perception about the role of the receiver as being an instrumental or strategic actor, the need for joint agreement, or the need to clarify messages not understood by the receiver. People engaged in communication constantly switch between these four modes to ensure understanding of their messages. Failure to switch between modes leads to communication breakdowns, which causes misinterpretations and misunderstandings (Habermas 1987), as outlined on page 1. Message senders (such as project sponsors or managers) should be aware that the validities of their messages are assessed by the receiver as outlined in Table 7-1, and messages are possibly rejected if not perceived as valid. Rejected messages should be re-phrased, so that common understandings can be achieved. These clarifying actions are especially difficult when using written communication, because of the media's lack of immediate feedback. Sponsors and managers should therefore use verbal communication as a complementary media to achieve shared understanding of their communication contents. This increases the effectiveness in communication and the satisfaction of both parties with the information provided.

Project sponsors and managers should aim for highest possible relational norms and shared understanding of the project objectives. For the seller firm this includes not only an understanding of the specification and the product to be delivered, but also an understanding how the product is used after the project is finished. For buyer firms this includes linking the project team with the overall organisational change process and other neighbouring projects, so that the seller firm's project manager is able to understand the purpose and 'big picture' of the project. Project execution should follow a clearly communicated project management methodology, which outlines the process, tasks and resources for project implementation, as well as clearly outline the organisational roles of the individual team members. Formal communication tends to stabilize at bi-weekly to monthly intervals in projects with high performance. Projects with higher or lower communication frequencies should be assessed using the Structure-Collaboration matrix outlined in section 6.4 to identify the reasons for the deviation from equilibrium frequencies. This allows to uncover risks and to counteract upcoming adverse trends in projects. Formal communication solely based on richer media is indicative of severely low levels of buyer - seller collaboration and structure in project execution. These projects should be closely investigated as to the project management practices used, as well as to the relationship between project sponsor and manager, in order identify ways to improve the project situation.

The following list of ten recommendations summarizes the managerial implications listed above, in order to increase communication effectiveness and thereby improve overall project results:

Project sponsors should:
- maintain a healthy level of scepticism about the project's performance and stay involved through communicative actions to ensure good understanding of project progress, issues and trends
- avoid relying too much on written status reports, especially those on past achievements and current status. These reports lack detailed discussion of potential and real issues, and should be used more as a backup to personal discussions with the project manager.
- reassure correct understanding of written reports through phone calls or informal meetings with the project manager.

Project managers should:

- go beyond written status reports and use complementary media to communicate project status, and also provide information on issues, open items, quality measures, next steps and trends
- constantly learn about their customer's expectations and experiences, as well as changes in these
- assess their customers satisfaction with the information provided in their progress reports and adapt their reporting practices accordingly
- encourage involvement of customers in the project, using rich communication media like personal meetings or phone calls, to have customers participate in the decision making processes and share parts of the responsibility for project success.

IT buyer and seller firms should:

- train their personnel on the different perspectives of buyers and sellers and the need for an upfront definition of communication frequency, contents and media in IT project implementation
- use the Structure – Collaboration Matrix as a tool to assess communication practices in projects. The identification of imbalances can then be further assessed using the underlying dimensions of relational norms, organisation structure, methodology and objective clearness.
- be aware of the importance of good communication for project outcomes and actively pursue the improvement of communication practices through joint work between industry and academia.

The competitive environment in the IT project business often requires selling organisations to take aggressive steps to promote their projects. This can lead to overpromising of project objectives. Here the project manager has the special responsibility to adjust customer expectations about project deliverables to realistic levels (Brown and Swartz 1989). This increases congruency of performance goals and perceptions in projects, which prevents from perceived project failure on the side of the buyer and improves word-of-mouth comments, which impacts current and future business of an IT supplier. Congruency in communication leads to mutually satisfying business relationships (Dance 1967), which are the building blocks for long-term buyer-seller relationships.

7.4 Strengths of the Study

The study addressed an often-cited weakness of project management research, i.e. the inward looking perspective of the existing normative project theories, and a general incoherence of project organisation theory (Ekstedt et al. 1999). For that the study was based on established and acknowledged theories and instruments originally developed in the context of permanent organisations.

Relevance is shown through the overall research approach, which identified the research topic through an initial research step. Here the analysis of the results of 36 IT project audits showed the significance of communication management for cost results in IT projects (Müller & Turner 2001). This result was further supported through the literature review and confirmed from the researcher's employer (a global IT firm).

Confidence in the study's results is also given through the mixed method approach with triangulated results from a quantitative and a qualitative study.

Content validity was addressed through an extensive literature review to identify the survey items, two focus groups were used to validate the research design and instrument, and accepted and validated multi-item measurement constructs were used wherever possible. Application of recommended web-survey design principles, which specifically addressed the error types of sampling, coverage, measurement and non-response also increase the validity of the instrument. Construct validity was given through the communication factors, derived from Factor Analysis, which show a consistency of media and contents in accordance with Media Richness Theory.

Reliability of the quantitative measurement constructs was achieved through purification by using accepted threshold levels for Cronbach Alpha and MSA. Development of new multi-item constructs followed Churchill's (1979) process, as recommended by Grover (1997).

A series of techniques was applied to identify outliers and influential responses. The resulting sample with a size of 200 responses, split into sub-samples of 138 project managers and 62 sponsors, as well as 122 high performing and 78 low performing projects, was large enough to fulfil the minimum requirements of variable-to-responses ratios to achieve reliable results from the quantitative techniques used. Quantitative results were assessed for statistical and practical significance.

The applied rigor in design and analysis, together with the triangulated results in a multi-method approach support generalizability of the results for IT projects in buyer-seller environments.

In accordance with the methodology outlined in chapter 4 the research results were continuously provided to the research community for scrutiny and evaluation. The publications in refereed journals as well as presentations at researcher and practitioner conferences were well received. Discussions at conferences and e-mail responses on journal publications did not question the validity of the results. A list of publications derived from this study is shown in Table 7-2, showing the state of the research and the associated publications as conference and refereed journal paper.

Stage	Conference Papers (10)	Refereed Journal Papers (8)
Initial research	"Project Management Knowledge Areas: Their Impact on Earned Value Results and Their Return on Investment ", in *Proceedings of the International Project Management Congress*, November 19 - 20, 2001, Tokyo, Japan. "The Impact of Performance in PM Knowledge Areas on Earned Value Results ", in *Proceedings of the PM Research Conference Vienna VIII*, November 21-22, 2001, Vienna, Austria.	"The impact of performance in project management knowledge areas on earned value results in information technology projects ", *Project Management: International Project Management Journal*, Finland, vol. 7, no. 1, Summer 2001.
Literature Review	"Managing Information Technology Projects - A Training and Communications Challenge", in *Proceedings (Key-note Address) of the First International Software Project Management Congress "IT Business in a New Light - The Projectised Way"*, May 20 -22, 2002, Bangalore, India "On the Nature of the Project as a Temporary Organization", in *Proceedings (Key-note Address) of IRNOP V, Fifth Congress of the International Research Network for Organization by Projects*, May 29 -31, 2002, Renesse, The Netherlands *	"Communication Between Buyer and Seller Organizations in the Context of Project Management", *Henley Working Paper Series HWP 0105*, Henley Management College, UK. "On the Nature of the Project as a Temporary Organization", *Henley Working Paper Series HWP 0206*, Henley Management College, Henley-on-Thames, UK * "On the Nature of the Project as a Temporary Organization", *International Journal of Project Management*, vol. 21, no.1 *
Differences in Project Sponsors and Managers communication preferences	"Improved Project Results through Alignment of IT Buyer and Seller Communications ", in *Proceedings of the First International Software Project Management Congress "IT Business in a New Light - The Projectised Way"*, May 20 -22, 2002, Bangalore, India "Communication Requirements and Capabilities of Project Sponsors and Project Managers in IT Projects ", in *Proceedings of the IPMA World Congress*, June 4-6, 2002, Berlin, Germany.	"Communication Requirements and Capabilities of Project Sponsors and Project Managers in IT Projects", *Indian Project Management Journal*, vol. 1, no. 2, APM India.
Drivers for Project Manager's communication	"The Impact of Organization Structure, Relational Norms and Project Risk on External Communication in IT Projects", in *Proceedings of IRNOP V, Fifth Congress of the International Research Network for Organization by Projects*, May 29 -31, 2002, Renesse, The Netherlands	"Determinants for External Communications of IT Project Managers", *International Journal of Project Management*, vol. 21, no. 7, (in print) "The Impact of Organization Structure, Relational Norms and Project Risk on External Communications of IT Project Managers", *Henley Working Paper Series HWP 0217*, Henley Management College, Henley-on-Thames, UK.
Model for Buyer-Seller Communication	"Communication Between IT Project Manager and Project Sponsor in a Buyer - Seller Relationship", in *Proceedings of the PMI Research Conference, Frontiers of Project Management Research and Application*, July 14 - 17, 2002 Seattle, USA, Project Management Institute, Newton Square, USA	"A Model for Project Manager and Sponsor Communications in IT Projects", *IEEE Transactions on Engineering Management*, IEEE, USA (in progress).
Detailed Gap Analysis of Communication Patterns	"A Model and Gap Analysis of Buyer - Seller Communications in IT Projects", in *Proceedings of the PM Research Conference Vienna IX*, November 27-28, 2002, Vienna, Austria "Bridging the Gap: A Model for Effective Buyer-Seller Communication during IT project Implementation", *Proceedings of the 17th World Congress on Project Management*, June 2-4, 2003, Moscow, Russia (to appear)	* = principal author J Rodney Turner

Table 7-37: Study Related Publications

7.5 Limitations of the Study

The study has a number of limitations, mainly related to the sampling approach, and the practical significance of the quantitative models.

The distribution of the survey through the professional institutions for project management did not allow for control over their distribution mechanisms to ensure the survey is delivered to all possible recipients. Furthermore it did not allow sending reminders to the final recipients. That possibly had a negative impact on the response rate and randomization of the sample.

The series of constraints imposed on possible respondents (IT projects only, at implementation stage, pairs of sponsor and manager etc.) potentially deterred some of the prospective respondents. It also did not allow quantifying the size of the real sampling frame, which, in turn, did not allow for calculation of a response rate. The 'hitrate' tracked by the survey provider does not indicate the number of recipients of the survey, only the number of those recipients who opened the survey versus the number of responses. The 29% response rate is therefore not equivalent to the traditional response rate in mail surveys. The possibility of non-response bias cannot be dispelled.

Low R^2 values from the regression models and the canonical correlation model were expected due to the variety of 'noise' that impacts communication between project sponsors and managers worldwide. However, that limits the practical significance of the established models and need to be taken into account during application of the models for practical purposes.

The advantages of easy access and preformatted sample data within a web based survey were balanced by a number of weaknesses. They are listed in Table 7-3. The majority of the disadvantages have an adverse effect on response rates, which lowers the sample size.

Advantages of web-surveys	Disadvantages of web-surveys
Automated questionnaire setup and processing.	Restricted control over layout of questions and answers on screen. Cumbersome development of 'work arounds' for question layouts that are not supported by the provider, e.g. for semantic differential scales.
Higher accuracy of data, e.g. by enforcing responses to all questions.	Respondents failing to answer all questions either ignore the associated error message or cannot find the answer they left out. Both prevents the questionnaire from being submitted to the database, leading to a lower response rate.
Ease of access for respondents.	Server downtimes, temporary geographical Internet access problems, firms blocking Internet access due to virus attacks and non-portability of the web-based surveys (e.g. to answer it on the airplane) have a potentially adverse effect on attractiveness of the survey and the associated response rates.

Table 7-38: Advantages and Disadvantages of web-based Surveys

7.6 Implications for Further Research

The majority of the study comprised empirical research. Even though the results were methodologically triangulated, they should be confirmed through further studies. These studies should preferably use different sampling approaches than the present study in order to identify possible influences due to the limitations stated above.

The results could be further enriched through a research on actual communication practices, as opposed to the preferred practices investigated in this study. This could also include contents analysis of existing documents or tape recordings from formal communication events between sponsors and managers. This would provide a further level of triangulation and contribute to the confidence in the overall results. A subsequent comparison of the three findings, namely literature suggestions, communication preferences, and actual practices allows for the development of a detailed list of recommendations for improvement. It also provides a basis for the development of a more generalizable theory about sponsor - manager communication.

Project sponsors assessment of validity claims in sponsor - manager interactions, as outlined in section 7.1, should be further assessed for its relationship with successful and less successful projects. This will allow for better understanding of the role of communication contents in influencing project sponsors perceptions about a project, and in determining communication efficiency.

The study identified a worldwide 'common denominator' in communications between project sponsors and managers. Further studies should be conducted to increase usability on a local basis through identification of local influences. A first test on geographical differences showed remarkable differences between America, Europe and other geographical areas on the drivers for communication (Table 7-4). Communication in Europe appears to be largely influenced by relational norms (Müller 2003), while communication in America seems to be driven by project risk. As shown in Table 7-4 experience appears to have contrary effects on preferences for project analysis and verbal updates. This should be used as starting point for research on communication differences caused by different cultures. Other factors that potentially impact communication are industry, project type or complexity.

| Independent Variables | Communication Frequency | | | | | | | | | Communication Contents | | | | | | | | | | | |
| | Variable Interval Communication | | | Fixed Interval Communication | | | Contiuous Communication | | | Personal Review | | | Project Analysis | | | Written Status | | | Verbal Update | | |
	Am	Eur	Oth	Am	Eur	Oth	Am	Eur	Oth	Am	Eur	Oth	Am	Eur	Oth	Am	Eur	Oth	Am	Eur	Oth
Demographic Variables																					
Work Experience	0	0	0	0	0	0	0	0	0	0	0	0	0	0	+*	0	0	0	0	0	0
Project Management Experience	0	0	0	0	0	0	0	0	0	0	0	0	+**	-**	-*	0	0	0	0	0	-*
Project Sponsor Experience	0	0	+*	0	0	0	0	0	0	0	0	-**	0	+*	0	0	+***	0	0	+*	-*
Project Variables																					
Relational Norms	0	0	0	0	+**	0	0	0	-*	0	+*	0	0	0	0	0	+***	0	0	0	0
Organization Structure	0	0	0	0	0	0	0	0	0	0	0	0	0	0	0	0	0	0	0	0	0
Objective Clearness	0	0	0	0	0	0	-**	0	-**	0	0	0	0	-****	+****	0	0	0	0	0	0
Methodology Clearness	0	0	0	0	0	0	+***	0	+*****	-**	0	0	0	0	0	0	0	0	0	0	0
Buyer - Seller Perspective	0	0	0	0	0	0	0	0	0	0	0	0	0	-**	-*	0	0	0	0	0	0

Note: 0 = not significant
* Significant at p < .10
**Significant at p < .05
***Significant at p < .01
****Significant at p < .005
*****Significant at p < .001

+/- = significant positive or negative correlation

n America = 65
n Europe = 92
n Other Areas = 41

Table 7-39: Differences in Communication Drivers by Geography

An underlying assumption of the present study was that communication is 'static' over the course of project implementation. Differences in communication preferences depending on the progress in the implementation stage should also be investigated, preferably using a longitudinal study to analyse the change in communication over the course of project implementation.

This will provide a further step towards a more holistic understanding of the communication between project sponsors and managers.

7.7 Summary

This chapter presented the conclusions of the study. Gaps in project sponsor – manager communication were discussed in the context of the study's underlying theories, and recommendations provided to close these gaps. The study's strength, mainly in the area of overall approach, relevance and methodological rigor were presented and balanced by the limitations caused by the sampling approach and use of web-based surveys.

In conclusion the study has reaffirmed some existing theories about organisational communication and shown that further improvements in communicational effectiveness are needed. This increase in effectiveness can be accomplished through a communication-about-communication, and well balanced operational structure and collaboration in project execution. Both together will provide for better project results through improved project performance.

References

Adler, T. R., Scherer, R. F., Barton, S. L., & Katerberg, R. 1998, "An empirical test of transaction cost theory: Validating contract typology", *Journal of Applied Management Studies*, vol. 7, no. 2, pp. 185-200.

Adriaenssens, C. & Cadman, L. 1999, "An adaptation of moderated e-mail focus groups to assess the potential for a new online (Internet) financial services offer in the UK", *Journal of Market Research Society*, vol. 41, no. 4, p. 417.

Alexander, E. R., Penley, L. E., & Jernigan, I. E. 1991, "The Effect of Individual Differences on Managerial Media Choice", *Management Communication Quarterly*, vol. 5, no. 2, pp. 155-173.

Allen, T. J., Lee, D. M. S., & Tushman, M. L. 1980, "R&D Performance as a Function of Internal Communication, Project Management, and the Nature of Work", *IEEE Transactions on Engineering Management*, vol. EM-27, no. 1, pp. 2-12.

Andersen, E. 2000, "Managing organization-structure and responsibilities," in *Gower Handbook of Project Management*, 3rd edn, J. R. Turner & S. J. Simister, eds., Gower Publishing Ltd., Hampshire, UK, pp. 277-292.

APM 2000, *APM Body of Knowledge*, Fourth edn, British Standards Institution, London, UK.

Archibald, R. D. 1976, "Evaluating and Directing the Project," in *Managing High-Technology Programs and Projects*, John Wiley & Sons, New York, USA, pp. 216-233.

Audi, R. 1998, *Epistemology: a contemporary introduction to the theory of knowledge*, Routledge, New York, USA.

Bacharach, S. B. & Lawler, E. J. 1980, *Power and Politics in Organizations*, Jossey-Bass Inc., San Francisco, USA.

Baker, C. D. 1984, "The search for adultness: membership work in adolescent - adult talk", *Human Studies*, vol. 7, pp. 301-323.

Barkowski, L. 1998, "Intranets for project and cost management in manufacturing", *Transactions of AACE International*, p. IT7-IT11.

Barney, J. B. & Hesterly, W. 1996, "Organizational Economics: Understanding the Relationship between Organizations and Economic Analysis," in *Handbook of Organization Studies*, S. R. Clegg, C. Hardy, & W. R. Nord, eds., Sage Publications, London, UK, pp. 115-147.

Barry, A. M. & Pascale, S. 1999, "Web Management and Integrative Procurement Communications", *Project Management Journal*, vol. 30, no. 1, pp. 6-10.

Barry, B. & Crant, J. M. 2000, "Dyadic Communication relationships in Organizations: An Attribution/Expectancy Approach", *Organization Science*, vol. 11, no. 6, pp. 648-664.

Bartunek, J. M. & Seo, M. G. 2001, "Qualitative research can add new meanings to quantitative research", *Journal of Organizational Behavior*, vol. 23, pp. 237-242.

Bashkar, R. 1975, *A Realist Theory of Science,* Leeds Books Ltd., Leeds, UK.

Bell, G. G., Oppenheimer, R. J., & Bastien, A. 2002, "Trust deterioration in an international buyer-seller relationship", *Journal of Business Ethics*, vol. 36, no. 1, pp. 65-78.

Bensaou, M. & Ventkatraman, N. 1996, "Inter-organizational relationships and information technology: a conceptual synthesis and a research framework", *European Journal of Information Systems*, vol. 5, pp. 84-91.

Bergen, M., Dutta, S., & Walker, O. C. 1992, "Agency Relationships in Marketing: A Review of the Implications and Applications of Agency and Related Theories", *Journal of Marketing*, vol. 56, no. 3, p. 1.

Bissett, L. L. & Weil, H. G. 1989, "Communicating for Desired Results," in *Project Management: A Reference for Professionals* , R. L. Kimmons & J. H. Loweree, eds., Marcel Dekker, Inc., New York, USA, pp. 895-898.

Blaikie, N. 1993, *Approaches to Social Enquiry,* Polity Press, Cambridge, UK.

Bloor, M., Frankland, J., Thomas, M., & Robson, K. 2001, *Focus Groups in Social Research,* SAGE Publications Ltd., London, UK.

Bogdan, R. & Taylor, S. J. 1975, *Introduction to Qualitative Research Methods,* John Wiley & Sons, Canada.

Booth-Kewley, S., Rosenfeld, P., & Edwards, J. E. 1993, "Computer-Administered Surveys in Organizational Settings: Alternatives, Advantages, and Applications," in *Improving Organizational Surveys*, P. Rosenfeld, J. E. Edwards, & M. D. Thomas, eds., SAGE Publications, Newbury Park, USA, pp. 73-101.

Brown, S. W. & Swartz, T. A. 1989, "A Gap Analysis of Professional Service Quality", *Journal of Marketing*, vol. 53, April, pp. 92-98.

Bryman, A. 1988, *Quantity and Quality in Social Research,* Unwin Hyman, Inc., UK.

Bunge, M. 1996, *Finding Philosophy in Social Science,* Yale University Press, Yale University.

Burns, T. & Stalker, G. M. 1994, *The Management of Innovation*, 2nd edn, Oxford University Press, USA.

BWB 1997, *V-Model: Development Standard for IT Systems of the Federal Republic of Germany,* IABG, Koblenz, Germany.

Calvert, S. 1995, "Managing Stakeholders," in *The Commercial Project Manager*, J. R. Turner, ed., McGraw-Hill, England, Maidenhead, England, pp. 214-222.

Cambridge 2001, *Cambridge International Dictionary of English.* http://dictionary.cambridge.org/. Cambridge University Press. Accessed 24-10-2002.

Carlson, P. J. & Davis, G. B. 1998, "An Investigation of Media Selection Among Directors and Managers: From 'Self' to 'Other' Orientation", *MIS Quarterly*, vol. 1998, no. September, pp. 335-362.

CCTA 2000, *Managing Successful Projects with PRINCE 2,* The Stationary Office, Norwich, UK.

Celestino, R. 1995, "Project Communications: Does High-tech Help or Hinder?", *Proceedings of the Project Management Institute's 26th Annual Seminar/Symposium, New Orleans, Louisiana, October 16 to 18, 1995* pp. 644-649.

Churchill, G. A. 1979, "A Paradigm for Developing Better Measures of Marketing Constructs", *Journal of Marketing Research*, vol. 14, no. February, pp. 64-73.

Churchill, G. A. 1999, *Marketing Research: Methodological Foundations,* fifth edn, The Dryden Press, Orlando, FL, USA.

Cleland, D. L. 1991, "The Age of Project Management", *Project Management Journal*, vol. 22, no. 1, pp. 19-24.

Cohen, J. 1988, *Statistical Power Analysis for the Behavioral Sciences*, 2nd edn, Lawrence Erlbaum Associates, Inc., Hillsdale, USA.

Cooper, J. M. 2000, "Collaborative Communication: Six Building Blocks for Conversations That Make Things Happen," in *Proceedings of the Project Management Institute Annual Seminars and Symposium*, PMI, September 7-16, 2000, Houston, Texas, USA.

Crawford, L. & Brett, C. 2000, "Exploring the Role of the Project Sponsor", *Proceedings of the 15th IPMA World Congress on Project Management,* London, UK.

Cronbach, L. J. 1951, "Coefficient Alpha and the Internal Structure of Tests", *Psychometrika*, vol. 16, no. 3, pp. 297-334.

Daft, R. L. & Lengel, R. H. 1986, "Organizational Information Requirements, Media Richness and Structural Design", *Management Science*, vol. 32, no. 5, pp. 554-571.

Dance, F. E. X. 1967, "Toward a Theory of Human Communication," in *Human Communication Theory*, F. E. X. Dance, ed., Holt, Rinehart and Winston Inc., New York, USA, pp. 288-309.

Denzin, N. K. 1978, *The Research Act*, 2nd edn, McGraw-Hill, New York, USA.

Dillman, D. A. & Bowker, D. K. 2001. *The Web Questionnaire Challenge to Survey Methodologists.* http://survey.sesrc.wsu.edu/dillman/papers.htm. Accessed 9-12-2002.

Dixon, T. 1996, *Communication, Organization and Performance*, Ablex Publishing Corporation, Norwood, USA.

Doll, W. J. & Torkzadeh, G. 1988, "The Measurement of End-User Computing Satisfaction", *MIS Quarterly*, vol. 1988, no. June 1988, pp. 259-274.

Donabedian, B., McKinnon, S. M., & Bruns, W. J. 1998, "Task Characteristics, Managerial Socialization, and Media Selection", *Management Communication Quarterly*, vol. 11, no. 3, pp. 372-400.

Donaldson, L. 1996, *For Positivist Organization Theory,* SAGE Publications, London, UK.

Doty, D. H., Glick, W. H., & Huber, G. 1993, "Fit, equifinality, and organizational effectiveness: A test", *Academy of Management Journal*, vol. 36, no. 6, p. 1196.

Duhig Berry 1993, *Project Control,* NCC Blackwell Ltd, Oxford, England.

Easterby-Smith, M., Thorpe, R., & Lowe, A. 1991, *Management Research,* SAGE Publication Ltd., UK.

Edwards, J. E., Thomas, M. D., Rosenfeld, P., & Booth-Kewley, S. 1996, *How to Conduct Organizational Surveys,* SAGE Publications, Inc., Thousand Oaks, California, USA.

Eisenberg, E., Farace, R. V., Monge, P. R., Bettinghaus, E. P., Kurchner-Hawkins, R., Miller, K. I., & Rothman, L. 1985, "Communication Linkages in Interorganizational Systems: Review and Synthesis," in *Progress in Communication Sciences*, B. Dervin & M. J. Voigt, eds., Ablex Publishing Corporation, Norwood, New Jersey, USA, pp. 231-261.

Ekstedt, E., Lundin, R. A., Soederholm, A., & Wirdenius, H. 1999, *Neo-Industrial Organising,* Routledge, UK.

Ericsson 1999, *PROPS: A General Model for Project Management in a Multiproject Organization,* Ericsson Project Management Institute, Karlstad, Sweden.

ESI 1994, *PMI Certification Exam Preparation Guide,* Educational Services Institute, Arlington, Virginia, USA.

ESI 1999, *Project Framework: A Project Management Maturity Model,* ESI International, Arlingtion, USA.

Fahy, J. 1998, "Improving Response Rates in Cross-Cultural Mail Surveys", *Industrial Marketing Management*, vol. 27, pp. 459-567.

Feyerabend, P. 1975. *Against Method*
http://www.marxists.org/reference/subject/philosophy/index.htm. Accessed 26-10-2002.

Fichman, M. & Goodman, P. 1996, "Customer-Supplier Ties in Interorganizational Relations", *Research in Organizational Behavior*, vol. 18, pp. 285-329.

Fornell, C. 1978, "Problems in the Interpretation of Canonical Analysis: The Case of Power in Distributive Channels", *Journal of Marketing*, vol. 15, no. August 1978, pp. 489-491.

Frame, J. D. 1987, *Managing Projects in Organizations*, Jossey-Bass, San Francisco, USA.

Frame, J. D. 1999, *Project Management Competence*, Jossey-Bass Inc., San Francisco, USA.

Frey, J. H. & Fontana, A. 1993, "The Group Interview in Social Research," in *Successful Focus Groups: Advancing the State of the Art*, D. L. Morgan, ed., Sage Publications, Newbury Park, California, USA, pp. 20-34.

Fulk, J. & Boyd, B. 1991, "Emerging Theories of Communication in Organizations", *Journal of Management*, vol. 17, no. 2, pp. 407-446.

Fulk, J. 1993, "Social construction of communication technology", *Academy of Management Journal*, vol. 36, no. 5, p. 921.

Gaddis, P. O. 1959, "The Project Manager", *Harvard Business Review*, vol. 1959, no. May-June, pp. 89-97.

Galbraith, J. R. & Lawler, E. E. 1993, "Effective Organizations: Using the New Logic of Organizing," in *Organizing for the Future*, Jossey-Bass Inc., San Francisco, USA, pp. 285-299.

Gareis, R. 1992, "Management of Networks of Projects", *American Association of Cost Engineers. Transactions of the American Association of Cost Engineers*, vol. 2, p. J.1.1.

Garvin, D. A. 1998, "The Process of Organization and Management", *Sloan Management Review*, vol. 1998, no. Summer, pp. 33-50.

Ghiselli, E. E. 1964, "Dr. Ghiselli comments on Dr. Tupes note", *Personnel Psychology*, vol. 17, pp. 61-63.

Griffin, S. D. 2002, "A Taxonomy of Internet Applications for Project Management Communication", *Project Management Journal*, vol. 33, no. 4, pp. 39-47.

Grover, V. 1997. *A Tutorial on Survey Research: From Constructs to Theory.*
http://dmsweb.badm.sc.edu/grover/survey/MIS-SUVY.html, last access 9-10-2002.

Gunnarson, S., Linde, A., & Loid, D. 2000, "Is Standardization Applicable to Project Managers of Multi-Project Companies," in *Proceedings of IRNOP IV: Fourth International Conference of the International Research Network on Organizing by Projects*, Sydney, Australia, pp. 136-146.

Habermas, J. 1987, *Theorie des Kommunikativen Handelns*, 4th edn, Suhrkamp Verlag, Frankfurt am Main, Germany.

Hair, J. F., Anderson, R. E., Tatham, R. L., & Black, W. C. 1998, *Multivariate Data Analysis*, fifth edn, Prentice Hall, USA.

Halinen, A. 1997, *Relationship Marketing in Professional Services,* Routledge, London, UK.

Hammer, M. & Stanton, S. 1999, "How Process Enterprises Really Work", *Harvard Business Review,* no. 11-12/1999, pp. 108-118.

Harpham, A. 2000, "Political, economic, social and technical influences - PEST," in *Gower Handbook of Project Management*, third edn, J. R. Turner & S. J. Simister, eds., Gower Publishing Limited, Hampshire, UK, pp. 165-184.

Harris, S. & Dibben, M. 1999, "Trust and Co-operation in Business Relationship Development: Exploring the Influence of National Values", *Journal of Marketing Management*, vol. 1999, no. 15, pp. 463-483.

Hartman, F. T. 2000, *Don't Park Your Brain Outside,* Project Management Institute, Newtown Square, USA.

Hartman, F. T., Herrero, J. C., & Ashrafi, R. A. 1995, "How to Identify and Communicate Customer Needs and Expectations," in *Proceedings from the Project Management Institute 36th Annual Seminar/Symposium* , PMI, October 16 to 18, 1995, New Orleans, Louisiana, USA, pp. 388-394.

Hastings, C. 1995, "Building the culture of organizational networking", *International Journal of Project Management*, vol. 13, no. 4, pp. 259-263.

Heide, J. B. & John, T. G. 1992, "Do Norms Matter in Marketing Relationships?", *Journal of Marketing*, vol. 56, no. 2, pp. 32-44.

Hirschheim, R. A. 1985, "Information Systems Epistemology: An Historical Perspective," in *Research Methods in Information Systems*, A. Mumford et al., eds., North-Holland, Amsterdam, pp. 13-35.

Huber, P. & Daft, R. L. 1987, "The Information Environments of Organizations," in *Handbook of Organizational Communication*, F. M. Jablin et al., eds., SAGE Publications Inc., Newbury Park, USA, pp. 130-164.

Hutinski, Z., Vrcek, N., & Bubas, G. 2001, "Communication in Complex Information System Development Projects", *Informing Science*, vol. 2001, no. June.

Ibbs, W. C. & Kwak, Y. H. 1997, *The Benefits of Project Management*, Project Management Institute, USA.

IPMA 1999, *IPMA Competence Baseline*, 2nd edn, International Project Management Association, Monmouth, UK.

Jensen, M. C. 2000, *A Theory of the Firm: Governance, Residual Claims, and Organizational Forms*, Harvard University Press, Cambridge, USA

Jiang, J. J., Klein, G., & Means, T. L. 2000, "Project Risk Impact on Software Development Team Importance", *Project Management Journal*, vol. 31, no. 4, pp. 19-26.

Jick, T. D. 1979, "Mixing Qualitative and Quantitative Methods: Triangulation in Action", *Administrative Science Quarterly*, vol. 24, pp. 602-611.

Jobber, D. & O'Reilly, D. 1998, "Industrial Mail Surveys: A Methodological Update", *Industrial Marketing Management*, vol. 27, pp. 95-107.

Johns, T. G. 1999, "On creating organizational support for the Project Management Method", *International Journal of Project Management*, vol. 17, no. 1, pp. 47-53.

Johnson, J. D. 1993, *Organizational Communication Structure*, Ablex Publishing Corp., Norwood, New Jersey, USA.

Johnson, J. D., Donohue, W. A., Atkin, C. K., & Johnson, S. 1994, "Differences between formal and informal communication channels", *Journal of Business Communication*, vol. 31, no. 2, p. 111.

Judgev, K. & Thomas, J. 2002, "Project Management Maturity Models: The Silver Bullets of Competitive Advantage", *Project Management Journal*, vol. 33, no. 4, pp. 4-14.

Katz, R. & Tushman, M. L. 1981, "An investigation into the managerial roles and career paths of gatekeepers and project supervisors in a major R&D facility", *R&D Management*, vol. 11, no. 3, pp. 103-110.

Keller, R. 2001, "Cross-Functional Project Groups in Research and New Product Development: Diversity, Communications, Job Stress, and Outcomes", *Academy of Management Journal*, vol. 44, no. 3, pp. 547-555.

Kerzner, H. 1982, *Project Management for Executives*, Van Nostrand Reinhold Company, New York, USA.

Kettinger, W. J. & Grover, V. 1997, "The Use of Computer-mediated Communication in an Organizational Context", *Decision Sciences*, vol. 28, no. 3, pp. 513-555.

Khandwalla, P. N. 1977, *The Design of Organizations*, Harcourt Brace Jovanovich, Inc., New York, USA.

Kraut, R. E. & Streeter, L. A. 1995, "Coordination in software development", *Communication of the ACM*, vol. 38, no. 3, p. 69.

Kreiner, K. 1992, "The Postmodern Epoch of Organization Theory", *International Studies of Management & Organization*, vol. 22, no. 2, p. 37.

Krone, K. J., Jablin, F. M., & Putnam, L. L. 1987, "Communication Theory and Organizational Communication: Multiple Perspectives," in *Handbook of Organizational Communication*, F. M. Jablin et al., eds., SAGE Publications, Newbury Park, USA, pp. 18-40.

Laffont, J. J. & Martimort, D. 2002, *The Theory of Incentives: The Principal-Agent Model,* Princeton University Press, Princeton, USA.

Lambert, Z. & Durand, R. 1975, "Some Precautions in Using Canonical Analysis", *Journal of Marketing Research*, vol. 12, no. November, pp. 468-475.

Lee, J. & Heath, R. L. 1999, "Managerial media selection and information evaluation from the receiver's perspective in decision making contexts", *Management Communication Quarterly*, vol. 13, no. 1, pp. 76-99.

Lengel, R. H. & Daft, R. L. 1988, "The Selection of Communication Media as an Executive Skill", *The Academy of Management Executive*, vol. 11, no. 3, pp. 225-232.

Levitt, B. & March, J. G. 1995, "Chester I. Barnard and the intelligence of learning," in *Organization Theory: from Chester Barnard to the Present and Beyond*, O. E. Williamson, ed., Oxford University Press, New York, USA, pp. 11-37.

Levitt, R. E., Thomsen, J., Christiansen, T. R., Kunz, J. C., Jin, Y., & Nass, C. 1999, "Simulating Project Work Processes and Organizations: Toward a Micro-Contingency Theory of Organizational Design", *Management Science*, vol. 45, no. 11, pp. 1479-1495.

Lipman, C. S. 1996, "Utilizing the Internet's Web Technology, HTML, to Facilitate Near-Real-Time Project Status Reporting and Team Collaboration," in *Proceedings of the Project Management Institute's 27th Annual Seminar / Symposium*, PMI, October 7 - 9, 1996, Boston, Massachusetts, USA.

Lock, D. 2000a, "Project Management Organization," in *Project Management*, seventh edn, GOWER Publishing, Vermont, USA, pp. 15-49.

Lock, D. 2000b, "Managing Cost," in *Gower Handbook of Project Management*, 3 edn, J. R. Turner & S. J. Simister, eds., Gower Publishing Ltd., Hampshire, UK, pp. 293-322.

Loo, R. 1995, "Effective Interpersonal Communications in Project Environments," in *Proceedings from the Project Management Institute 26th Annual Seminar/Symposium*, PMI, pp. 508-512.

Lucas, J. J. 1997, "The Corporate Intranet for Project Management," in *Proceedings of the Project Management Institute's 28th Annual Seminars & Symposium*, PMI, September 29 to October 1, 1997, Chicago, Illinois, USA.

Luthans, F., Welsh, D. H. B., & Taylor III, L. E. 1988, "A Descriptive Model of Managerial Effectiveness", *Group & Organization Studies*, vol. 13, no. 2, pp. 148-162.

Mattessich, P. W. & Monsey, B. R. 1992, *Collaboration: What makes it work*, Amherst H. Wilder Foundation, St. Paul, USA.

Maturana, H. R. & Varela, F. J. 1980, *Autopoiesis and Cognition,* D. Reidel, Dordrecht, Holland.

McGrath, J. E. 1982, "Dilemmatics: The Study of Research Choices and Dilemmas," in *Judgement Calls in Research*, J. E. McGrath, J. Martin, & R. A. Kulka, eds., SAGE Publications, USA, Beverly Hills, California.

McPhee, R. D. & Poole, M. S. 2000, "Organizational Structures and Configurations," in *The New Handbook of Organizational Communication: Advances in Theory, Research, and Methods*, F. M. Jablin & L. L. Putnam, eds., SAGE Publications, London, UK, pp. 503-543.

McPhee, R. D. 1985, "Formal structure and organizational communication," in *Organizational Communication: Traditional themes and new directions*, R. D. McPhee & P. K. Tompkins, eds., Sage Publications, Beverly Hills, USA, pp. 149-177.

McPhee, R. D. 1989, "Giddens' conception of personal relationships and its relevance to communication theory," in *The meaning of "relationship" in interpersonal communication*, R. Conville & E. Rogers, eds., Praeger, Westport, USA, pp. 83-106.

Mead, R. 1990, *Cross-Cultural Management Communication,* John Wiley & Sons Ltd., Chichester, UK.

Miles, M. B. & Huberman, A. M. 1994, *Qualitative Data Analysis*, 2 edn, SAGE Publications, USA.

Miles, M. B., Covin, J. C., & Heeley, M. B. 2000, "The Relationship Between Environmental Dynamism and Small Firm Structure, Strategy, and Performance", *Journal of Marketing Theory and Practice*, vol. 8, no. Spring 2000, pp. 63-78.

Milinusic, M. 1999, "Cost Reporting by Simultaneous Multiple Breakdown Structures", *AACE International Transactions*, vol. 1999, p. CSC.03.1-CSC.03.7.

Miller, K. 2001, "Quantitative Research Methods," in *The New Handbook of Organizational Communication: Advances in Theory, Research, and Methods,* F. M. Jablin & L. L. Putnam, eds., Sage Publications, Thousand Oaks, California, USA, pp. 137-160.

Miller, K. 2002, *Communication Theories: Perspectives, Processes and Contexts.* McGraw Hill, Boston, USA.

Mintzberg, H. & Van der Heyden, L. 1999, "Organigraphs: Drawing How Companies Really Work", *Harvard Business Review*, vol. 1999, no. September-October, pp. 87-94.

Mintzberg, H. 1982, "Organisationsstruktur: modisch oder passend?," in *Harvard Manager Band 2: Führung und Organization*, Manager Magazin Verlagsgesellschaft, Hamburg, Germany, pp. 9-21.

Mitchell, J. C. 1973, "Networks, norms and institutions," in *Network Analysis*, J. Boissevain & J. C. Mitchell, eds., Mouton, The Hague, France.

Mohrman, S. A., Gibson, C. B., & Mohrman, A. M. 2001, "Doing Research that is Useful to Practice: A Model and Empirical Exploration", *Academy of Management Journal*, vol. 44, no. 2, pp. 357-375.

Morand, D. A. 1995, "The role of behavioral formality and informality in the enactment of bureaucratic versus organic organizations", *Academy of Management. The Academy of Management Review*, vol. 20, no. 4, p. 831.

Morgan, D. L. 1993, *Successful Focus Groups,* Sage Publications, London, UK.

Morgan, G. 1996, *Images of Organization*, 2nd edn, SAGE Publications, Inc., USA.

Morgeson, F. P. & Hofmann, D. A. 1999, "The structure and function of collective constructs: Implications for multilevel research and theory development", *Academy of Management Review*, vol. 24, no. 2, pp. 249-265.

Morris, P. 2000, "Researching the Unanswered Questions of Project Management", *Proceedings of the PMI Research Conference*, June 21 - 24, 2000, Paris, France, pp. 87-101.

Morris, P. 1998, "Why Project Management Doesn't Always Make Business Sense", *Project Management: International Project Management Journal*, Finland, vol. 4, no. 1, pp. 12-16.

Morris, P. W. G. 1994, "The Management of Projects: the new model," in *The management of projects*, Thomas Telford Services Ltd., London, England, pp. 213-272.

Möbius, M. 2002, "Gaining Knowledge about Extranet Technology - An Epistemological Journey," in *European Conference on Research Methodology for Business and Management Studies*, D. Remenyi, ed., Blackhorse House, Reading University, Reading, UK, pp. 245-260.

Mullins, L. J. 1999a, "The Nature of Organisations," in *Management and Organisational Behaviour*, 5th edn, L. J. Mullins, ed., Financial Times Management, London, UK, pp. 87-114.

Mullins, L. J. 1999b, "Organisation Structure and Design," in *Management and Organisational Behaviour*, 5th edn, L. J. Mullins, ed., Financial Times Management, London, UK, pp. 519-553.

Mullins, L. J. 1999c, "Group Processes and Behavior," in *Management and Organisational Behaviour*, 5th edn, L. J. Mullins, ed., Financial Times Management, London, UK, pp. 483-516.

Müller, R. 2001, "Communication between Buyer and Seller Organizations in the Context of Project Management", *Henley Working Paper Series*, vol. HWP 0105, Henley Management College, Henley-on-Thames, UK

Müller, R. 2003, "Determinants for external communications of IT project managers", *International Journal of Project Management*, vol. 21, no. 7, p. (to appear).

Müller, R. & Turner, J. R. 2001, "The Impact of Performance in Project Management Knowledge Areas on Earned Value Results in Information Technology Projects", *Project Management: International Project Management Journal,* Project Management Association Finland, Norwegian Project Management Forum, vol. 7, no. 1, pp. 44-51.

NASA. 2002. *Mishap Investigation Board, Mars Climate Orbiter, Phase 1 Report.* Internet: ftp://ftp.hq.nasa.gov/pub/pao/reports/1999/MCO_report.pdf . 1999. Accessed 20-12-2002.

NCR 1997, *GlobalPM Project Management Methodology,* NCR Corporation, Dayton, USA.

Ngwenyama, O. K. & Lee, A. S. 1997, "Communication Richness in Electronic Mail: Critical Social Theory and the Contextuality of Meaning", *MIS Quarterly*, vol. 1997, no. June, pp. 145-167.

Nonaka, I. & Takeuchi, H. 1995, *The knowledge-creating company,* Oxford University Press, USA.

Norusis, M. J. 2000, "Building Multiple Regression Models," in *SPSS 10.0 Guide to Data Analysis*, SPSS Inc., Upper Saddle River, NJ, USA, pp. 455-488.

O'Reilly, C. A., Chatman, J. A., & Anderson, J. C. 1987, "Message Flow and Decision Making," in *Handbook of Organizational Communication*, F. M. Jablin et al., eds., Sage Publications, Newbury Park, USA, pp. 600-623.

Orlikowski, W. & Yates, J. 1994, "Genre Repertoire: The Structuring of Communicative practices in Organizations", *Administrative Science Quarterly*, vol. 1994, no. 39, pp. 541-574.

Orlikowski, W. & Yates, J. 1998. *Genre Systems: Structuring Interaction through Communicative Norms.* http://ccs.mit.edu/papers/CCSWP205. MIT, USA. Accessed 29-10-2001.

Oxford University Press 1996, *Concise Oxford Dictionary*, ninth edn, Oxford University Press, Oxford, UK.

Oz, E. & Sosik, J. 2000, "Why Information Systems Projects are Abandoned: A Leadership and Communication Theory and Exploratory Study", *Journal of Computer Information Systems*, vol. 2000, no. Fall, pp. 66-78.

Parry, J. 1967, *The psychology of human communication*, third edn, University of London Press, London, UK.

Partington, D. 2000, "Implementing strategy through programmes of projects," in *Gower Handbook of Project Management*, third edn, J. R. Turner & S. J. Simister, eds., Gower Publishing Limited, Hampshire, UK, pp. 33-46.

Partington, D. 1997, *Management processes in projects of organizational change: case studies from four industries*, PhD Thesis, Cranfield University, UK.

Payne, J. H. & Turner, J. R. 1999, "Company-wide project management: the planning and control of programmes of projects of different type", *International Journal of Project Management*, vol. 17, no. 1, pp. 55-59.

Payne, J. H. 1995, "Management of multiple simultaneous projects: a state-of-the-art review", *International Journal of Project Management*, vol. 13, no. 3, pp. 163-168.

Pettigrew, A. M., Ferlie, E., & McKee, L. 1992, "Understanding the Process of Organizational Change," in *Shaping Strategic Change*, Sage Publications, London, UK, pp. 5-60.

Pinto, J. K. 1998, "Project Scope Management," in *The Project Management Institute: Project Management Handbook*, J. K. Pinto, ed., Jossey-Bass Publishers, San Francisco, USA, pp. 109-118.

Pinto, J. K. & Kharbanda, O. M. 1996, "Project Implementation Profile (PIP)", *Business Horizons*, vol. 39, no. 4, pp. 45-54.

Pinto, J. K. & Slevin, D. P. 1989, "The Project Champion: Key to Implementation Success", *Project Management Journal*, vol. 20, no. 4, pp. 15-20.

PMI 2000, *Guide to the Project Management Body of Knowledge*, 2000 edn, Project Management Institute, Newton Square, USA.

PMI 1987, *Project Management Body of Knowledge,* Project Management Institute, Upper Darby, PA, USA.

PMI 1999, *The Future of Project Management,* Project Management Institute, Newton Square, Pennsylvania, USA.

Popper, K. 1959, *The Logic of Scientific Discovery*, Basic Books, New York, USA.

Putnam, L. L., Phillips, N., & Chapman, P. 1996, "Metaphors of Communication and Organization," in *Handbook of Organization Studies*, S. R. Clegg, C. Hardy, & W. Nord, eds., SAGE Publications, London, UK, pp. 375-408.

Remenyi, D., Williams, B., Money, A., & Swartz, E. 1998, *Doing Research in Business and Management,* SAGE Publications, UK.

Rice, R. E. & Shook, D. E. 1990, "Relationship of Job Categories and Organizational Levels to Use of Communication Channels, Including Electronic Mail: A Meta Analysis and Extension", *Journal of Management Studies*, vol. 27, no. 2, pp. 195-229.

Rindfleisch, A. & Heide, J. B. 1997, "Transaction Cost Analysis: Past, Present, and Future Applications", *Journal of Marketing*, vol. 61, no. October 1997, pp. 30-54.

Runkel, P. J. & McGrath, J. E. 1972, *Research on Human Behavior: A Systematic Guide to Method*, Holt, Rinehart & Winston, New York, USA.

Russ, G. S., Daft, R. L., & Lengel, R. H. 1990, "Media Selection and Managerial Characteristics in Organizational Communications", *Management Communication Quarterly*, vol. 4, no. 2, pp. 151-175.

Samouel, P. 1996, *Power, Relational Norms and Transaction Cost Analysis: Theory and Empirical Investigation,* DBA Thesis, Henley Management College, Henley-on-Thames, UK.

Schmitz, J. & Fulk, J. 1991, "Organizational Colleagues, Media Richness, and Electronic Mail", *Communication Research*, vol. 18, no. 4, pp. 487-523.

Schneider, G. P., Teplitz, C. J., & Bruton, C. M. 1995, "Project Cost Control: Improving the Communication of Accounting Information," in *Proceedings from the Project Management Institute 26th Annual Seminar/symposium*, PMI, October 16 to 18, 1995, New Orleans, Louisiana, USA, pp. 353-355.

SEI 1993. Capability *Maturity Model (SW-CMM) for Software*, http://www.sei.cmu.edu/cmm/cmm.html. Software Engineering Institute, Carnegie Mellon University. Accessed. 4-7-2001.

SEI 2002, *Capability Maturity Model Integration (CMMI)*, 1.1 edn, Carnegie Mellon University, USA.

Selin, G. 1991, "Project management in decentralized organizations", *International Journal of Project Management*, vol. 9, no. 4, pp. 216-221.

Sharma, S. 1996, *Applied Multivariate Techniques,* John Wiley & Sons, Inc, USA.

Shulman, A. 1996, "Putting Group Information Technology in its Place: Communication and Good Work Group Performance," in *Handbook of Organization Studies*, S. R. Clegg, C. Hardy, & W. Nord, eds., SAGE Publications, London, UK, pp. 357-374.

Silverman, D. 1993, *Interpreting Qualitative Data,* Sage Publications, London, UK.

Sitkin, S. B., Sutcliffe, K. M., & Barrios-Choplin, J. R. 1992, "A Dual-Capacity Model of Communication Media Choice in Organizations", *Human Communication Research*, vol. 18, no. 4, pp. 563-598.

Standish Group. CHAOS '98: A Summary Review. A Standish Group Research Note 1998, 1-4. 1998. The Standish Group, USA.

Stewart, D. W. & Shamdasani, P. N. 1998, "Focus Group Research," in *Handbook of Applied Social Research Methods*, L. Bickman & D. J. Rog, eds., SAGE Publications, Inc., Thousand Oaks, California, USA, pp. 505-526.

Surveypro. 2001. www.surveypro.com, last access October 25, 2002 .

Symons, J. 1996, "Realism: Recapturing the Middle Ground," in *Theory-Building in the Business Sciences*, T. Elfring, H. S. Jensen, & A. Money, eds., Handelshojskolens Forlag, Copenhagen, Denmark, pp. 155-170.

Tan, R. R. 1996, "Success Criteria and Success Factors for External Technology Transfer Projects", *Project Management Journal*, vol. 27, no. 2, pp. 45-56.

Tashakkori, A. & Teddlie, C. 1998, *Mixed Methodology,* Sage Publications, Thousand Oaks, California, USA.

Taylor, J. 1999, "The other side of rationality", *Management Communication Quarterly*, vol. 13, no. 2, pp. 317-326.

Timmons, J. 2000, "Web-Enabled Project Management - Your Ticket to Success," in *Proceedings of the Project Management Institute Annual Seminars & Symposium*, PMI, September 7-16, 2000, Houston, Texas, USA.

Trevino, L. K., Webster, J., & Stein, E. W. 2000, "Making Connections: Complementary Influences on Communication Media Choices, Attitudes, and Use", *Organization Science*, vol. 11, no. 2, pp. 163-182.

Trevino, L. K., Lengel, R. H., & Daft, R. L. 1987, "Media Symbolism, Media Richness, and Media Choice Organizations", *Communication Research*, vol. 14, no. 5, pp. 553-574.

Trevino, L. K., Lengel, R. H., Bodensteiner, W., Gerloff, E. A., & Muir, N. K. 1990, "The Richness Imperative and Cognitive Style", *Management Communication Quarterly*, vol. 4, no. 2, pp. 176-197.

Tse, A. C. B. 1999, "Conducting electronic focus group discussions among Chinese respondents", *Journal of the Market Research Society*, vol. 41, no. 4, p. 407.

Turner, J. R. & Cochrane, R. A. 1993, "Goals-and-methods matrix: coping with projects with ill defined goals and/or methods of achieving them", *International Journal of Project Management*, vol. 11, no. 2, pp. 93-102.

Turner, J. R. 1993, *Handbook of Project-based Management: Improving the Process for Achieving Strategic Objectives*, 1 edn, McGraw-Hill, UK.

Turner, J. R. 1999, *Handbook of Project-based Management: Improving the Process for Achieving Strategic Objectives,* 2nd edn, McGraw-Hill, UK.

Turner, J. R. & Simister, S. J. 2000, *Handbook of Project Management*, 3rd edn, Gower Publishing Ltd., Hampshire, UK.

Turner, J. R. & Keegan, A. 2001, "Mechanisms of governance in the project-based organization: Roles of the broker and steward", *European Management Journal*, vol. 19, no. 3, pp. 254-267.

Turner, J. R. & Müller, R. 2003, "On the nature of the project as a temporary organization", *International Journal of Project Management*, vol. 21, no. 1, pp. 1-8.

Turner, J. R. 2000, "The global body of knowledge, and its coverage by referees and members of the international editorial board of this journal", *International Journal of Project Management*, vol. 18, no. 2000, pp. 1-5.

Turner, J. R. 1997, "The Versatile Organisation: Achieving Centuries of Sustainable Growth", *European Management Journal*, vol. 15, no. 5, pp. 509-522.

Turner, J. R. 2003, "Farsighted project contract management: incomplete in its entirety", *Construction Management and Economics* (to appear).

Tushman, M. L. & Scanlan, T. J. 1981, "Boundary Spanning Individuals: Their Role in Information Transfer and Their Antecedents", *Academy of Management Journal*, vol. 24, no. 2, pp. 289-305.

Tushman, M. L. & Katz, R. 1980, "External Communication and Project Performance: An Investigation into the Role of Gatekeepers", *Management Science*, vol. 26, no. 11, pp. 1071-1085.

Tushman, M. L. & Nadler, D. A. 1978, "Information Processing as an Integrating Concept in Organizational Design", *Academy of Management Review,* no. July 1978, pp. 613-624.

Tushman, M. L. 1979a, "Managing Communication Networks in R&D Laboratories", *Sloan Management Review*, vol. Winter 1979, pp. 39-49.

Tushman, M. L. 1979b, "Work Characteristics and Subunit Communication Structure: A Contingency Analysis", *Administrative Science Quarterly*, vol. 24, no. March 1979, pp. 82-98.

Warner, M. 1996, "Organization paradigms," in *International encyclopedia of business and management*, M. Warner, ed., Routledge, London,UK, pp. 3866-3880.

Wateridge, J. 1998, "How can IS/IT projects be measured for success?", *International Journal of Project Management*, vol. 16, no. 1, pp. 59-63.

Weick, K. E. 1987, "Theorizing About Organizational Communication," in *Handbook of Organizational Communication*, F. M. Jablin, ed., Sage Publications, Beverly Hills, USA, pp. 97-122.

Wicks, A. C. & Freemean, R. E. 1998, "Organization Studies and the New Pragmatism: Positivism, Anti-positivism, and the Search for Ethics", *Organization Science*, vol. 9, no. 2, pp. 123-140.

Wideman, R. M. 1991, *A Framework for Project and Program Management Integration*, Preliminary edn, PMI, Drexel Hill, USA.

Wideman, R. M. 2000. *IS/IT Project Sponsor.* http://www.maxwideman.com/issacons/iac1020/sld001.htm . Accessed 30-11-2000.

Williamson, O. E. 1975, *Markets and Hierarchies: Analysis and Antitrust Implications,* Collier Macmillan, Canada, Ltd., New York, USA.

Williamson, O. E. 1985, *The Economic Institutions of Capitalism,* The Free Press, New York, USA.

Williamson, O. E. 1995, "Transaction Cost Economics and Organization Theory," in *Organization Theory*, O. E. Williamson, ed., Oxford University Press, New York, USA, pp. 207-256.

Wright, J. N. 1997, "Time and budget: the twin imperatives of a project sponsor", *International Journal of Project Management*, vol. 15, no. 3, pp. 181-186.

Yin, R. K. 1994, *Case Study Research: Design and Methods*, 2nd edn, SAGE Publications Ltd., London, UK.

Yoo, Y. & Alavi, M. 2001, "Media and Group Cohesion: Relative Influences on Social Presence, Task Participation, and Group Consensus", *MIS Quarterly*, vol. 25, no. 3, pp. 371-390.

Appendix A-1: Relationship between Research Questions, Constructs and Hypotheses

Research Questions	Construct	Hypotheses
Questions 1: How do organisational structure, relational norms and project risk impact preferences for communication frequency, contents and media of project sponsors and managers in their formal communication during implementation of IT projects?	Communication frequency, contents and media from Literature Review	H1: There will be a significant difference between communications preferences of project sponsors from IT seller firms and those of project managers from IT seller firms, in terms of communication frequency, contents and media.
	Organisation Structure (Burns & Stalker 1994)	H2: There will be a positive relationship between the extent of organic organisation structure and communication frequency. The more organic the organisation, the higher the frequency in communication. H3: There will be a negative relationship between the level of organic organisation structure and the use of lean media. Bureaucratic organisation structures will favour written reports, while organic structures favour more interactive media like verbal communication or face-to-face meetings. H4: There will be a negative relationship between the extent of organic organisation structure and the use of quantitative measures, like quality metrics and earned value numbers. Bureaucratic structures will favour quantitative data.
	Relational Norms (Heide & John 1992)	Exploratory investigation
	Risk (Turner & Cochrane 1993) Media Richness Theory (Russ, Daft & Lengel 1990)	Exploratory investigation H5: There will be a positive relationship between project goal equivocality and media richness; rich media (e.g. face-to-face meetings) will be selected for communication in projects with unclear goals, and lean media (i.e. written communication) for projects with clearly defined goals.
		H6: There will be a positive relationship between clearness of methodology and use of written media for communication.
Question 2: How effective is the formal communication between project sponsors and project managers during IT project implementation?	Project Performance (Wateridge 1998)	Exploratory investigation

Appendix A

Appendix A-2: Definition of Research Variables

Level of Variable	Variable	Definition
Independent Variables: Situational Variables	Organisation Structure	Level of mechanistic to organic organisation structure. Higher values indicate higher levels of organic structures.
	Methodology Clearness	Level of methodology clearness. Higher levels indicate lower risk.
	Objective Clearness	Level of objective clearness. Higher levels indicate lower risk.
	Relational Norms	Level of individual buyer's and seller's interest in maintaining their relationship and curtailing behaviors that promote the goals of the individual party (Heide & John 1992). Higher values indicate higher levels of interest in maintaining the relationship.
Dependent Variables: Communication Variables	Communication Frequency	The number of formal communication events between project sponsor and manager. It includes all media and possible communication contents.
	Communication Contents	The information exchanged between project manager and sponsor at each formal communication event
		The way a message is physically conveyed between project manager and sponsor.
Structural Variable: Buyer - Seller Perspective	Buyer - Seller	Role of the respondent: project sponsors represent buyer firms, project managers represent IT seller firms
Structural Variable: Project Performance	Project Performance	Level of perceived project success. Higher values indicate higher perceived success of the project

Appendix A

Appendix A-3: Questionnaire Design

Variable	Item	Question	Variable	Scale	Author
Buyer - Seller	1	Role as Project Manager or Sponsor	ROLE	Nominal	Internal or external projects	New
Project Type	2	Project Type	PTYPE	Nominal	Research, development, technical service	Tushman (1979a)
	3	Project type's representation of objectives	PTDEF	Ordinal	small to large extend	Tushman (1979a)
Risk	4	Objectives clearly defined	OBJCLR			New, developed from Turner & Cochrane (1993) and Wateridge (1998)
	5	Objectives well documented	OBJDOC			
	6	Objectives agreed with customer	OBJAGR	Interval	7 point Likert, Strongly Disagree - Strongly Agree	
	7	Methodology clearly defined	METCLR			
	8	Methodology well documented	METDOC			
	9	Methodology agreed with customer	METAGR			
Relational Norms	10	Keep each other informed	INFO1			
	11	Problems treated as joint responsibility	SOL1			
	12	Flexibility in response	FLEX1			
	13	Adjust relationship to changing circumstances	FLEX2			Heide & John (1992)
	14	In unexpected situation work out a new deal	FLEX3	7 point Likert, Completely Inaccurate - Completely Accurate		
	15	Any information that helps is provided	INFO2	Interval		
	16	Frequent and informal information exchange	INFO3			
	17	Parties provide proprietary information	INFO4			
	18	Committed to improve the relationship	SOL2			
	19	Parties don't mind owing each other favors	SOL3			
Media importance	20	Importance of Written communication	MIMWRI			New, developed from results of literature review (Müller 2001)
	21	Importance of Verbal communication	MIMVER	Interval	7 point Likert, Not At All Important - Very important	
	22	Importance of Personal communication	MIMPER			
Frequency in written communication	23	Written daily communication	FQWDAY			
	24	Written weekly communication	FQWWEK			
	25	Written bi-weekly communication	FQW2WK			New, developed from results of literature review (Müller 2001)
	26	Written monthly communication	FQWMON	Interval	7 point Likert, Strongly Disagree - Strongly Agree	
	27	Written communication at milestone achievement	FQWMIL			
	28	Written communication at phase or project end	FQWPHA			
	29	No formal written communication	FQWNON			
Frequency in verbal communication	30	Verbal daily communication	FQVDAY			
	31	Verbal weekly communication	FQVWEK			
	32	Verbal bi-weekly communication	FQV2WK			New, developed from results of literature review (Müller 2001)
	33	Verbal monthly communication	FQVMON	Interval	7 point Likert, Strongly Disagree - Strongly Agree	
	34	Verbal communication at milestone achievement	FQVMIL			
	35	Verbal communication at phase or project end	FQVPHA			
	36	No formal Verbal communication	FQVNON			
Frequency in personal communication	37	Personal daily communication	FQPDAY			
	38	Personal weekly communication	FQPWEK			
	39	Personal bi-weekly communication	FQP2WK			New, developed from results of literature review (Müller 2001)
	40	Personal monthly communication	FQPMON	Interval	7 point Likert, Strongly Disagree - Strongly Agree	
	41	Personal communication at milestone achievement	FQPMIL			
	42	Personal communication at phase or project end	FQPPHA			
	43	No formal Personal communication	FQPNON			

Variable	Item	Question	Variable	Scale		Author
Contents in written communication	44	Written contents: status and achievements	COWSTA			New, developed from results of literature review (Müller 2001)
	45	Written contents: measures and quality metrics	COWMEA			
	46	Written contents: issues or 'open items'	COWISS			
	47	Written contents: project changes	COWCHA	Interval	7 point Likert, Strongly Disagree - Strongly Agree	
	48	Written contents: trends	COWTRE			
	49	Written contents: next steps	COWNXT			
	50	Written contents: other	COWOTH			
Contents in verbal communication	51	Verbal contents: status and achievements	COVSTA			New, developed from results of literature review (Müller 2001)
	52	Verbal contents: measures and quality metrics	COVMEA			
	53	Verbal contents: issues or 'open items'	COVISS			
	54	Verbal contents: project changes	COVCHA	Interval	7 point Likert, Strongly Disagree - Strongly Agree	
	55	Verbal contents: trends	COVTRE			
	56	Verbal contents: next steps	COVNXT			
	57	Verbal contents: other	COVOTH			
Contents in personal communication	58	Personal contents: status and achievements	COPSTA			New, developed from results of literature review (Müller 2001)
	59	Personal contents: measures and quality metrics	COPMEA			
	60	Personal contents: issues or 'open items'	COPISS			
	61	Personal contents: project changes	COPCHA	Interval	7 point Likert, Strongly Disagree - Strongly Agree	
	62	Personal contents: trends	COPTRE			
	63	Personal contents: next steps	COPNXT			
	64	Personal contents: other	COPOTH			
Project Performance	65	Project performs well	PRFALL			New, developed from Wateridge (1998)
	66	Project meets the user's requirements	PRFREQ	Interval	7 point Likert, Strongly Disagree - Strongly Agree	
	67	Project will achieve its purpose	PRFPUR			
Organisation Structure	68	Channels of communication	ORGSTR1			
	69	Managerial style	ORGSTR2			
	70	Decision making	ORGSTR3			Khandwalla (1977)
	71	Management style	ORGSTR4	Interval	7 point Likert, semantic difference	
	72	Level of control	ORGSTR5			
	73	Formal procedures	ORGSTR6			
	74	Adherence to job descriptions	ORGSTR7			
Project information	75	Project name	PNAME			New
	76	E-mail address of counterpart (Project Manager or Sponsor)	PARTNAME	Nominal	text entry field	
	77	Respondent's name	RESPNAME	Nominal		
	78	Respondent's e-mail address	RESPMAIL	Nominal		
	79	Respondent's country	CNTRY	Nominal		
Demographics	80	Respondent's age	AGE	Ordinal	text entry field	New
	81	Respondent's years of work experience	BUSEXP	Ordinal		
	82	Respondent's years of experience in project management	PMEXP	Ordinal		
	83	Respondent's years as sponsor (Sponsors only)	PSEXP	Ordinal		
Incentive	84	Copy of summary of the results	RESULTS	Nominal	text entry field	New

Appendix A-4: Survey Introduction Letter

Dear PMI Chapter President,

Communication between project managers and their customers is THE major determinant for cost variances in IT projects. Improvements in communication capabilities will have a positive impact on the costs of IT projects and will directly add to the bottom-line results. This was found in many recent research studies.

But how can the communication between project managers and their customer be improved? What is the 'best' communication, given the differences in project types and organizations that come together in a project?

To answer these questions a research project was launched together with a UK University. It investigates best practices and develops recommendations for improvements in the communication practices between project managers and their customers. This will eventually lead to lower costs in IT projects.

Results from a small pre-test in this research showed significant differences between customers and project managers in desired communication media, frequency and contents. There is potential for large savings. However, the results cannot be disclosed, they must first be confirmed through a larger study. For that I need your help.

I kindly ask you to send the attached questionnaire to your Chapter members, so that IT project managers or sponsors can fill it in and forward this e-mail to their customers / suppliers. A high response rate is crucial for the generalizability of the results. So every respondent counts. Please take the approx. 15 Minutes to answer the questions.

I am happy to send you a summary of the results if you are interested. Please mark the appropriate field in the questionnaire.

Thank you for your help and best regards

Ralf Mueller

rjmueller@CompuServe.com

Appendix A-5: Introduction Letter for Respondents

Dear Study Participant,
Attached you will find a questionnaire which is part of a research project on:

Communication between Information Technology (IT) buyer and seller firms during project implementation

The main objective of the research is to identify factors for better communication in project implementation to achieve an overall improvement of efficiency in project delivery.

I kindly ask you to answer the questionnaire, which should take no more than 20 minutes to complete. Most of the questions can be answered very quickly based on your experience in managing IT projects.

Information obtained from you will be held in strict confidence. No references will be made to specific individuals or names of organizations in future reports. The overall summary of the results will be shared with you if you so indicate at the end of the questionnaire.

Thank you very much for your time and consideration for this study. If you have any questions or concerns please contact me using the e-mail address stated below my signature.

Below you will find Internet-links to two different questionnaires. One for Project Managers in firms **selling** IT projects. The other for Project Sponsors in firms **buying** IT projects. Please select the one questionnaire that represents your work by clicking on the underlined Internet web-address (it may take a few seconds to load the survey).

Questionnaire for firms selling IT projects – click here: http://www.surveypro.com/cgi-bin/surveypro/run_survey.cgi?id=777
Questionnaire for firms buying IT projects - click here: http://www.surveypro.com/cgi-bin/surveypro/run_survey.cgi?id=1116

Thank you in advance and best regards,

Ralf Mueller
rjmueller@CompuServe.com

PS: This part-time doctoral research study is conducted together with a UK University. The researcher is employed by NCR Corporation. However, no names, e-mail addresses or phone numbers of individuals or organizations will be provided to NCR or any other organization within this study.

Appendix A-6: Seller Questionnaire

A Research Project on Buyer-Seller Communication in Information Technology Project Implementation

- Questions marked with * require a Valid Response

This questionnaire is structured to obtain data about your preferences in formal communication with a Project Sponsor during the implementation of Information Technology (IT) projects.

Within this questionnaire, the Project Sponsor is the owner of a project in a firm buying IT projects, i.e. the manager with ultimate responsibility for project success. The Project Manager manages the implementation of the project and is often a representative of the organization selling the project.

Formal communication between the Project Manager of a selling firm and a Project Sponsor of a buying firm takes place at contractually or otherwise pre-specified intervals and is

- a way to communicate project progress to the customer, and also
- an opportunity to officially remind or notify customers of their obligations in a project.

The questionnaire collects data on media, contents and frequency for this communication. There are no right or wrong answers. Participation is voluntarily.

Please answer the questions in relation to the implementation stage of your current project. Implementation stage is the time after the contract is signed, when work on the project deliverables has commenced, but before the operational use of the project deliverables. In case you are currently not managing a project, then please answer the questions in relation to the implementation stage of the last project you managed.

YOUR ROLE AS PROJECT MANAGER

Please indicate whether you manage (or recently managed) a project that is delivered to customers that are internal or external to your organization. Please mark one box.

○ I am an IT Project Manager delivering a project to an external firm
○ I am an IT Project Manager delivering projects within the firm I am employed with
○ Other (Please Specify)

THE NATURE OF YOUR PROJECT

Please select one category that best characterizes the objectives of your project.

○ RESEARCH: The project is intended to develop new knowledge about an area. Work involves creation and evaluation of new concepts or components but not development for operational use.

○ DEVELOPMENT: The combination of existing feasible concepts, perhaps with new knowledge, to provide a distinctly new product, service or process for operational use. The application of known facts and theory to solve a particular problem through exploratory study, design, development, and testing of new components or systems.

○ TECHNICAL SERVICE: Recombination, modification and testing of systems using existing knowledge. Cost/performance improvement to existing products, processes or systems. This includes installation, parametrization, and modification of existing hardware and software that does not provide a distinctly new product.

	To a small extent	To a moderate extent	To a great extent
Related to the question above, please indicate how completely the project's objectives are represented by the selected category	○	○	○

In the project you selected above the project objectives are...

	Strongly disagree	Disagree	Slightly disagree	Neither agree nor disagree	Slightly agree	Agree	Strongly agree
Clearly defined	○	○	○	○	○	○	○
Well documented	○	○	○	○	○	○	○
Agreed with the customer	○	○	○	○	○	○	○

In the project you selected above the work methods for the project team are...

	Strongly disagree	Disagree	Slightly disagree	Neither agree nor disagree	Slightly agree	Agree	Strongly agree
Clearly defined	○	○	○	○	○	○	○
Well documented	○	○	○	○	○	○	○
Agreed with the customer	○	○	○	○	○	○	○

THE RELATIONSHIP BETWEEN BUYER AND SELLER FIRM

Please rate how accurate the following descriptions are for the relationship between buyer and seller firm in your project.
Select one of the following ratings:

1 = Completely inaccurate description
2 = Inaccurate description
3 = Slightly accurate description
4 = Neither accurate nor inaccurate description
5 = Slightly accurate description
6 = Accurate description
7 = Completely accurate description

	1	2	3	4	5	6	7
It is expected that we keep each other informed about events or changes that may affect the other party.	○	○	○	○	○	○	○
Problems that arise in the course of this relationship are treated by the parties as joint rather than individual responsibilities.	○	○	○	○	○	○	○
Flexibility in response to requests for changes is a characteristic of this relationship.	○	○	○	○	○	○	○
The parties expect to be able to make adjustments in the ongoing relationship to cope with changing circumstances.	○	○	○	○	○	○	○
When some unexpected situation arises, the parties would rather work out a new deal than hold each other to the original terms.	○	○	○	○	○	○	○
In this relationship, it is expected that any information that might help the other party will be provided to them.	○	○	○	○	○	○	○
Exchange of information in this relationship takes place frequently and informally, and not only according to a pre-specified agreement.	○	○	○	○	○	○	○
It is expected that the parties will provide proprietary information if it can help the other party.	○	○	○	○	○	○	○
The parties are committed to improvements that may benefit the relationship as a whole, and not only the individual parties.	○	○	○	○	○	○	○
The parties in this relationship do not mind owing each other favors.	○	○	○	○	○	○	○

PROJECT COMMUNICATION

Communication between Project Manager and Project Sponsor can be informal, e.g. in ad-hoc conversations, but can also take place at formal status reporting events, i.e. at contractually agreed intervals and with pre-specified contents. The official information exchanged at these formal events may have an impact on the further progress of the project, or the relationship between the project seller and the buyer firm.

The following blocks of questions ask about YOUR preferences for formal communication at the implementation stage of your project. Ignore the current practices in your project and answer only what you think is appropriate.

IMPORTANCE OF MEDIA

How important is written, verbal, and personal communication in formal communication between Project Manager and Project Sponsor during project implementation?
(Please rate all questions. Same ratings for different media are possible)

	Not at all important	Not important	Slightly unimportant	Neither important nor unimportant	Slightly important	Important	Very important
Written communication, e.g. written reports, letters, e-mails, fax, is ...	○	○	○	○	○	○	○
Verbal communication, e.g. telephone, voice-mail, or net-meeting, is ...	○	○	○	○	○	○	○
Personal communication, e.g. face-to-face discussion, group meeting, video-conference, is ...	○	○	○	○	○	○	○

FREQUENCY OF COMMUNICATION

Rate each of the following questions according to your own preference.
Same ratings for different questions are possible.

Frequency in formal written communication
That includes letters, notes, e-mails, faxes etc.

At the current state of my project the following frequency in formal <u>written</u> communication between Project Manager and Project Sponsor is appropriate.....

	Strongly disagree	Disagree	Slightly disagree	Neither agree nor disagree	Slightly agree	Agree	Strongly agree
Daily	○	○	○	○	○	○	○
Weekly only	○	○	○	○	○	○	○
Every 2nd week only	○	○	○	○	○	○	○
Monthly only	○	○	○	○	○	○	○

	Strongly disagree	Disagree	Slightly disagree	Neither agree nor disagree	Slightly agree	Agree	Strongly agree
At milestone achievements only	○	○	○	○	○	○	○
At phase end, phase transition or project end only	○	○	○	○	○	○	○
No formal written communication	○	○	○	○	○	○	○

Frequency in formal verbal communication.
That includes telephone, voice-mail, net-meeting etc.

At the current state of my project the following frequency for formal <u>verbal</u> communication between Project Manager and Project Sponsor is appropriate ...

	Strongly disagree	Disagree	Slightly disagree	Neither agree nor disagree	Slightly agree	Agree	Strongly agree
Daily	○	○	○	○	○	○	○
Weekly only	○	○	○	○	○	○	○
Every 2nd week only	○	○	○	○	○	○	○
Monthly only	○	○	○	○	○	○	○
At milestone achievements only	○	○	○	○	○	○	○
At phase end, phase transition or project end only	○	○	○	○	○	○	○
No formal verbal communication	○	○	○	○	○	○	○

Frequency in formal personal communication.
That includes face-to-face meetings, group meetings, video-conferences etc.

At the current state of my project the following frequency for formal <u>personal</u> communication between Project Manager and Project Sponsor is appropriate ...

	Strongly disagree	Disagree	Slightly disagree	Neither agree nor disagree	Slightly agree	Agree	Strongly agree
Daily	○	○	○	○	○	○	○
Weekly only	○	○	○	○	○	○	○
Every 2nd week only	○	○	○	○	○	○	○
Monthly only	○	○	○	○	○	○	○
At milestone achievements only	○	○	○	○	○	○	○
At phase end, phase transition or project end only	○	○	○	○	○	○	○
No formal personal communication	○	○	○	○	○	○	○

CONTENTS IN FORMAL COMMUNICATION

Rate each of the following questions according to your own preferences at the current state of your project.
Same ratings for different questions are possible.

Contents in formal written communication between Project Manager and Project Sponsor.

That is for written reports, letters, e-mails etc.

At the current state of my project the following contents for formal <u>written</u> communication between Project Manager and Project Sponsor is appropriate ...

	Strongly disagree	Disagree	Slightly agree	Neither agree nor disagree	Slightly agree	Agree	Strongly agree
Status and achievements, e.g. related to functionality, schedule and/or budget	○	○	○	○	○	○	○
Measures, e.g. earned value measures, quality metrics etc.	○	○	○	○	○	○	○
Issues or "open item" list	○	○	○	○	○	○	○
Changes to project scope, plan, risks, quality etc.	○	○	○	○	○	○	○
Trend analysis	○	○	○	○	○	○	○
Next steps	○	○	○	○	○	○	○
Other contents (not listed above)	○	○	○	○	○	○	○

Contents in formal verbal communication between Project Manager and Project Sponsor. That is in telephone calls, voice-mail, net-meeting etc.

At the current state of my project the following contents in formal <u>verbal</u> communication between Project Manager and Project Sponsor is appropriate ...

	Strongly disagree	Disagree	Slightly disagree	Neither agree nor disagree	Slightly agree	Agree	Strongly agree
Status and achievements, e.g. related to functionality, schedule and/or budget	○	○	○	○	○	○	○
Measures, e.g. earned value measures, quality metrics etc.	○	○	○	○	○	○	○
Issues or "open item" list	○	○	○	○	○	○	○
Changes to project scope, plan, risks, quality etc.	○	○	○	○	○	○	○
Trend analysis	○	○	○	○	○	○	○
Next steps	○	○	○	○	○	○	○
Other contents (not listed above)	○	○	○	○	○	○	○

Contents in formal personal communication between Project Manager and Project Sponsor. That is in face-to-face discussions, group meetings, video-conference etc.

At the current state of my project the following contents for formal <u>personal</u> communication between Project Manager and Project Sponsor is appropriate ...

	Strongly disagree	Disagree	Slightly disagree	Neither agree nor disagree	Slightly agree	Agree	Strongly agree
Status and achievements, e.g. related to functionality, schedule and/or budget	○	○	○	○	○	○	○

	Strongly disagree	Disagree	Slightly disagree	Neither agree nor disagree	Slightly agree	Agree	Strongly agree
Measures, e.g. earned value measures, quality metrics etc.	○	○	○	○	○	○	○
Issues or "open item" list	○	○	○	○	○	○	○
Changes to project scope, plan, risks, quality etc.	○	○	○	○	○	○	○
Trend analysis	○	○	○	○	○	○	○
Next steps	○	○	○	○	○	○	○
Other contents (not listed above)	○	○	○	○	○	○	○

PROJECT PERFORMANCE AND SUCCESS

	Strongly disagree	Disagree	Slightly disagree	Neither agree nor disagree	Slightly agree	Agree	Strongly agree
Altogether, the project performs well in terms of functionality, budget and timing.	○	○	○	○	○	○	○
The project meets the user's requirements.	○	○	○	○	○	○	○
The project will achieve its purpose.	○	○	○	○	○	○	○

The following seven questions ask about the management philosophy of your project team. Please rate on the seven point scale what best approximates the actual conditions within your project team.

In general the operating management philosophy <u>in my project team</u> favors...

Highly structured channels of communication and a highly restricted access to important financial and operating information.						Open channels of communication with important financial and operating information flowing quite freely throughout the organization.
1	2	3	4	5	6	7
○	○	○	○	○	○	○

In general the operating management philosophy in my project team favors...

A strong insistance on a uniform managerial style throughout the team						Operating styles are allowed to range freely from the very formal to the very informal.
1	2	3	4	5	6	7
○	○	○	○	○	○	○

In general the operating management philosophy in my project team favors...

A strong emphasis on giving the most say in decision making to formal line managers.						A strong tendency to let the expert in a given situation have the most say in decision making even if this means temporary bypassing of formal line authority.

	1	2	3	4	5	6	7
	○	○	○	○	○	○	○

In general the operating management philosophy in my project team favors...

A strong emphasis on holding fast to tried and true management principles despite any changes in business.

A strong emphasis on adapting freely to changing circumstances without too much concern for past practice.

	1	2	3	4	5	6	7
	○	○	○	○	○	○	○

In general the operating management philosophy in my project team favors...

Tight formal control of most operations by means of sophisticated control and information systems.

Loose, informal control; heavy dependence on informal relationships and the norm of cooperation for getting things done.

	1	2	3	4	5	6	7
	○	○	○	○	○	○	○

In general the operating management philosophy in my project team favors...

A strong emphasis on always getting personnel to follow the formally laid down procedures.

A strong emphasis on getting things done even if it means disregarding formal procedures.

	1	2	3	4	5	6	7
	○	○	○	○	○	○	○

In general the operating management philosophy in my project team favors...

A strong emphasis on getting line and staff personnel to adhere closely to formal job descriptions.

A strong tendency to let the requirements of the situation and the individual's personality define proper on-job behavior.

	1	2	3	4	5	6	7
	○	○	○	○	○	○	○

To properly analyze the results it is necessary to send a similar questionaire to the Project Sponsor of the project you had in mind when answering the questions. Therefore please enter the project name and the e-mail address of the Project Sponsor in the fields below. No information from this questionnaire will be passed on to your customer or vice versa. Confidentiality is guaranteed.

Project name:

E-mail address of Project Sponsor:

The data below are collected for demographic purposes and in case of questions arising from incomplete or corrupted data within the questionnaire. All personal data will be separated from answers prior to analysis of the questionnaire.

Your name:

* Your e-mail address (required):

Your country (for USA, please add state)

Your age (in years)

Number of years of work experience

Number of years with experience in project management

Results of the study are expected to be available in early 2002.

◯ **Please click here if you would like to receive a copy of the final study**

Thank you for taking the time to complete the questionnaire.

Please click on the "Submit" button now

[Submit Query]

Appendix A-7: Buyer Questionnaire

A Research Project on Buyer-Seller Communication in Information Technology Project Implementation

- Questions marked with * require a Valid Response

This questionnaire is structured to obtain data about your preferences in formal communication with your Information Technology (IT) supplier during the implementation of IT projects.

Within this questionnaire, the Project Sponsor is the owner of a project in a firm buying IT projects, i.e. the manager with ultimate responsibility for project success. The Project Manager manages the implementation of the project and is often a representative of the organization selling the project.

Formal communication between a Project Manager of a selling firm and a Project Sponsor of a buying firm takes place at contractually or otherwise pre-specified intervals and is

- a way to obtain information on project progress from the supplier, and also
- an opportunity to officially remind on mutual obligations within a project.

The questionnaire collects data on media, contents and frequency of this communication. There are no right or wrong answers. Participation is voluntarily.

Please answer the questions in relation to the current situation in the implementation stage of one of your IT projects. Implementation stage is the time after the contract is signed, when work on the project deliverables has commenced, but before the operational use of the project deliverables. In case you are currently not sponsoring a project, then please answer the questions in relation to the implementation stage of the last project you sponsored.

YOUR ROLE AS PROJECT SPONSOR
Please indicate whether you are a Sponsor, or act on behalf of a Sponsor, for a project that is delivered by an organization internal or external to your firm. Check one answer.

- ○ I am a Sponsor, or act on behalf of a Sponsor, for an IT project that is delivered by an external firm.
- ○ I am a Sponsor, or act on behalf of a Sponsor, for an IT project that is delivered by an organization from within my firm.
- ○ Other (Please Specify)

THE NATURE OF YOUR PROJECT
Please select one category that best characterizes the objectives of your project.

- ○ RESEARCH: The project is intended to develop new knowledge about an area. Work involves creation and evaluation of new concepts or components but not development for operational use.
- ○ DEVELOPMENT: The combination of existing feasible concepts, perhaps with new knowledge, to provide a distinctly new product,

service or process for operational use. The application of known facts and theory to solve a particular problem through exploratory study, design, development and testing of new components or systems. That is hardware or software development for new products.

○TECHNICAL SERVICE: Recombination, modification and testing of systems using existing knowledge. Cost/performance improvement to existing products, processes or systems. Includes installation, parameterization, modification and roll-out of existing hardware or software that does not provide a distinctly new product.

	To a small extent	To a moderate extent	To a great extent
Related to the question above, please indicate how completely the projects' objectives are represented by the selected category.	○	○	○

In the project you selected above the project objectives are....

	Strongly disagree	Disagree	Slightly disagree	Neither agree nor Disagree	Slightly agree	Agree	Strongly agree
Clearly defined	○	○	○	○	○	○	○
Well documented	○	○	○	○	○	○	○
Agreed with the supplier	○	○	○	○	○	○	○

In the project you selected above the work methods for the project team are....

	Strongly disagree	Disagree	Slightly disagree	Neither agree nor disagree	Slightly agree	Agree	Strongly agree
Clearly defined	○	○	○	○	○	○	○
Well documented	○	○	○	○	○	○	○
Agreed with the supplier	○	○	○	○	○	○	○

THE RELATIONSHIP BETWEEN BUYER AND SELLER FIRM

Please rate how accurate the following descriptions are for the relationship between buyer and seller firm in your project.
Use the follwing ratings for the next block of questions:

1 = Completely inaccurate description
2 = Inaccurate description
3 = Slightly inaccurate descrition
4 = Neither accurate nor inaccurate description
5 = Slightly accurate description
6 = Accurate description
7 = Completely accurate description

	1	2	3	4	5	6	7
It is expected that we keep each other informed about events or changes that may affect the other party.	○	○	○	○	○	○	○
Problems that arise in the course of this relationship are treated by the parties as joint rather than individual responsibilities.	○	○	○	○	○	○	○
Flexibility in response to requests for changes is a characteristic of this relationship.	○	○	○	○	○	○	○
The parties expect to be able to make adjustments in the ongoing relationship to cope with changing circumstances.	○	○	○	○	○	○	○
When some unexpected situation arises, the parties would rather work out a new deal than hold each other to the original terms.	○	○	○	○	○	○	○
In this relationship, it is expected that any information that might help the other party will be provided to them.	○	○	○	○	○	○	○
Exchange of information in this relationship takes place frequently and informally, and not only according to a pre-specified agreement.	○	○	○	○	○	○	○
It is expected that the parties will provide proprietary information if it can help the other party.	○	○	○	○	○	○	○
The parties are committed to improvements that may benefit the relationship as a whole, and not only the individual parties.	○	○	○	○	○	○	○
The parties in this relationship do not mind owing each other favors.	○	○	○	○	○	○	○

PROJECT COMMUNICATION

Communication between the Project Sponsor and the supplier's Project Manager can be informal, e.g. in ad-hoc conversations, but can also take place at formal status reporting events, i.e. at contractually agreed intervals and with pre-specified contents. The official information exchanged at these formal events may have an impact on the further progress of the project, or the relationship between the project seller and the buyer firm.

The following blocks of questions ask about YOUR preferences for formal communication at the implementation stage of your project. Ignore the current practices in your project and answer only what YOU think is appropriate.

IMPORTANCE OF MEDIA

How important is written, verbal, and personal communication in formal communication with the supplier's Project Manager.
For each question select one of the following ratings:

1 = Not at all important
2 = Not important
3 = Slightly unimportant
4 = Neither important nor unimportant
5 = Slightly important
6 = Important

7 = Very important

Same ratings for different media are possible

	1	2	3	4	5	6	7
Written communication, e.g. written reports, letters, e-mails, fax.	○	○	○	○	○	○	○
Verbal communication, e.g. telephone, voice-mail, net-meeting.	○	○	○	○	○	○	○
Personal communication, e.g. face-to-face discussion, group meeting, video-conference.	○	○	○	○	○	○	○

FREQUENCY OF COMMUNICATION

Rate each of the following questions according to YOUR preference. Same ratings for different questions are possible.

Frequency in formal written communication.
That includes letters, notes, e-mails, faxes etc.

At the current state of my project the following frequency in formal <u>written</u> communication between Project Manager and Project Sponsor is appropriate ...

	Strongly disagree	Disagree	Slightly disagree	Neither agree nor disagree	Slightly agree	Agree	Strongly agree
Daily	○	○	○	○	○	○	○
Weekly only	○	○	○	○	○	○	○
Every 2nd week only	○	○	○	○	○	○	○
Monthly only	○	○	○	○	○	○	○
At milestone achievement only	○	○	○	○	○	○	○
At phase end, phase transition or project end only	○	○	○	○	○	○	○
No formal written communication	○	○	○	○	○	○	○

Frequency in formal verbal communication.
That includes telephone, voice-mail, net-meeting etc.

At the current state of my project the following frequency in formal <u>verbal</u> communication between Project Manager and Project Sponsor is appropriate ...

	Strongly disagree	Disagree	Slightly disagree	Neither agree nor disagree	Slightly agree	Agree	Strongly agree
Daily	○	○	○	○	○	○	○
Weekly only	○	○	○	○	○	○	○
Every 2nd week only	○	○	○	○	○	○	○

	Strongly disagree	Disagree	Slightly disagree	Neither agree nor disagree	Slightly agree	Agree	Strongly agree
Monthly only	○	○	○	○	○	○	○
At milestone achievement only	○	○	○	○	○	○	○
At phase end, phase transition or project end only	○	○	○	○	○	○	○
No formal verbal communication	○	○	○	○	○	○	○

Frequency in formal personal communication.
That includes face-to-face discussions, group meetings, video-conferences etc.

At the current state of my project the following frequency in formal <u>personal</u> communication between Project Manager and Project Sponsor is appropriate ...

	Strongly disagree	Disagree	Slightly disagree	Neither agree nor disagree	Slightly agree	Agree	Strongly agree
Daily	○	○	○	○	○	○	○
Weekly only	○	○	○	○	○	○	○
Every 2nd week only	○	○	○	○	○	○	○
Monthly only	○	○	○	○	○	○	○
At milestone achievement only	○	○	○	○	○	○	○
At phase end, phase transition or project end only	○	○	○	○	○	○	○
No formal personal communication	○	○	○	○	○	○	○

CONTENTS IN FORMAL COMMUNICATION

Rate each of the following questions according to your own preferences at the current state of your project.
Same ratings for different questions are possible.

Contents in formal written communication.
That includes letters, written reports, e-mails, faxes etc.

At the current state of my project the following contents in formal <u>written</u> communication between Project Manager and Project Sponsor is appropriate ...

	Strongly disagree	Disagree	Slightly disagree	Neither agree nor disagree	Slightly agree	Agree	Strongly agree
Status and achievements, e.g. related to functionality, schedule and/or budget.	○	○	○	○	○	○	○

	Strongly disagree	Disagree	Slightly disagree	Neither agree nor disagree	Slightly agree	Agree	Strongly agree
Measures, e.g. earned value measures, quality metrics etc.	○	○	○	○	○	○	○
Issues or "open item" list	○	○	○	○	○	○	○
Changes to project scope, plan, risks, quality etc.	○	○	○	○	○	○	○
Trend analysis	○	○	○	○	○	○	○
Next steps	○	○	○	○	○	○	○
Other contents (not listed above)	○	○	○	○	○	○	○

Contents in formal verbal communication.
That includes telephone, voice-mail, net-meeting etc.

At the current state of my project the following contents in formal <u>verbal</u> communication between Project Manager and Project Sponsor is appropriate ...

	Strongly disagree	Disagree	Slightly disagree	Neither agree nor disagree	Slightly agree	Agree	Strongly agree
Status and achievements, e.g. related to functionality, schedule and/or budget	○	○	○	○	○	○	○
Measures, e.g. earned value measures, quality metrics etc.	○	○	○	○	○	○	○
Issues or "open item" list	○	○	○	○	○	○	○
Changes to project scope, plan, risks, quality etc.	○	○	○	○	○	○	○
Trend analysis	○	○	○	○	○	○	○
Next steps	○	○	○	○	○	○	○
Other contents (not listed above)	○	○	○	○	○	○	○

Contents in formal personal communication.
That includes face-to-face discussions, group meetings, video-conference etc.

At the current state of my project the following contents in formal <u>personal</u> communication between Project Manager and Project Sponsor is appropriate ...

	Strongly disagree	Disagree	Slightly disagree	Neither agree nor disagree	Slightly agree	Agree	Strongly agree
Status and achievements, e.g. related to functionality,	○	○	○	○	○	○	○

	Strongly disagree	Disagree	Slightly disagree	Neither agree nor disagree	Slightly agree	Agree	Strongly agree
schedule and/or budget							
Measures, e.g. earned value measures, quality metrics etc.	○	○	○	○	○	○	○
Issues or "open item" list	○	○	○	○	○	○	○
Changes to project scope, plan, risks, quality etc.	○	○	○	○	○	○	○
Trend analysis	○	○	○	○	○	○	○
Next steps	○	○	○	○	○	○	○
Other contents (not listed above)	○	○	○	○	○	○	○

PROJECT PERFORMANCE AND SUCCESS

	Strongly disagree	Disagree	Slightly disagree	Neither agree nor disagree	Slightly agree	Agree	Strongly agree
Altogether, the project performs well in terms of functionality, budget and timing	○	○	○	○	○	○	○
The project meets the user's requirements	○	○	○	○	○	○	○
The project will achieve its purpose	○	○	○	○	○	○	○

The following seven questions ask about the management philosophy of your organization. Please rate each question on the seven point scale. Rate what best approximates the actual conditions in your organization.

In general the operating management philosophy in my organization favors...

Highly structured channels of communication and a highly restricted access to important financial and operating information.						Open channels of communication with important financial and operating information flowing quite freely throughout the organization.
1	2	3	4	5	6	7
○	○	○	○	○	○	○

In general the operating management philosophy in my organization favors...

A strong insistance on a uniform managerial style throughout the organization

Managers' operating styles allowed to range freely from the very formal to the very informal

1	2	3	4	5	6	7
○	○	○	○	○	○	○

In general the operating management philosophy in my organization favors...

A strong emphasis on giving the most say in decision making to formal line managers

A strong tendency to let the expert in a given situation have the most say in decision making even if this means temporary bypassing of formal line authority

1	2	3	4	5	6	7
○	○	○	○	○	○	○

In general the operating management philosophy in my organization favors...

A strong emphasis on holding fast to tried and true management principles despite any changes in business

A strong emphasis on adapting freely to changing circumstances without too much concern for past practice

1	2	3	4	5	6	7
○	○	○	○	○	○	○

In general the operating management philosophy in my organization favors...

A strong emphasis on always getting personnel to follow the formally laid down procedures

A strong emphasis on getting things done even if it means disregarding formal procedures

1	2	3	4	5	6	7
○	○	○	○	○	○	○

In general the operating management philosophy in my organization favors...

Tight formal control of most operations by means of sophisticated control and information systems

Loose, informal control; heavy dependence on informal relationships and the norm of cooperation for getting things done

1	2	3	4	5	6	7
○	○	○	○	○	○	○

In general the operating management philosophy in my organization favors...

A strong emphasis on

A strong tendency to let the requirements of the

getting line and staff personnel to adhere closely to formal job descriptions 1	2	3	4	5	6	situation and the individual's personality define proper on-job behavior 7
○	○	○	○	○	○	○

To properly analyze the results it is necessary to send a similar questionnaire to your supplier's Project Manager of the project you had in mind when answering the questions. Therefore please enter the project name and the e-mail address of your supplier's Project Manager in the fields below. No information from this questionnaire will be passed on to your supplier or vice versa. Confidentiality is guaranteed.

Project name:

E-mail address of your supplier's Project Manager:

The data below are collected for demographic purposes and in case of questions arising from incomplete or corrupted data within the questionnaire. All personal data from below will be separated from your answers prior to analysis of the questionnaire.

Your name:

*Your e-mail address (required):

Your country (for USA, please add state)

Your age (in years)

Number of years of work experience

Number of years with experience in project management

Number of years with experience in project sponsoring

Results of the study are expected to be available early 2002.

○ Please click here if you would like to receive a summary of the final study

Thank you for taking the time to complete the questionnaire.

Please click on the "Submit" button now

[Submit Query]

Appendix A-8: Differences by Internal or External Role

ANOVA analysis on situational variables and demographics:

ANOVA

		Sum of Squares	df	Mean Square	F	Sig.
BUSEXP	Between Groups	220.864	1	220.864	2.843	.093
	Within Groups	14372.315	185	77.688		
	Total	14593.179	186			
PMEXP	Between Groups	22.443	1	22.443	.533	.466
	Within Groups	7783.682	185	42.074		
	Total	7806.126	186			
PSEXP	Between Groups	8.860	1	8.860	.314	.578
	Within Groups	1241.053	44	28.206		
	Total	1249.913	45			
METCLEAR	Between Groups	4.061	1	4.061	2.316	.130
	Within Groups	343.699	196	1.754		
	Total	347.760	197			
OBJCLEAR	Between Groups	2.196	1	2.196	1.726	.190
	Within Groups	249.322	196	1.272		
	Total	251.518	197			
RELNOM	Between Groups	2.543	1	2.543	3.151	.077
	Within Groups	158.155	196	.807		
	Total	160.697	197			
ORGSTRUC	Between Groups	3.968	1	3.968	3.666	.057
	Within Groups	211.041	195	1.082		
	Total	215.009	196			

ANOVA analysis on extracted communication factors (see also Chapter 4)

ANOVA

		Sum of Squares	df	Mean Square	F	Sig.
Personal Reviews	Between Groups	2.372E-02	1	2.372E-02	.023	.879
	Within Groups	198.776	196	1.014		
	Total	198.800	197			
Project Analysis	Between Groups	.426	1	.426	.427	.514
	Within Groups	195.738	196	.999		
	Total	196.164	197			
Written Status Report	Between Groups	.446	1	.446	.441	.508
	Within Groups	198.524	196	1.013		
	Total	198.970	197			
Verbal Update	Between Groups	6.188E-02	1	6.188E-02	.061	.805
	Within Groups	198.708	196	1.014		
	Total	198.770	197			
Variable Interval Communication	Between Groups	5.308E-02	1	5.308E-02	.052	.819
	Within Groups	198.559	196	1.013		
	Total	198.612	197			
Fixed Interval Communication	Between Groups	.371	1	.371	.367	.545
	Within Groups	198.246	196	1.011		
	Total	198.618	197			
Continuous Communication	Between Groups	.592	1	.592	.590	.443
	Within Groups	196.670	196	1.003		
	Total	197.262	197			

Appendix A-9: Interview Instructions and Questions

A. Introduction

1. Thank interviewees for participation

2. Explain research purpose
   - Identification of differences in project manager - sponsor communication
   - Developing a model of project manager- sponsor communication
   - Identification of communication differences in projects of higher / lesser performance

3. Explain purpose of the interview
   - Find evidence to confirm or reject hypotheses
   - Understand some of the survey results

4. Explain process
   - 60 min. taped interview with open questions
   - write-up and verification by interviewees
   - Analysis as part of methodological triangulation

5. Motivate interviewees to express their opinions freely (no right or wrong answers)

At the end of the interview:

Thank the participants again and remind them that they will receive a transcript for verification.

B.   **Interview Questions** (obtain answer from each participant)

1. Please give a short summary of the project and its performance

2. Each of you independently, please explain your preferred mutual communication, in terms of media, frequency and contents.

3. Each of you independently, why do you prefer this 'pattern'?

4a. The survey results show a significantly higher preference on the side of project sponsors for verbal media like phone calls or voice mails. Why do you think project sponsors prefer verbal media?

4b. Why do you think project managers don't prefer verbal media as much as project sponsors?

5a. The survey results show a significantly higher preference on the side of project sponsors for trend data, quality measures and earned value results. Why do you think project sponsors prefer quantitative results more than their project managers?

5b. Why do you think project managers prefer quantitative measures significantly less?

6a. The survey results show that project sponsors are more interested in forward looking information, like trends and issues. What do you think are the reasons for that?

6b. What are the reasons for project managers to be more interested in backward looking information, like e.g. status and achievements?

7. The survey results show that high performing projects use written status reports at bi-weekly or monthly intervals. Less well performing projects don't show that pattern. What are the reasons that this particular mix of contents and frequency is preferred in these projects?

Appendix A-10: Item to Total Correlations of Situational Variables

Situational Variables		
Construct	Variable	Item to Total Correlation
Objective Clearness		
	OBJCLR	.71
	OBJDOC	.70
	OBJAGR	.60
Methodology Clearness		
	METCLR	.81
	METDOC	.76
	METAGR	.66
Relational Norms		
	INFO1	.61
	SOL1	.73
	FLEX1	.63
	FLEX2	.61
	FLEX3	.46
	INFO2	.68
	INFO3	.59
	INFO4	.54
	SOL2	.67
	SOL3	.61
Organisation Structure		
	ORGSTR1	.45
	ORGSTR2	.64
	ORGSTR3	.59
	ORGSTR4	.50
	ORGSTR5	.51
	ORGSTR6	.52
	ORGSTR7	.54
Performance		
	PRFALL	.48
	PRFREQ	.68
	PRFPUR	.64

Appendix B-1: Correlation Matrix Original Four Factor Frequency Model

	FQWDAY	FQWWEK	FQW2WK	FQWMON	FQWMIL	FQWPHA	FQVDAY	FQVWEK	FQV2WK	FQVMON	FQVMIL	FQVPHA	FQPDAY	FQPWEK	FQP2WK	FQPMON	FQPMIL
FQWDAY																	
FQWWEK	.216*																
FQW2WK	-.363*	.021															
FQWMON	-.339*	-.276*	.452*														
FQWMIL	-.252*	-.251*	.075	.528*													
FQWPHA	-.203*	-.231*	.020	.445*	.859*												
FQVDAY	.393*	.344*	-.147	-.174*	-.161	-.147											
FQVWEK	-.134	.321*	.281*	.153	.106	.060	-.006										
FQV2WK	-.280*	-.223*	.572*	.570*	.317*	.248*	-.305*	.212*									
FQVMON	-.181*	-.209*	.315*	.614*	.416*	.420*	-.286*	.011	.658*								
FQVMIL	-.133	-.209*	.111	.407*	.691*	.675*	-.244*	.006	.396*	.596*							
FQVPHA	-.152	-.209*	.025	.296*	.634*	.661*	-.234*	-.030	.296*	.504*	.898*						
FQPDAY	.181*	.266*	-.072	-.026	.016	.012	.486*	.101	-.109	-.068	-.068	-.024					
FQPWEK	.093	.279*	.125	-.015	-.130	-.093	.356*	.275*	-.091	-.271*	-.179*	-.193*	.355*				
FQP2WK	.007	.099	.393*	.195*	.001	.031	.076	.336*	.400*	.161	.058	.018	-.088	.210*			
FQPMON	-.025	-.066	.274*	.402*	.230*	.231*	-.082	.081	.439*	.503*	.338*	.237*	-.205*	-.220*	.333*		
FQPMIL	-.061	-.022	.071	.268*	.598*	.559*	-.150	.116	.345*	.403*	.651*	.651*	-.169*	-.211*	.058	.381*	
FQPPHA	-.048	-.089	.073	.260*	.618*	.626*	-.154	.041	.290*	.382*	.645*	.686*	-.219*	-.201*	.009	.376*	.819*

* Indicates correlations significant at the .01 level

Appendix B-2: Anti-image Correlations of Original Four Factor Frequency Model

	FQWDAY	FQWWEK	FQW2WK	FQWMON	FQWMIL	FQWPHA	FQVDAY	FQVWEK	FQV2WK	FQVMON	FQVMIL	FQVPHA	FQPDAY	FQPWEK	FQP2WK	FQPMON	FQPMIL	FQPPHA
FQWDAY	.696*																	
FQWWEK	-.016	.688*																
FQW2WK	.301	-.146	.746*															
FQWMON	.111	.194	-.245	.835*														
FQWMIL	.115	.071	.092	-.317	.805*													
FQWPHA	.070	.073	.085	.003	-.644	.835*												
FQVDAY	-.205	-.109	.004	-.064	-.068	.062	.724*											
FQVWEK	.089	-.308	-.039	-.051	-.110	.026	.169	.664*										
FQV2WK	.047	.260	-.324	-.045	-.070	.165	.183	-.084	.798*									
FQVMON	-.065	-.146	.071	-.377	.192	-.140	.079	.102	-.414	.827*								
FQVMIL	-.192	-.053	-.099	.030	-.272	.008	.015	.022	-.055	-.195	.802*							
FQVPHA	.210	.124	.100	.070	.154	-.082	.097	.052	.119	-.049	-.768	.763*						
FQPDAY	-.134	-.192	-.019	.002	-.054	-.117	-.435	-.102	-.055	-.080	.159	-.275	.504*					
FQPWEK	-.014	-.086	-.040	-.183	.134	-.094	-.147	-.154	-.102	-.160	-.124	.081	-.191	.714*				
FQP2WK	-.163	-.096	-.174	.049	.059	-.152	-.195	-.208	-.032	.081	.230	-.187	.295	-.177	.552*			
FQPMON	-.036	-.001	-.003	-.171	.120	-.012	-.105	-.007	-.004	-.189	.107	.183	.063	.200	-.256	.833*		
FQPMIL	-.002	-.173	.110	.031	-.134	.077	-.039	-.095	-.164	.042	-.140	-.045	.053	.093	.023	-.075	.868*	
FQPPHA	-.179	-.066	-.152	.075	-.084	-.201	-.089	.014	-.064	.038	-.099	-.338	.294	-.066	.215	-.183	-.541	.796*

* Measures of Sampling Adequacy (MSA)

Appendix B

Appendix B-3: Correlation Matrix Final Frequency Factors

	FQWDAY	FQWWEK	FQW2WK	FQWMON	FQWMIL	FQWPHA	FQVDAY	FQV2WK	FQVMON	FQVMIL	FQVPHA	FQPWEK	FQP2WK	FQPMON	FQPMIL
FQWDAY															
FQWWEK	.219*														
FQW2WK	-.324*	.027													
FQWMON	-.311*	-.234*	.436*												
FQWMIL	-.253*	-.232*	.062	.511*											
FQWPHA	-.191*	-.189*	.007	.427*	.846*										
FQVDAY	.393*	.355*	-.098	.152	-.133	-.119									
FQV2WK	-.222*	-.199*	.549*	.546*	.278*	.216*	-.290*								
FQVMON	-.150	-.192*	.322*	.603*	.408*	.404*	-.245*	.650*							
FQVMIL	-.098	-.154	.105	.403*	.673*	.657*	-.195*	.388*	.598*						
FQVPHA	-.130	-.145	.036	.324*	.620*	.667*	-.181*	.284*	.512*	.889*					
FQPWEK	.092	.251*	.115	-.015	-.134	-.089	.346*	-.102	-.261*	-.184*	-.164*				
FQP2WK	-.011	.093	.398*	.178*	-.010	.013	.055	.378*	.150	.031	.003	.219*			
FQPMON	-.018	-.065	.270*	.417*	.228*	.227*	-.089	.433*	.507*	.328*	.235*	-.239*	.316*		
FQPMIL	-.040	-.002	.057	.273*	.593*	.553*	-.134	.320*	.395*	.637*	.617*	-.247*	.033	.390*	
FQPPHA	-.048	-.075	.051	.264*	.618*	.636*	-.144	.269*	.366*	.603*	.650*	-.226*	-.013	.380*	.799*

* Indicates correlations significant at the .01 level

Appendix B-4: Anti-image Correlations Final Frequency Factors

	FQWDAY	FQWWEK	FQW2WK	FQWMON	FQWMIL	FQWPHA	FQVDAY	FQV2WK	FQVMON	FQVMIL	FQVPHA	FQPWEK	FQP2WK	FQPMON	FQPMIL	FQPPHA
FQWDAY	.638*															
FQWWEK	-.032	.730*														
FQW2WK	.305	-.148	.729*													
FQWMON	.102	.116	-.223	.844*												
FQWMIL	.179	.109	.070	-.299	.798*											
FQWPHA	.022	.009	.095	-.017	-.631	.841*										
FQVDAY	-.346	-.220	-.059	-.040	-.118	.019	.720*									
FQV2WK	-.015	.151	-.316	-.113	-.013	.107	.170	.824*								
FQVMON	-.070	-.052	.009	-.311	.123	-.106	.010	-.393	.859*							
FQVMIL	-.188	-.020	-.077	.076	-.297	.050	.079	-.083	-.176	.794*						
FQVPHA	.167	.039	.084	-.006	.211	-.184	-.032	.105	-.088	-.764	.780*					
FQPWEK	-.046	-.158	-.087	-.186	.072	-.109	-.227	-.044	.209	-.033	-.015	.671*				
FQP2WK	-.070	-.057	-.204	.098	.005	-.087	-.025	-.270	.100	.088	-.091	-.208	.615*			
FQPMON	-.037	.009	.000	-.223	.146	-.013	-.070	.026	-.205	-.130	.196	.218	-.305	.792*		
FQPMIL	-.012	-.201	.077	.027	-.161	.103	.003	-.124	.053	-.163	.016	.109	-.020	-.087	.850*	
FQPPHA	-.125	.014	-.117	.107	-.097	-.198	.057	-.047	.072	.216	-.296	.143	-.223	.143	-.565	.813*

* Measures of Sampling Adequacy (MSA)

Appendix B

Appendix B-5: Correlation Matrix Contents Factors

	COWSTA	COWMEA	COWISS	COWCHA	COWTRE	COWNXT	COWOTH	COVSTA	COVMEA	COVISS	COVCHA	COVTRE	COVNXT	COVOTH	COPSTA	COPMEA	COPISS	COPCHA	COPTRE	COPNXT
COWSTA																				
COWMEA	.272*																			
COWISS	.342*	.230*																		
COWCHA	.398*	.351*	.455*																	
COWTRE	.309*	.575*	.219*	.264*																
COWNXT	.253*	.065	.305*	.272	.271*															
COWOTH	.118	.273*	.180*	.176*	.315*	.251*														
COVSTA	.119	-.053	.089	.163*	-.040	-.029	-.162													
COVMEA	.013	.366*	.099	.102	.342*	.007	.110	.339*												
COVISS	.049	-.079	.252*	.070	-.038	.126	.030	.415*	.263*											
COVCHA	.192*	-.037	.144	.156*	.049	.127	-.042	.444*	.273*	.613*										
COVTRE	.135	.357*	.082	.140	.452*	.056	.054	.186*	.632*	.089	.216*									
COVNXT	.105	-.072	.120	.171*	.083	.374*	.136	.267*	.196*	.366*	.384*	.220*								
COVOTH	.073	.175*	.159*	.120	.169*	.146	.363*	.010	.202*	.125	.012	.263*	.299*							
COPSTA	.181*	-.027	.066	.007	.117	.048	.068	.297*	.029	.179*	.117	.046	.140	.005						
COPMEA	.113	.335*	.029	.112*	.415*	.053	.164*	.047	.337*	.042	.117	.330*	.145	-.008	.497*					
COPISS	.132	.121	.291*	.239*	.212*	.201*	.226*	.072	.046	.244*	.087	.115	.169*	.132	.505*	.272				
COPCHA	.158*	.064	.139	.209*	.239*	.152	.064	.165*	.121	.268*	.342*	.141	.331*	.065	.490*	.397*	.539*			
COPTRE	.113	.277*	.066	.141	.459*	.048	.210*	.044	.359*	-.005	.004	.446*	.096	.140	.343*	.656*	.326*	.360*		
COPNXT	.182*	.111	.154	.130	.264*	.323*	.294*	-.116	.055	.086	.049	.135	.436*	.280*	.382*	.303*	.584*	.558*	.409*	
COPOTH	.143	.209*	.158*	.171*	.255*	.168*	.496*	-.089	.103	.023	-.076	.260*	.175*	.672*	.253*	.251*	.363*	.240*	.373*	.481*

* Indicates correlations significant at the .01 level

Appendix B-6: Anti-image Correlations Contents Factors

	COWSTA	COWMEA	COWISS	COWCHA	COWTRE	COWNXT	COWOTH	COVSTA	COVMEA	COVISS	COVCHA	COVTRE	COVNXT	COVOTH	COPSTA	COPMEA	COPISS	COPCHA	COPTRE	COPNXT	COPOTH
COWSTA	.741*																				
COWMEA	-.122	.748*																			
COWISS	-.174	-.046	.793*																		
COWCHA	-.220	-.227	-.289	.708*																	
COWTRE	-.134	-.381	-.037	.053	.835*																
COWNXT	-.083	.127	-.147	-.109	-.230	.779*															
COWOTH	.016	-.092	-.003	-.022	-.158	-.099	.797*														
COVSTA	-.062	.016	.043	-.185	.043	.089	.138	.596*													
COVMEA	.155	-.185	-.046	.067	-.002	.022	-.131	-.303	.712												
COVISS	.062	.033	-.212	.148	.086	-.015	-.010	-.119	-.159	.693*											
COVCHA	-.169	.047	.055	-.042	-.005	-.014	-.044	-.142	-.019	-.480	.711*										
COVTRE	-.069	-.049	.035	.049	-.215	.033	.254	.035	-.142	.151	-.162	.725*									
COVNXT	.061	.182	-.050	-.116	.052	-.246	-.073	-.238	.035	-.135	-.109	-.178	.841*								
COVOTH	.023	-.084	.031	.031	-.020	.055	-.070	.036	.064	-.091	.066	-.042	-.257	.657*							
COPSTA	-.164	.137	-.003	.217	.015	.021	.002	-.073	-.121	.009	.053	.066	.106	.005	.673*						
COPMEA	.051	-.235	.061	-.027	-.059	.004	.005	.002	.136	-.032	.040	.032	-.215	.226	-.443	.781*					
COPISS	.150	-.040	-.147	-.164	.003	-.025	-.071	-.009	.230	-.032	-.291	-.122	.170	.085	-.289	-.165	.698*				
COPCHA	.065	.057	.040	-.140	-.116	.060	.090	.016	-.009	.008	.004	.123	-.047	.043	-.165	-.195	.110	.848*			
COPTRE	.027	.163	.005	-.061	-.170	.086	-.035	-.101	.025	-.081	.048	.061	.171	.017	.043	-.111	-.459	-.025	.806*		
COPNXT	-.123	-.072	.026	.141	.012	-.115	.029	.276	-.080	.102	.048	.130	-.441	.032	.017	-.017	.066	-.017	-.236	.739*	
COPOTH	-.018	.032	.016	-.073	.083	-.008	-.287	-.006	.159	.002	.062	-.183	.173	-.615	-.090	-.102	.151	-.345	-.201	-.089	.730*

* Measures of Sampling Adequacy (MSA)

Appendix B

Appendix B-7: Normal Distribution of Dependent Variables

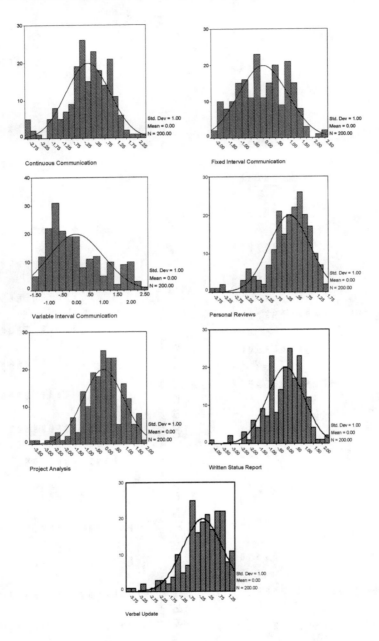

Appendix B-8: Heteroscedasticity and Normal Probability of the Error Term

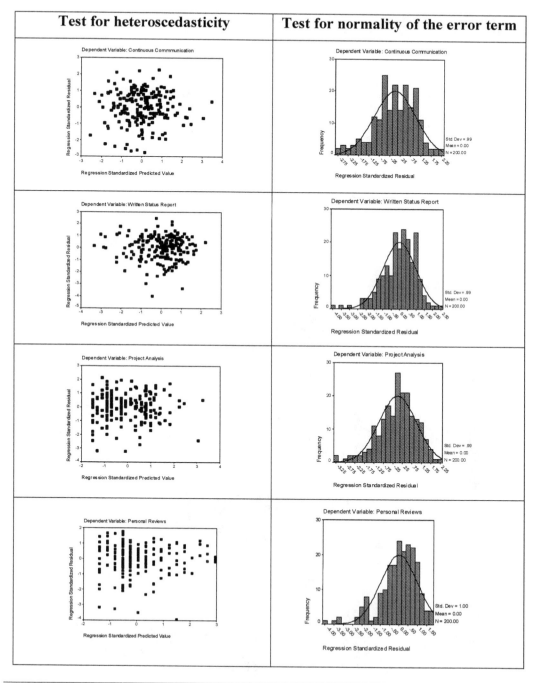

Test for heteroscedasticity	Test for normality of the error term

Appendix B-9: Correlation Matrix of Dependent and Independent Variables.

	Personal Reviews	Project Analysis	Written Status Report	Verbal Update	Variable Interval Communication	Fixed Interval Communication	Continuous Communication	Age	BUSEXP	PMEXP	PSEXP	METCLEAR	OBJCLEAR	RELNOM
Personal Reviews														
Project Analysis	.198													
Written Status Report	-.089	.060												
Verbal Update	-.039	.161	.160											
Variable Interval Com.	-.032	.240	-.120	-.006										
Fixed Interval Com.	-.062	.102	-.036	.048	-.036									
Continuous Com.	-.099	-.031	.283	.108	-.437	.112								
AGE	-.287	-.063	.168	-.139	.026	-.162	.131							
BUSEXP	-.271	.026	.218	.023	.014	-.200	.138	.910						
PMEXP	-.160	.037	.332	.102	.072	.039	.069	.645	.665					
PSEXP	-.172	.187	.160	-.027	.261	.055	-.051	.537	.534	.650				
METCLEAR	.101	.065	.087	-.022	-.066	.250	.053	.369	.316	.339	.288			
OBJCLEAR	.018	.008	.292	-.103	.162	.024	.086	.370	.376	.307	.355	.354		
RELNOM	.139	.249	.319	-.098	.014	-.008	-.001	.231	.235	.143	.311	.297	.526	
ORGSTRUC	.043	.004	-.144	-.032	.011	-.072	-.039	-.108	-.106	.048	.026	.120	.111	.088

Appendix B

Appendix B-10: Advanced Diagnostics Results

Diagnostic Measure	Threshold Value Specification	Calculated Threshold Value	Observations Exceeding Thresholds in Regression Model for:			
			Continuous Communication	Personal Review	Project Analysis	Written Status Report
Residuals						
Standardized, Studentized, Studentized Deleted	t-value at specified confidence level	±1.96	2, 52, 42 72, 92, 100, 105, 108, 185, 187	135, 141, 152, 163, 176, 200	26, 68, 108, 132, 146, 175, 179, 185, 190, 197	5, 7, 15, 22, 63, 115, 136, 193
Leverage						
Hat values	2p/n	various	Threshold 0.04 — 42	Threshold 0.02 — 44, 69, 70, 72, 117, 127, 128, 179, 181	Threshold 0.03 — 26, 44, 72, 180, 182	Threshold 0.03 — 23, 25, 66, 72, 117, 180
Mahalanobis Distance	Evaluate the distribution of values	Top 10 observations	128, 61, 182, 180, 26, 44, 67, 157, 171, 23	44, 182, 179, 127, 72, 26, 128, 117, 160	44, 26, 180, 182, 20, 128, 117, 23, 45,160	180, 182, 66, 44, 23, 184, 72, 25, 71, 117
Single Case Measures						
SDFBETA	±2√n	±0.14	Intercept: 2, 42, 60, 71, 72, 92, 100,105, 129, 130, 184 — ORGSTRUC 42, 60, 177, 100, 120, 157, 158, 159, 185 — OBJCLR 6, 26, 61, 73, 92, 100, 105, 108, 119, 120, 157, 199 — METCLR 2, 9, 12, 42, 61, 72, 100, 105, 157, 184, 185	Intercept: 70, 83, 117, 200 — OBJCLR 70, 72, 83, 96, 163, 200	Intercept: 26, 68, 96, 127, 132, 146, 160,175, 180, 182 — OBJCLR 12, 26, 68, 84, 90, 127, 132, 161, 175, 180, 182, 190 — BUYSEL 12, 26, 58, 68	Intercept: 7, 22, 70, 115, 127, 129, 130, 182, 190 — ORGSTRUC 7, 69, 70, 99, 115, 127, 180 — BUYSEL 22, 95, 137, 182
Cook's Distance	generally accepted practices	1.0				
COVRATIO	1±3p/n		Upper threshold: 1.06 — 23, 26, 151,171, 180, 184 — Lower threshold: 0.94 — 42, 100, 108, 187	Upper threshold: 1.045 — 44, 127, 182 — Lower threshold: 0.955 — 120, 200	Upper threshold: 1.045 — 20, 44, 117, 128 — Lower threshold: 0.955 — 68, 132	Upper threshold: 1.045 — 12, 23, 25, 40, 44, 57, 66, 72, 161, 171, 180, 182 — Lower threshold: 0.955 — 5, 7, 63,, 64, 115
SDFFIT	2√((k+1)/(n-k-1))	0.35	2, 42, 72, 92, 157, 185	176, 200	26, 190	26, 115

Appendix B

Appendix B-11: Description of Dyadic Sample

Descriptives

		N	Mean	Std. Deviation	Std. Error	95% Confidence Interval for Mean		Minimum	Maximum
						Lower Bound	Upper Bound		
AGE	0	113	42.20	7.84	.74	40.74	43.67	28	62
	1	67	42.13	8.70	1.06	40.01	44.26	27	62
	Total	180	42.18	8.15	.61	40.98	43.38	27	62
BUSEXP	0	121	20.36	8.70	.79	18.80	21.93	5	42
	1	68	19.79	9.23	1.12	17.55	22.02	5	40
	Total	189	20.16	8.87	.65	18.88	21.43	5	42
PMEXP	0	121	10.33	6.15	.56	9.22	11.43	2	30
	1	68	10.14	7.06	.86	8.43	11.85	0	31
	Total	189	10.26	6.47	.47	9.33	11.19	0	31
PSEXP	0	21	7.00	6.45	1.41	4.06	9.94	1	22
	1	27	4.96	3.85	.74	3.44	6.49	1	18
	Total	48	5.85	5.19	.75	4.35	7.36	1	22
METCLEAR	0	124	4.9946	1.3495	.1212	4.7547	5.2345	1.00	7.00
	1	76	5.1272	1.2858	.1475	4.8334	5.4210	1.67	7.00
	Total	200	5.0450	1.3240	9.362E-02	4.8604	5.2296	1.00	7.00
OBJCLEAR	0	124	5.3199	1.1542	.1037	5.1147	5.5251	2.00	7.00
	1	76	5.5088	1.1424	.1310	5.2477	5.7698	2.33	7.00
	Total	200	5.3917	1.1506	8.136E-02	5.2312	5.5521	2.00	7.00
PERFORM	0	123	5.7344	.8589	7.744E-02	5.5811	5.8877	2.00	7.00
	1	76	5.6053	1.1098	.1273	5.3517	5.8589	1.00	7.00
	Total	199	5.6851	.9618	6.818E-02	5.5506	5.8195	1.00	7.00
RELNOM	0	124	5.3720	.8758	7.865E-02	5.2163	5.5276	2.70	7.00
	1	76	5.5750	.9298	.1067	5.3625	5.7875	2.60	7.00
	Total	200	5.4491	.8998	6.363E-02	5.3236	5.5746	2.60	7.00
ORGSTRUC	0	124	4.4634	1.0437	9.373E-02	4.2779	4.6489	1.57	6.43
	1	75	4.7666	1.0313	.1191	4.5293	5.0039	1.86	7.00
	Total	199	4.5777	1.0469	7.421E-02	4.4313	4.7240	1.57	7.00
Personal Reviews	0	124	-4.9E-02	1.0572469	9.49E-02	-.2371001	.1387699	-3.70859	1.69045
	1	76	8.02E-02	.8998176	.1032162	-.1254003	.2858339	-2.14929	1.67179
	Total	200	-1.9E-16	1.0000000	7.07E-02	-.1394384	.1394384	-3.70859	1.69045
Project Analysis	0	124	-3.6E-02	1.0779005	9.68E-02	-.2279960	.1552166	-3.44957	2.11641
	1	76	5.94E-02	.8614557	9.88E-02	-.1374784	.2562237	-2.76723	1.86482
	Total	200	1.15E-16	1.0000000	7.07E-02	-.1394384	.1394384	-3.44957	2.11641
Written Status Report	0	124	-7.0E-03	.9802105	8.80E-02	-.1812725	.1672097	-4.02625	2.26810
	1	76	1.15E-02	1.0379718	.1190635	-.2257145	.2486590	-3.07939	2.36039
	Total	200	6.55E-17	1.0000000	7.07E-02	-.1394384	.1394384	-4.02625	2.36039
Verbal Update	0	124	4.83E-02	1.0449907	9.38E-02	-.1375027	.2340100	-3.83486	1.57910
	1	76	-7.9E-02	.9232084	.1058993	-.2896918	.1322325	-3.45124	1.50272
	Total	200	-7.1E-17	1.0000000	7.07E-02	-.1394384	.1394384	-3.83486	1.57910
Variable Interval Communication	0	124	3.53E-02	.9866797	8.86E-02	-.1400719	.2107102	-1.49260	2.40610
	1	76	-5.8E-02	1.0253319	.1176136	-.2919244	.1766724	-1.54285	2.30909
	Total	200	7.11E-17	1.0000000	7.07E-02	-.1394384	.1394384	-1.54285	2.40610
Fixed Interval Communication	0	124	-4.0E-02	1.0191479	9.15E-02	-.2207981	.1415270	-1.99503	2.47374
	1	76	6.47E-02	.9711291	.1113961	-.1572440	.2865810	-2.08934	2.39554
	Total	200	-4.4E-18	1.0000000	7.07E-02	-.1394384	.1394384	-2.08934	2.47374
Continuous Communication	0	124	-3.3E-02	1.0023502	9.00E-02	-.2109583	.1453949	-2.72083	2.18682
	1	76	5.35E-02	1.0004699	.1147618	-.1751312	.2821031	-2.63877	2.42405
	Total	200	8.44E-17	1.0000000	7.07E-02	-.1394384	.1394384	-2.72083	2.42405

Appendix B-12: ANOVA of Dyadic Sample and Total Sample

ANOVA

		Sum of Squares	df	Mean Square	F	Sig.
AGE	Between Groups	.201	1	.201	.003	.956
	Within Groups	11888.110	178	66.787		
	Total	11888.311	179			
BUSEXP	Between Groups	14.487	1	14.487	.183	.669
	Within Groups	14785.158	187	79.065		
	Total	14799.646	188			
PMEXP	Between Groups	1.518	1	1.518	.036	.850
	Within Groups	7873.278	187	42.103		
	Total	7874.796	188			
PSEXP	Between Groups	49.016	1	49.016	1.853	.180
	Within Groups	1216.963	46	26.456		
	Total	1265.979	47			
METCLEAR	Between Groups	.828	1	.828	.471	.493
	Within Groups	347.989	198	1.758		
	Total	348.817	199			
OBJCLEAR	Between Groups	1.681	1	1.681	1.272	.261
	Within Groups	261.750	198	1.322		
	Total	263.431	199			
PERFORM	Between Groups	.784	1	.784	.846	.359
	Within Groups	182.371	197	.926		
	Total	183.155	198			
RELNOM	Between Groups	1.943	1	1.943	2.416	.122
	Within Groups	159.180	198	.804		
	Total	161.122	199			
ORGSTRUC	Between Groups	4.296	1	4.296	3.979	.047
	Within Groups	212.695	197	1.080		
	Total	216.991	198			
Personal Reviews	Between Groups	.789	1	.789	.788	.376
	Within Groups	198.211	198	1.001		
	Total	199.000	199			
Project Analysis	Between Groups	.432	1	.432	.431	.512
	Within Groups	198.568	198	1.003		
	Total	199.000	199			
Written Status Report	Between Groups	1.613E-02	1	1.613E-02	.016	.899
	Within Groups	198.984	198	1.005		
	Total	199.000	199			
Verbal Update	Between Groups	.760	1	.760	.759	.385
	Within Groups	198.240	198	1.001		
	Total	199.000	199			
Variable Interval Communication	Between Groups	.407	1	.407	.406	.525
	Within Groups	198.593	198	1.003		
	Total	199.000	199			
Fixed Interval Communication	Between Groups	.513	1	.513	.511	.475
	Within Groups	198.487	198	1.002		
	Total	199.000	199			
Continuous Communication	Between Groups	.351	1	.351	.350	.555
	Within Groups	198.649	198	1.003		
	Total	199.000	199			

Appendix B-13: Mean Gap in Project Sponsor and Manager Scores

Factor Variable	N	Mean	S.D
Frequency Factor 1: Variable Interval Communication			
Written communication at milestone achievement	35	0.57	2.91
Written communication at phase or project end	36	0.19	3.45
Verbal monthly communication	33	0.82	2.88
Verbal communication at milestone achievement	34	0.50	2.19
Verbal communication at phase or project end	35	0.57	2.43
Personal communication at milestone achievement	35	0.74	2.84
Personal communication at phase or project end	36	0.58	3.18
Frequency Factor 2: Fixed Interval Communication			
Written bi-weekly communication	34	0.00	2.17
Written monthly communication	35	0.74	2.68
Verbal bi-weekly communication	32	0.41	2.64
Verbal monthly communication	33	0.82	2.88
Personal bi-weekly communication	34	-0.18	2.69
Personal monthly communication	26	-0.40	2.78
Frequency Factor 3: Continuous Communication			
Written daily communication	36	-0.42	2.05
Written weekly communication	26	-0.23	2.25
Verbal daily communication	36	0.83	2.51
Personal weekly communication	37	-0.24	2.44
Contents Factor 1: Personal Review			
Personal contents: status and achievements	35	-0.06	2.20
Personal contents: measures and quality metrics	35	0.09	2.05
Personal contents: issues or 'open items'	36	-0.22	1.61
Personal contents: project changes	35	-0.20	1.49
Personal contents: trends	35	0.29	2.33
Personal contents: next steps	35	-0.17	1.62
Personal contents: other	28	-0.21	2.11
Contents Factor 2: Project Analysis			
Written contents: measures and quality metrics	37	0.43	2.12
Written contents: trends	36	0.19	1.55
Verbal contents: measures and quality metrics	34	0.85	2.45
Verbal contents: trends	36	0.86	1.88
Personal contents: measures and quality metrics	35	0.09	2.05
Personal contents: trends	35	0.29	2.33
Contents Factor 3: Written Status with possible follow-up			
Written contents: status and achievements	37	-0.11	1.26
Written contents: issues or 'open items'	36	-0.06	1.76
Written contents: project changes	37	-0.30	1.76
Written contents: next steps	37	-0.46	1.45
Written contents: other	29	-0.59	1.92
Verbal contents: other	28	0.25	1.92
Personal contents: other	28	-0.21	2.11
Contents Factor 4: Verbal Update			
Verbal contents: status and achievements	36	0.25	2.37
Verbal contents: issues or 'open items'	36	0.39	2.28
Verbal contents: project changes	37	0.16	2.30
Verbal contents: next steps	36	-0.03	1.78

Appendix B-14: Tests for Normality and Heteroscedasticity in Regressions of Dyadic Sample

Histogram

Dependent Variable: DPERF

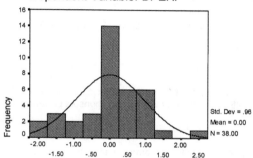

Regression Standardized Residual

Scatterplot

Dependent Variable: DPERF

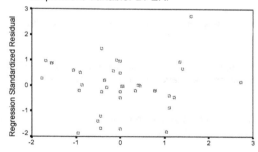

Regression Standardized Predicted Value

Appendix B-15: Summary of Explanatory Results

Question 1:

The survey results show that significantly higher preference on the side of the project sponsors prevail for verbal media, like phone calls or voice mails. Why do you think project sponsors prefer verbal media?

- Sponsor has a wider perspective than project manager, because of the integration of the project in the overall organisation.

- Project manager tries to establish track record of achievements.

Question 2:

The survey results show a significantly higher preference on the side of the Project Sponsor for trend data, quality measures, and Earned Value results. Why do you think project sponsors prefer quantitative results more than their project managers?

- facts needed by sponsor for external communication to show progress, value and quality of the project

- project managers are contract focused, perceive calculation of quantitative data as waste of time, make no use of these data.

Question 3:

The survey results show that project sponsors are more interested in forward looking information, like trends and issues. What do you think are the reasons for that?

- Project Sponsors are looking ahead to see how the project outcome will fit the overall organisational change and its objectives. They have a high stake, as well as financial and career exposure with the project.

- Project managers are contract focused and interested in showing a track record of succesful delivery.

Question 4:

The survey results show that high performing projects use written status reports at bi-weekly or monthly intervals. Less well performing projects don't show these patterns. What are the reasons for that particular mix of contents and frequency, and why is it preferred in these projects?

- Bi-weekly or monthly status report is a good balance between formal overhead and risk of missing plan deviations at the earliest possible stage.

- Forces rigor and discipline

- Formal, auditable reports needed for management

Appendix B-16: Summary of Exploratory Results

	Informal Communication		Formal Communication	
Preferences				
- Frequency	Daily to weekly		Weekly status meeting with minutes	Bi-weekly or monthly report
- Contents	"How things going. What's coming up"	Issues, changes, possible escalations	Issues, task achievements and plans for next week	Issues, risk, time, cost, people, progress to plan
- Media	Face-to-face, e-mail for documentation only		Written (minutes)	Face-to-dace plus written report
Reasons for Preferences				
- Trust building	Trust is most important. Not to expect any negative surprises. To have a trustful relationship ...for the project members, and the stakeholders, so that everybody knows how things are going.			
- Surprise avoidance	To have the feeling that I know what's going on at the other side. Don't be negatively surprised. ...enables visibility in the progress and to the project sponsor. And it gives an early warning for any kind of potential issues or delays.		I felt that the short weekly status report was adequate and good for. It was a good balance between burden on my time versus keeping the status moving.	
- Enhanced controlability	It gives me more control over the project, when it comes to meeting the deadline, meeting the deliverables. Otherwise I don't – when problems happen, it will become a disaster, it will be dragged on along with the project.		And also once a month we have this monthly status meeting with upper level management. One category the overall project, then another category talked about costs, the other one talked about schedule. So there was three categories and in different colors. And the reason being that it could be a red or it could be good red, because if you are under budget then that is good, but it stays red. So red definition was when you had ten percent variance on the original plan, then it's red Towards the end of the project we actually stopped the weekly communication, because at that time our Project Management Office introduced a more formal procedure of a formalized monthly status report on all projects, with red, green, yellow status, tracks against budget, and a lot more content. But the contents of the weekly status was also incorporated in the monthly status. We went very briefly to that towards the end of the project. That there is evidence for everything you do. A lot of things were just said and weren't put on paper, they weren't documented. There wasn't that bit of control that goes with a project. So, I think, you come across problems if there isn't delivered what the customer wants.	